SPSS

A User-Friendly Approach

Jeffery E. Aspelmeier
Radford University

Thomas W. Pierce
Radford University

WORTH PUBLISHERS

Publisher: Catherine Woods

Acquisitions Editor: Sarah Berger

Associate Managing Editor: Tracey Kuehn

Project Editor: Leigh Renhard

Marketing Manager: Amy Shefferd

Production Manager: Laura Hakala, Pre-PressPMG

Cover Designer: Kevin Kall

Composition: Pre-PressPMG

Printing and Binding: RR Donnelley

Library of Congress Control Number: 2008942259

ISBN-13: 978-1-4292-2418-5

ISBN-10: 1-4292-2418-5

© 2009 by Worth Publishers

Printed in the United States of America

First printing

Worth Publishers

41 Madison Avenue

New York, NY 10010

www.worthpublishers.com

Brief Table of Contents

CHAPTER 1   Introduction to SPSS: A User-Friendly
            Approach   1

CHAPTER 2   Basic Operations   10

CHAPTER 3   Finding Sums   26

CHAPTER 4   Frequency Distributions and Charts   36

CHAPTER 5   Describing Distributions   57

CHAPTER 6   Compute Statements: Reversing Scores,
            Combining Scores, and Creating Z-Scores   68

CHAPTER 7   Comparing Means in SPSS (*t*-Tests)   81

CHAPTER 8   One-Way ANOVA: Means Comparison
            with Two or More Groups   95

CHAPTER 9   Factorial ANOVA   106

CHAPTER 10   Repeated-Measures Analysis of Variance   126

CHAPTER 11   Regression and Correlation   152

CHAPTER 12   Multiple Regression   166

CHAPTER 13   Chi-Square   187

CHAPTER 14   Reliability   202

CHAPTER 15   Factor Analysis   217

Table of Contents

CHAPTER 1 Introduction to SPSS: A User-Friendly Approach   **1**

Don't Panic!   1
How to Use this Book   2
Data Analysis as a Decision-Making Process   2
Summary   8
Practice Exercises   8

CHAPTER 2 Basic Operations   **10**

Three Windows   10
Data Editor   10
Syntax Files   18
Output Files   21
Summary   24
Practice Exercises   25
Notes   25

CHAPTER 3 Finding Sums   **26**

Setting Up the Data   26
Running the Analysis   28
Reading the Output   30
Finding ΣX^2, ΣY^2, and Other Complex Summations   31
Find the Sums and Interpret the Output   34
More Compute Operators   34
Summary   35
Practice Exercises   35

CHAPTER 4 Frequency Distributions and Charts   **36**

Setting Up the Data   36
Obtaining Frequency Tables   37
Obtaining Frequency Charts   42
Obtaining Charts of Means   51
Summary   55
Practice Exercises   55

CHAPTER 5 Describing Distributions   **57**

Setting Up the Data   57
Measures of Central Tendency: Mean, Median, and Mode   59

Measures of Variability: Range, Variance, and
   Standard Deviation   61
Measures of Normality: Skewness and Kurtosis   64
Summary   66
Practice Exercises   67

**CHAPTER 6   Compute Statements: Reversing Scores,
Combining Scores, and Creating Z-Scores   68**

Setting Up the Data   68
Reverse Scoring Variables   69
Generating Multi-Item Scale Scores   72
Generating Z-Scores   75
Summary   79
Practice Exercises   80

CHAPTER 7   Comparing Means in SPSS (*t*-Tests)   81

Setting Up the Data   82
One-Sample *t*-test   83
Independent-Samples *t*-Test   87
Paired-Samples *t*-Test   90
Summary   93
Practice Exercises   93

**CHAPTER 8   One-Way ANOVA: Means Comparison
with Two or More Groups   95**

Setting Up the Data   95
Running the Analyses   98
Reading the One-Way ANOVA Output   100
Summary   104
Practice Exercises   105

CHAPTER 9   Factorial ANOVA   106

Setting Up the Data   108
Running the Analysis   111
Reading the Output for a Two-Way ANOVA   114
Simple Effects Testing   119
Summary   124
Practice Exercises   125
References   125

CHAPTER 10   Repeated-Measures Analysis of Variance   126

One-Way Repeated-Measures ANOVA   128
Mixed-Model Repeated-Measures ANOVA   138
Summary   150
Practice Exercises   150

CHAPTER 11 Regression and Correlation 152

Setting Up the Data   152
Correlation   153
Simple Linear Regression   157
Obtaining the Scatterplot   160
Summary   164
Practice Exercises   164

CHAPTER 12 Multiple Regression 166

Setting Up the Data   166
Simultanesous Entry of Two Predictor Variables   169
Varying the Order of Entry: Hierarchical Multiple Regression 175
Using Automated Strategies for Selecting Predictor Variables 180
Summary   184
Practice Exercises   185

CHAPTER 13 Chi-Square 187

Setting Up the Data   188
Goodness-of-Fit Chi-Square   190
Pearson's Chi-Square   196
Summary   201
Practice Exercises   201
References   201

CHAPTER 14 Reliability 202

Setting Up the Data   202
Test–Retest and Parallel Forms Reliability   203
Split–Half Reliability   207
Cronbach's Alpha   211
Concluding Comments on the GSR Scale   214
Summary   215
Practice Exercises   215

CHAPTER 15 Factor Analysis 217

Setting Up the Data   217
Goals of Factor Analysis   218
Running a Factor Analysis in SPSS   222
Reading the SPSS Output for Factor Analysis   226
Summary   230
Practice Exercises   230

Preface

The user-friendly approach to statistics was originally developed for the average student of statistics—the anxious and trepidatious. My friend and colleague Steve Schacht developed this cartoon-based approach to combat the paralyzing math and statistics anxiety that he saw among his students. I was introduced to this method after using Steve's book—*Statistics: A User-Friendly Approach*—in the first statistics classes I taught. I have spent the past 11 years using this approach to teach statistical concepts at both the graduate and undergraduate levels. In 2005, Steve and I co-authored *Social and Behavioral Statistics: a User-Friendly Approach*. Unfortunately, very shortly after the book was contracted, Steve discovered that his cancer, which had been in remission, returned, and he passed away before the book was released.

Steve and I had always intended to develop a user-friendly guide for teaching computer-based approaches to data analysis, and our work together forms the foundation upon which *SPSS: A User-Friendly Approach* is built. It embodies that same commitment to making statistics fun and accessible to students and to helping them to develop a sense of empowerment.

While planning *SPSS: A User-Friendly Approach*, I invited my friend Tom Pierce to join the project. I asked Tom for his help largely because in my opinion he is a gifted statistics teacher, and I owe a very large portion of my understanding of statistics and the teaching of statistics to him. I also asked him to be a part of this project because he shares my appreciation for absurd humor. Together Tom and I have more than 27 years of teaching experience. I think you will see that our collaboration has been quite fruitful and, though it may be hard to believe, we have had tremendous fun writing this book.

Although Tom and I are both psychologists, *SPSS: A User-Friendly Approach* should be attractive to anyone teaching or taking research courses in the social, behavioral, and educational sciences. This book was written to be a compendium to the traditional statistics texts in undergraduate and graduate courses that use SPSS as a data analysis tool. Our intent is to teach students to conduct statistical analyses typically found in statistics and research methods courses. We also focus on reinforcing the basic statistical concepts that students encounter in these courses. This text covers basic data management techniques, descriptive analyses, and hypothesis testing approaches along with more advanced topics like factorial designs, multiple regression, reliability analysis, and factor analysis. We have approached these topics with cartoons and humor, but our main goal is to provide substantive and thorough coverage of these procedures. Both anxious and confident students should find this text to be compelling and informative.

It is our sincerest hope that you have as much fun using this book as Tom and I have had writing it.

Jeff Aspelmeier

ACKNOWLEDGMENTS

We would like to thank Lisa Underwood, who on behalf of Steve Schacht's estate has allowed us to keep Steve's work alive. We would also like to thank our editor Sarah Berger and all the staff at Worth for their creativity and expertise and for producing a book we are all very proud of.

Thanks to Kim for tolerating and indulging an obsession with statistics and cartoons.

J.A.

Thanks to Ann, Bethany, and Luna. Thanks also to Tom's parents for modeling and encouraging curiosity as a lifelong core value.

T.W.P.

ABOUT THE AUTHORS

Jeff Aspelmeier is currently an associate professor in the Department of Psychology at Radford University, where he has been teaching since 1999. He earned his B.S.Ed. in Secondary Education from Southwest Missouri State University, and his M.A. and Ph.D. in Social Psychology from Kent State University. His research interests focus on attachment and adult romantic relationships. When not writing statistics textbooks for fun, he likes to travel and ski with his wife Kim, canoe in the New River with his dog Cassidy, and play guitar (which is typically not appreciated by either Kim or Cassidy).

Tom Pierce is a professor in the Department of Psychology at Radford University. He has been teaching statistics and research methods since coming to Radford in 1992. He has a B.A in Psychology from McGill University and a Ph.D. in Psychology from the University of Maine. He was also a postdoctoral fellow in the Center for the Study of Aging at Duke University Medical Center. His research interests are in the areas of aging and cognitive function, stress and human performance, and time series analysis of behavioral and physiological data.

Introduction to SPSS: A User-Friendly Approach

DON'T PANIC!

Douglas Adams wrote a very funny and insightful series of novels that center around an electronic book called the *Hitchhiker's Guide to the Galaxy*. The *Guide* contains all relevant information in the known universe, which is nice, but perhaps the most useful piece of advice is featured on the cover: the words "*DON'T PANIC.*" This is a great suggestion for any occasion, but is especially pertinent as you open a textbook dedicated to two topics likely to strike feelings of fear, boredom, or both into the hearts of students and faculty members alike: *statistics* and *software*. We recognize that many of you are less than thrilled at the prospect of starting a course involving the use of statistical software and that some of you experience a sizable amount of anxiety at the mere thought of this stuff. To you, especially, we would like to offer the same sage words of advice: don't panic! You're going to be okay.

We have written this book as a very friendly introduction to SPSS (Statistical Package for the Social Sciences). The central goal of the book is to make potentially complicated concepts and procedures easy to understand, easy to complete, and (when humanly possible) *fun* to work with. We have found that if you are having fun, it is hard to be anxious. Humor can often distract students from the anxiety they feel, and this in turn gives them a chance to develop their skills as statistical thinkers and develop a sense of confidence in their own abilities. As an example of our approach, every chapter features a cartoon on which humorous (hopefully) and absurd (certainly) data sets are based. A cursory flip through the book will reveal penguin-soliciting pilgrims, college professors from other dimensions, questionnaires for lions, cow poetry, and anti-social one-eared bunnies on Prozac.

However, this book was not written solely for stats-anxious students. As Cartoon 1.1 clearly shows, some of you will find that SPSS represents a clear path to "Nerdvana."

▶ **Cartoon 1.1**

Whether you are totally comfortable with quantitative topics (and come to SPSS in an altered state of geeky bliss) or you are completely stressed out when sitting in front of a computer, we will tell you what you need to know in as clear and concise a manner as we can. A careful reading will reveal that behind the goofy cartoons and examples, you have purchased a very comprehensive introduction to SPSS. It covers the procedures traditionally included in introductory level statistics courses and a number of more advanced topics typically covered in courses at the upper-level undergraduate and Master's levels. In addition, we have organized this book so that it can serve as both an initial introduction to SPSS now and a useful reference tool in the future. Finally, this book was written to reinforce the concepts you are likely to cover in statistics courses in the social, behavioral, and educational sciences. In conjunction with a more traditional statistics textbook, this book will help you to develop a firm conceptual and applied understanding of quantitative techniques using one of the most user-friendly software packages available for statistical analysis—SPSS!

HOW TO USE THIS BOOK

Generally speaking, the chapters in this book are all organized in the same way. Each chapter opens with a brief introduction to the procedure(s) of interest. These introductions focus on the organizational themes for the book: (a) deciding when procedures are appropriate to use, and (b) the types of research questions each procedure is typically used to address. These themes are described in more detail later in this chapter.

Following the introduction, we present the steps you need to take in SPSS to conduct the procedures. In each chapter, we will walk you through SPSS procedures using an at-a-glance, step-by-step approach. Usually, a single figure visually presents the windows and dialogue boxes you will encounter when running a particular procedure. In addition, the steps are outlined in greater detail within procedure boxes. This approach is intended to make the procedures easy to learn, easy to use, and easy to review. Our goal is to ensure that when you are sitting at your computer doing the analysis, you will always know what to do next.

This book emphasizes more than just the mechanics of conducting data analysis in SPSS. For each procedure, we offer a detailed discussion of how to read the generated results (i.e., the *Output*). Specifically, we direct your attention to the information you need in order to answer your research questions. We also offer a clear description of what the results tell us about the participants in our data set and their behavior. Furthermore, many instructors require their students to learn the hand calculations associated with basic statistical procedures. Where appropriate, we illustrate ways in which the results obtained from SPSS can be used to check the results obtained from hand calculations.

Finally, a major part of learning is practice. Each chapter concludes with a set of Practice Exercises. These problems are designed to reinforce the major concepts presented in the chapter.

DATA ANALYSIS AS A DECISION-MAKING PROCESS

Like Calvin in Cartoon 1.2, many students are disappointed to discover that computers will not just do the work for you. When using SPSS, you still have to create variables, enter data, request the appropriate procedures, and interpret the results. More importantly, you need

to make decisions about what to do with your data. The value of SPSS is that once you know what to do with your data, it becomes quite easy to get the information you want.

Unfortunately, there is no simple mnemonic device or road map approach we can provide that will tell you what to do in every data analysis situation. In large part students develop this knowledge over time by working with different types of data. However, we do offer a simplified framework for making common statistical decisions. The rules of thumb we offer here will help you make decisions about the statistical procedures you will likely encounter in statistics and research courses at the undergraduate and Master's level. This decision-making framework serves as the core organizing theme for the chapters that follow. We strongly encourage you to familiarize yourself with this framework and to periodically return to this section as you begin to learn new statistical procedures.

WHAT TYPE OF DATA DO YOU HAVE?

When choosing an appropriate procedure, keep in mind that *each statistical procedure answers a particular kind of question*, and the kind of question you ask depends on the type of data you have. The first step in choosing a statistic is deciding what type of data you have. Over the years, statisticians have classified data in a variety of ways. A common approach is based on a hierarchy of levels or scales of measurement: *nominal, ordinal, interval,* and *ratio*. Many books also refer to a distinction between *discrete* and *continuous* data. These and other organizational approaches certainly have their place, and having a fully developed understanding of statistics requires you to make use of these distinctions at various times. However, in the interest of keeping things simple, we focus on a distinction between variables that represent *groups* and variables that represent *scores*. As you familiarize yourself with the group/score distinction, you will likely find variables that seem to straddle both categories. In most cases, however, these conflicts can be resolved by considering how you intend to use the measurement. Regardless, in a vast majority of the data analysis problems you will face, this simple distinction is enough to make good decisions about how to analyze your data.

By *Group Variable*, we mean any way of assigning different types of people, events, or outcomes to a particular category. Returning to Cartoon 1.2, assume that we want to study children's beliefs about computers. We can employ a great variety of group-based variables for this task. We could separately evaluate female children and male children. A group of children (ages 6 to 11) could be compared with a group of adolescents (ages 14 to 17). We could look at children with computers at home and children without. Or we could design an experiment where one group of children is given an opportunity to work with computers while a control group performs a similar task without the use of computers.

With respect to children's beliefs about computers, we could use group-based variables as well. For example, we could create categories of beliefs about computers within which the children could be classified. The Youth Inventory of Personal Computer Attitudes and Beliefs—Long Edition (YIPe-CompAttABLE) asks children to pick the statement that best describes their attitudes toward computers, and it groups respondents based on the statements they pick. The groupings are as follows:

> Which of the following statements is most like you?
> 1. I think computers are a tool for solving problems more efficiently.
> 2. I think computers do work that humans do not have the time or motivation to do.
> 3. I think computers make simple tasks too complicated.
> 4. I think computers were created by a society of underground mole people in order to distract us so they can steal all the prizes from our boxes of breakfast cereal.

Alternatively, a simple yes/no format could be utilized, which asks children whether they like using computers. This too would represent a group variable.

Group variables can also be used to represent random discrete outcomes (either/or). For example, if we had children flip a coin, then the outcomes can be grouped as either heads or tails. Similarly, children rolling six-sided die would give us six possible outcomes or groupings: either a 1 or a 2 or a 3 etc. For the most part, variables like this should also be classified as group variables.

Score Variables are used when we want to represent how much or how many of something you have. The value of a score variable represents the location of a participant along a numerical range of possible values. With respect to the characteristics of the children in our study, we could use age as a variable. Whether we measure age in months or years, it would represent a numerical range of possible values. Other scores we could use might include height, weight, IQ, score on an educational achievement test, grade point average, classroom teacher-to-student ratios, hours per week spent using a computer, family income, number of computers in the home, or the number of tasks correctly completed in a basic computer skills test. Another type of score, which is of particular interest to social and behavioral scientists, consists of attitude and personality ratings. For example, we could ask participants to rate the statement "I like to use computers" using a 5-point scale; (1) Strongly Disagree, (2) Disagree, (3) Neither Disagree nor Agree, (4) Agree, or (5) Strongly Agree. Most attitude/personality measures consist of multiple items, and the ratings for each item are combined to form a single score (usually through averaging or summing; this is covered in Chapters 6 and 14).

Now that we have defined group and score variables, it should be noted that variables representing *rankings* do not really fit into this framework. Ranked variables (also called *ordinal variables*) reflect categories which have a logical order to them. For example, we could rank the height of 10 children, where 1 is the tallest and 10 is the shortest. Similarly, if we ranked the computer skills of the students in Calvin's classroom from most skilled to least skilled, then we would have an ordinal level of measurement. Ranked variables typically require special statistical procedures that lie beyond the scope of this text.

MATCHING VARIABLES WITH STATISTICS

Once you have identified the type of data you are working with, you can begin the process of selecting a statistical procedure. Different procedures are available depending on the type of data you have and whether you are describing one variable or the relationship between two or more variables. Figure 1.1 shows the statistical procedures

▶ **Figure 1.1** Matching Variables with Statistics

Group Variables		
One Variable		
Frequencies (%)		Ch. 4
Mode		Ch. 5
Goodness-of-Fit Chi-Square		Ch. 13
Two Variables		
Pearson's Chi-Square		Ch. 13

Score Variables	
One Variable	
Sum	Ch. 3
Frequencies (%)	Ch. 4
Central Tendency	Ch. 5
Variability	Ch. 5
Normality	Ch. 5
Z-Scores	Ch. 6
Single-Sample t-Tests	Ch. 7
Two Variables	
Correlation	Ch. 11
Simple Regression	Ch. 11
Two or More Variables	
Combined Scores	Ch. 6
Multiple Regression	Ch. 12
Reliability	Ch. 14
Factor Analysis	Ch. 15

Group Variables with Score Variables	
One Group and One Score Variable	
2 Groups: Independent Sample t-Tests	Ch. 7
2 or More Groups: One-Way ANOVA	Ch. 8
Two or More Group Variables and One Score Variable	
Factorial ANOVA	Ch. 9

Repeated-Measures Variables	
2 Time Points: Paired-Samples t-Test	Ch. 7
2 or More Time Points: Repeated-Measures ANOVA	Ch. 10
Within-Subjects & Between-Subjects: Mixed Model ANOVA	Ch. 10

included in this book along with the chapters in which they are presented. The first column applies to situations where group variables are of interest, the second column applies to variables representing scores, and the third column applies to situations where we are interested in assessing the influence that group variables have on scores. The third column also lists a group of statistics that apply to *Repeated-Measures Variables*. Repeated-measures procedures represent a unique set of analyses and will be described in a separate section later in this chapter.

Evaluating a single variable. Typically, describing or summarizing the characteristics of individual variables is the first step in a larger data analysis plan for a study. For example, if we have a single group variable that classifies children into two groups—those who have computers at home and those who do not—we could obtain the frequency (number) or percentage of children in each group. We could then use this information to construct tables and charts to visually summarize the number of participants in each category (Chapter 4). We could also determine which group had the most children in it (the modal group; Chapter 5). More ambitiously, we use the *Goodness-of-Fit Chi-Square* (Chapter 13) to determine whether the ratio of children with computers to children without computers in our sample meaningfully differs from the ratio found (or expected) in the population.

A very different set of procedures is available to describe a single variable representing scores. For example, if we had a variable representing the number of hours per week that each child uses a computer, the *sum* procedure (Chapter 3) will calculate the total number of hours that the children as a group use a computer each week. Obtaining the sum of a set of scores is a common first step in completing many other statistical procedures. *Frequency Tables* or *Charts* will visually summarize the computer data (Chapter 4). *Measures of Central Tendency* (*Mean*, *Median*, and *Mode*; Chapter 5) will tell us what amount of time is most representative of how long children use a computer each week. Similarly, measures of *Variability* (*Standard Deviation*, *Variance*, and *Range*; Chapter 5) and *Z-scores* (Chapter 6) can help us determine how representative a given score is based on how much children differ in the amount of time they spend using a computer each week. *Measures of Normality* (*Skewness* and *Kurtosis*; Chapter 5) will determine whether the shape of the distribution of scores for Children's Computer Use resembles the shape of distributions typically collected from populations (e.g., the *Normal Curve*). Finally, a *Single-Sample t-Test* (Chapter 7) can determine whether the average amount of time children in our sample use a computer each week differs from some comparison value, like the population average.

Evaluating associations between two variables. Although describing the characteristics of a single variable is an important first step, frequently the goal of research is to demonstrate how two variables are related to or influence one another. With respect to group variables, we can use *Pearson's Chi-Square* (also called the *Test of Independence;* Chapter 13) to determine whether male and female children differ with respect to the likelihood that they have a computer in their home. Alternatively, with respect to score variables, we can use a *Correlation Coefficient* (e.g., *Pearson's r*) or *Simple Linear Regression* (Chapter 11) to determine whether children who use computers more frequently also tend to score higher on tests of computer skills (a positive correlation).

We can also assess the relationship between one group variable and one variable representing scores. First, if we have a group variable which is comprised of two groups (e.g., children with and without computers at home), we can use an *Independent Samples t-Test* (Chapter 7) or *One-Way ANOVA (Analysis of Variance;* Chapter 8). These tests will determine whether there is a meaningful difference between the two groups with respect to their weekly amount of computer use. However, if the group variable represents more than two groups (e.g., children, adolescents, and adults), then a one-way ANOVA should be used to determine whether significant differences are observed among the groups.

Questions with more than two variables. The ability to include more than two variables in a particular analysis allows researchers to address a wide range of complex and interesting questions. *Multiple Regression* (Chapter 12) can be used to answer a variety of questions regarding how two or more score variables are related to (or predict) the scores of another variable. Alternatively, multiple score variables can be combined to form a single score, such as an average or summed score (Chapter 6). Furthermore, *Reliability* (Chapter 14) and *Factor Analysis* (Chapter 15) can be used to determine which combinations of scores make the most useful groupings. Factor analysis, reliability analysis, and the ability to form combined scores are all commonly used when working with multi-item measures like achievement tests, clinical assessments, or attitude and personality measures.

When you have two or more group variables and a single variable representing scores, you can use *Factorial ANOVA* (Chapter 9) to answer questions very similar to the ones asked in one-way ANOVA and *t*-tests. For example, in a single procedure we could determine whether children who have computers at home differ from children who do not and whether males differ from females with respect to scores on a computer skills test. In addition, factorial ANOVA can address the more complex question of whether the two group variables interact with one another. For example, this same analysis can determine whether differences found between children with and without computers depend on whether the child is male or female. Among other potential patterns of results, it may be that males who have computers at home demonstrate greater skill than do males who do not have computers at home, but among females computer skills are high regardless of whether they have a computer.

REPEATED-MEASURES VARIABLES

As the name implies, you have repeated-measures variables when you collect the same measurements from the same group (or groups) of people at different points in time. For example, we could give our sample of children a measure of computer skills before training (pre-test), administer a training program, and then measure their computer skills again (post-test). This is generally referred to as a *Within-Subjects Design.* Had we measured computer skills among two different groups of participants, one that has received training and one that has not, then we would have a *Between-Subjects Design.* Further, had we taken pre-test and post-test computer skills measurements (within-subjects variable) from one group that receives training and another that does not (between-subjects variable), then we would have a *Mixed Design* (i.e., the design contains a mixture of within- and between-subjects variables).

When you have two measurements taken at different times, then a *Paired-Sample t-Test* (Chapter 7) or a *One-Way Repeated-Measures ANOVA* (Chapter 10) can tell you whether the average score taken during the first point in time meaningfully differs from the average score taken during the second point in time. One-way repeated-measures ANOVA can also be used when measurements have been collected from more than two time points. For example, we could compare the computer skills scores of children prior to training (time 1), after one training session (time 2), and after two training sessions (time 3). Finally, the *Mixed-Model Repeated-Measures ANOVA* (Chapter 10) can be used with mixed (between-within) designs. Like factorial ANOVA the mixed-model ANOVA provides a single procedure that will determine whether there are any differences between the groups for the between-subjects variable and whether there are any differences between the times for the within-subjects variable. Further, the procedure will test the interaction of the two independent variables. For example, we can ask whether the size of the differences found in children's pre-test and post-test scores on a computer skills assessment depends on whether the children are male or female.

SUMMARY

Making good decisions about what statistical procedures are appropriate for a given situation is a matter of knowing what kind of data you have. If you want to compare groups with groups, then you can evaluate frequencies and chi-square statistics. If you want to compare scores with other scores then correlation, regression, and multiple regression may be appropriate. If you want to compare the scores of different groups, then *t*-tests, ANOVA, or factorial ANOVA may be appropriate. Finally, if you have given the same measure for the same people on more than one occasion and you want to compare those scores, then a repeated-measures analysis of some sort is called for. We realize this will seem like a lot to cover all at once; after all, you are going to take at least a semester to work your way through these things. *Don't panic!* This scheme is intended to help you place each new topic you cover within a relatively simple framework. Do not bother trying to commit the framework to memory, but go back to it periodically until you become more familiar with it. Hopefully, it will come in handy later on when you need to pick the right procedure to answer a particular kind of question with a particular type of variable (group or score) or variables. For now, we just want you to be aware of the big picture; different statistical procedures answer different kinds of questions about different kinds of data.

PRACTICE EXERCISES

The following exercises are meant to reinforce the concepts we have introduced in this chapter. If this is your first statistics course, parts B and C of these exercises will probably be quite challenging, especially at the start of the semester. You may want to return to these problems later on in the semester to evaluate how much you have learned about how to pick the correct statistical procedure.

A. Determine whether the variables described below reflect group variables or score variables.

1. Ethnicity/race.

2. Time spent showering per day.

3. Hair color.

4. Average ratings on a 10-item measure of depression.

5. Political affiliation.

     6. Religious affiliation.

     7. Years of education.

     8. Attitude toward statistics rated using a 7-point scale.

     9. Number of pets a person owns.

B. For the following, determine whether the design of the study is between-participants, within-participants, or a mixed (between-within) design.

    10. In an experiment, one-third of the participants are asked to read cartoons for 30 minutes. Another one-third of the participants are asked to watch a cartoon TV show for 30 minutes. The final one-third are asked to sit quietly for 30 minutes.

    11. In an experiment, all participants completed a measure of attitudes toward statistics. Half of the participants then received a 30-minute review of statistics instruction using a cartoon approach. The other half of the participants read cartoons for 30 minutes. All participants were then asked to complete the measure of attitudes toward statistics for the second time.

    12. Researchers asked participants (all currently enrolled in a statistics course) to complete a measure of attitudes toward statistics once a week for the entire semester in which they were enrolled in the course.

    13. Researchers asked participants (all currently enrolled in a statistics course) to complete a measure of attitudes toward statistics once a week for the entire semester in which they were enrolled in the course. The researchers are interested in testing whether male and female participants differ at and across the various time points.

C. For the following, indicate which statistical procedure would be appropriate.

    14. Researchers want to know whether male and female children differ in the number of hours per week they use a computer.

    15. Researchers want to know whether the age of participants is related to the number of hours per week they use a computer.

    16. Researchers want to describe a variable representing the number of different computers participants use in a week.

    17. Researchers want to describe a variable representing the type of operating system children use most often (e.g., Mac OS versus Windows).

    18. Researchers want to know whether participants' gender/sex (male versus female) is related to the type of operating system children use most often.

    19. Researchers want to compare the computer skills test scores for students from third-, fourth-, and fifth-grade classes.

    20. Researchers want to compare the computer skills test scores for male and female students that come from third-, fourth-, and fifth-grade classes.

    21. Researchers want to know whether the number of hours per week children use computers and the number of students in the children's classrooms are associated with the children's scores on a computer skills test.

Basic Operations

hapter 1 presented a very conceptual overview of SPSS. The present chapter will walk you through the routine procedures that you will use nearly every time you work with SPSS. Specifically, you will learn how to navigate the SPSS environment; how to enter, save, and retrieve data sets; create, modify, and save text-based records of the procedures you perform (syntax); and generate, navigate, save, and print the results of your data analyses (output).

THREE WINDOWS

The base version of SPSS can be split up into three major parts: the *Data Editor* (where we enter data and create new variables), the *Syntax Editor* (where we store and create syntax for our analyses and procedures), and the *SPSS Viewer* (where we view the output/results our statistical analyses have generated). The student version of SPSS does not include the Syntax Editor, but the Data Editor and SPSS Viewer operate in the same manner as the base version. Each of the major parts of SPSS have their own program window in SPSS. When more than one SPSS window is open, there will be separate buttons for SPSS on the Windows task bar (see Figure 2.1). You can navigate between the different windows of SPSS by left-clicking on the appropriate buttons on the task bar. When working in the SPSS windows, if you close either the SPSS Viewer or the Syntax Editor the remaining windows will not be affected. However, closing the Data Editor closes the entire SPSS program, and the SPSS Viewer and Syntax Editor will close as well.

▶ **Figure 2.1** Windows Task Bar

DATA EDITOR

The first step in any data analysis process is to set up the data file in the Data Editor (You can create variables and enter data in the Syntax Editor, but that is beyond the scope of this text). The SPSS Data Editor is split into two parts (or views): the **Variable View** and the **Data View**. The Data View allows you to view and input data. The columns in the Data View represent variables and the rows represent observations/participants/subjects (often referred to as cases). The Variable View allows you to edit variables and add new variables to the data set. Note that in the Variable View, the rows represent each variable and correspond to the columns in the Data View. The columns in the Variable View represent different aspects of each variable. Figure 2.2 presents the Variable View and the Data View for a blank Data Editor file. Window Ⓐ shows the Variable View and window Ⓑ shows the Data View. To toggle back and forth between the two views, click on the labeled buttons located at the bottom left-hand corner of the Data Editor spreadsheet: in Figure 2.2 the buttons are marked with the letter Ⓒ.

▶**Figure 2.2** Variable View and Data View for a Blank Data File

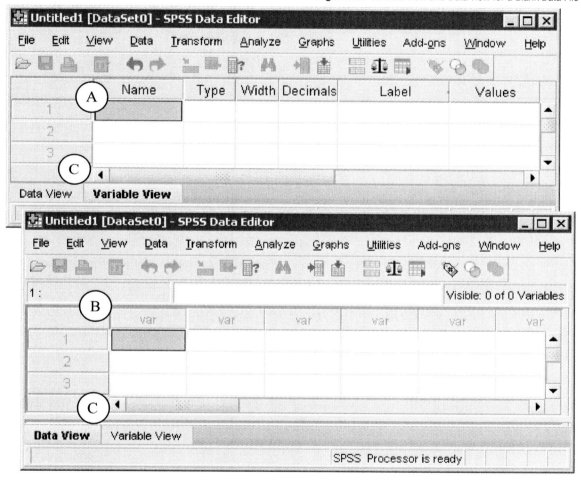

CREATING NEW VARIABLES

Cartoon 2.1 inspired the data set that you will work with for this chapter. Helga's statement about Hagar implies that he would not know what the well water tastes like because he only drinks beer. Beer holds a special place in the hearts of most statisticians as some of the basic statistical procedures and assumptions used today were developed by William Gossett, an employee of the Guinness brewery in Ireland. In the early 1900s, Gossett developed the student *t*-distribution so that he could select the best varieties of barley for producing beer. Thus, without beer there would be no statistics, although you

may argue that without statistics there would be little need for beer. It seems likely that both statements are true.

Assume that a researcher is interested in the drinking habits of different cartoon characters. Specifically, she is interested in the types and amounts of beer consumed by cartoon characters. The type of beer would be considered a group variable. The amount in this case is operationalized as the number of beers (12 oz. cans) consumed per week, and this variable represents a set of scores. If the distinction between variables representing groups and scores is unclear to you, then go back and review the discussion in Chapter 1. Table 2.1 displays the result of the study. The first column lists the participant number by which each cartoon character is identified. Hagar is participant number 15. The second column presents the number of beers consumed per week by each character. The third column presents the brand of beer preferred by each character.

▶**Table 2.1** Amount and Brands of Beer Consumed by Cartoon Characters

Participant #	# of Beers Per Week	Brand
1	1	Bongo Beer
2	2	Swiller Light
3	4	Swiller Light
4	4	Lights-Out-Lager
5	5	Lights-Out-Lager
6	6	Lights-Out-Lager
7	7	Lights-Out-Lager
8	7	Lights-Out-Lager
9	9	Budget Brew
10	10	Budget Brew
11	11	Budget Brew
12	12	Belcher's Pride
13	12	Cirrhosis Light
14	12	Cirrhosis Light
(Hagar's Data) 15	15	Cirrhosis Light

▶**Table 2.2** Guidelines for Naming Variables

Things you cannot do:
Names cannot start with a number (1, 2, 3,…), though they can have numbers in them.
Names cannot have spaces or the following symbols: - !%^&*+~ ( ) { }[ ] ?/><.
The following names are reserved and cannot be used: ALL, AND, BY, EQ, GE, GT, LE, LT, NE, NOT, OR, TO, and WITH.
Things you can do:
Names can consist of upper and lower case letters.
Names can use periods (or decimal points), but variable names cannot end with periods.
You can use #, $, @, and _, but avoid using symbols at the end of variable names as SPSS may mistake the name for certain types of commands.

Variable Names. To create new variables on a blank data file, select the Variable View. Give each variable a variable name by typing the desired name in the first open row of the first column, labeled Name. Older versions of SPSS limited variable names to eight characters. Newer versions allow for much longer variable names (approximately 60 characters), though it is a good idea to keep them as short as possible; eight or fewer is ideal. Table 2.2 offers other guidelines for naming variables. For our example, we have named the first variable, representing the number of beers each cartoon character drinks a week, **beerweek.** Similarly, we have named the second variable, representing the brand of beer that each cartoon character drinks, **beerbrnd**. Figure 2.3 presents the variable view with the variable names entered for our example.

Variable Labels. The next step is to give each variable a variable label by left-clicking the appropriate cell in the Label column. In our example, we have given the **beerweek** variable the variable label "Weekly Beer Consumption Data Set," and we have given the **beerbrnd** variable the variable label "Brands of Beer Data Set." Variable labels are more flexible than variable names. You can have more than 200 characters, and you can use spaces and symbols. The variable label allows you to give variables a more descriptive name so you do not forget what the variable measures. Be as precise as possible when labeling your variables. When you provide variable labels, they appear on the output of your analyses, which makes your output easier to read. However, the output will only present the first 40 or so characters of the variable label, so put the most unique and descriptive information first. Variable labels can also be used to identify variables when requesting statistical analyses, but only the first 20 characters are displayed in the analysis windows. You can choose whether the analysis windows display variable names or variable labels by doing the following: left-click **Edit** => select **Options…** => left-click the **General** tab => select **Display Labels** or **Display Names** from the **Variable Lists** options.

Value Labels. If the variable represents groups or categories (a discrete/nominal variable; e.g., sex/gender, ethnicity, treatment versus no treatment, brands of beer, etc.), SPSS requires each group or category to be represented with numerical values (e.g., 1 = male, 2 = female; treatment = 1, no treatment = 0). This does make data entry easier and less prone to error, but it can be hard to remember what the numbers represent. Value labels are category names that we can assign to values representing each group. When included, value labels can appear in the Data Editor and will be used in any output you generate. In our

▶ **Figure 2.3** Defining New Variables in the Variable View

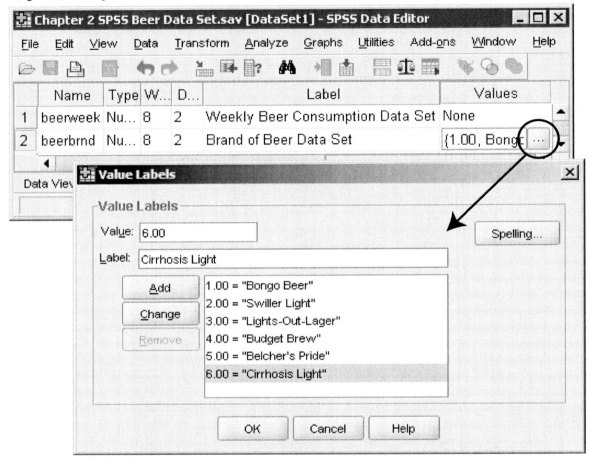

example, we used the numbers 1 through 6 to represent our six brands of beer. In Figure 2.3, the following values are paired with the following labels: 1 = Bongo Beer, 2 = Swiller Light, 3 = Lights-Out-Lager, 4 = Budget Brew, 5 = Belcher's Pride, and 6 = Cirrhosis Light. The steps for creating value labels are presented in the procedures box on p. 15.

ENTERING DATA

Once the variables have been named and the values labeled, you can begin data entry. To do this, return to the Data Editor and select Data View. Remember that the rows in the Data View represent cases/observations/subjects/participants, while the columns represent the variables you have defined. Notice that once variables are defined, the columns are labeled with the variable names. To enter data for a given case of a given variable, simply left-click the cell you want to begin with, type the appropriate value into that cell, and then either press "enter" or one of the directional arrow keys on your keyboard. If entering data on the right-hand numeric keypad, be sure that the number lock has been turned on and be careful not to turn it off when reaching for the 7 key. Data can be corrected by left-clicking the desired cell and typing in the new value and pressing either enter or a directional arrow key.

PROCEDURE FOR CREATING VALUE LABELS:

- In the **Values** column of the Variable View, left-click on the row that corresponds to the variable with values you want to label.
- When you left-click on this cell, a small gray box will appear. Left-click on the box to open the **Value Labels** dialogue box.
  - This window can be closed by clicking **OK**, **Cancel**, or the small red **X** in the upper right-hand corner of the window.
- In the **Val<u>u</u>e:** field of the dialogue box, type the lowest value (e.g., 0 or 1) you will be using to represent the groups or categories. For the most part, you can use any numbers you want.
- Then in the **<u>L</u>abel:** field, type the name of the category (e.g., Bongo Beer) and left-click the **<u>A</u>dd** button.
- In the **Val<u>u</u>e:** field, type the next highest value (e.g., 2). Then in the **<u>L</u>abel:** field, type the name for the next desired group or category (e.g., Swiller Light), and left-click the **<u>A</u>dd** button.
- Continue this process until all the values for all the groups or categories have been named.
- When this is complete, left-click **OK** and you will return the Variable View of the Data Editor.

Figure 2.4 shows the Data View for our example. Here, we have entered the data for each of our 15 cartoon characters. The first column lists the number of beers consumed by each character per week. The second column lists the brand of beer consumed by each character per week. In our example, the first cartoon character drinks one beer per week and drinks Bongo Beer. Similarly, the fifteenth cartoon character (Hagar) drinks 15 beers per week and drinks Cirrhosis Light.

Value Labels in the Data View. You should note that for our **beerbrnd** variable, the value label appears in the cell. However, when we entered the data for this variable, we used the numerical values assigned to each brand of beer. For example, for subject 15 we did not type out the words "Cirrhosis Light;" we simply typed 6 on the numeric keypad. It is possible to change the settings of the Data Editor so that the Data View shows the numerical values instead of the value labels. This can be accomplished by selecting the **Value Labels** option from the **<u>V</u>iew** pull-down menu. Alternatively, you can use the Value Labels icon on the toolbar, which is circled in black in Figure 2.4. When this option is checked, the value labels will appear in the Data View spreadsheet. When this option is not checked, the values will appear in the Data View spreadsheet. We recommend that you turn off the value labels when entering the data (especially if you are entering larger amounts of numbers), as it requires several more keystrokes to enter each data point.

Missing data. As a note of caution, through the course of data entry it is possible to activate data cells that you do not intend to use. For example, you may have data for 10 people, but accidentally activate 11 rows. When this occurs, the active cells without data will have a decimal point in them and nothing else. When a cell is activated and there is no data

► Figure 2.4 Example for Entering Data

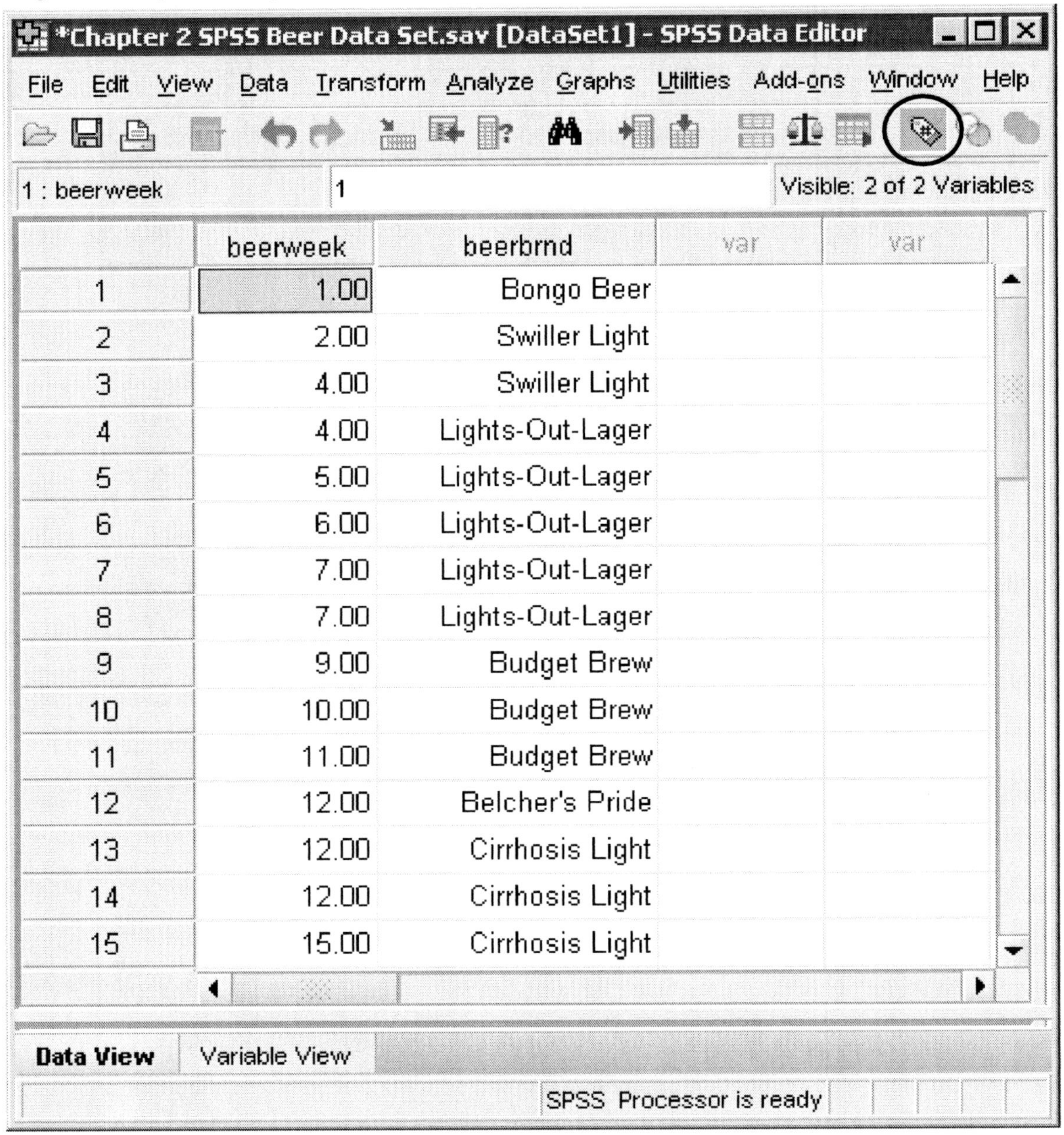

	beerweek	beerbrnd	var	var

*Chapter 2 SPSS Beer Data Set.sav [DataSet1] – SPSS Data Editor

File   Edit   View   Data   Transform   Analyze   Graphs   Utilities   Add-ons   Window   Help

1 : beerweek   1   Visible: 2 of 2 Variables

	beerweek	beerbrnd	var	var
1	1.00	Bongo Beer		
2	2.00	Swiller Light		
3	4.00	Swiller Light		
4	4.00	Lights-Out-Lager		
5	5.00	Lights-Out-Lager		
6	6.00	Lights-Out-Lager		
7	7.00	Lights-Out-Lager		
8	7.00	Lights-Out-Lager		
9	9.00	Budget Brew		
10	10.00	Budget Brew		
11	11.00	Budget Brew		
12	12.00	Belcher's Pride		
13	12.00	Cirrhosis Light		
14	12.00	Cirrhosis Light		
15	15.00	Cirrhosis Light		

Data View   Variable View

SPSS Processor is ready

entered for that cell, SPSS considers this *missing data*. Having these extra missing data cases is usually not a major problem, but it can make reading the results of certain analyses a little more complicated. It is a good idea to delete missing data cases when you notice that you have them. To do this, left-click on the row number (located to the far left of the data editor spreadsheet) that contains the missing case; this will highlight the whole row. Pushing the delete button on the keyboard will deactivate all of the cells in that row. When you delete cells, be sure that you are not deleting any data that you intend to keep.

SAVING AND OPENING YOU DATA FILES

You should periodically save your data file in order to avoid losing all of the work you have just completed.

PROCEDURE FOR SAVING DATA:

1. Select **File** from the pull-down menu.
2. Select the **Save** or **Save as...** option. This will open the **Save Data As** dialogue box.
3. Left-click the boxed arrow on the right of the **Look in:** field and navigate through the file tree to select the drive [e.g., C: (the hard drive) or E: (external storage device)] and the directory (folder) in which you want to save your data.
4. Type the name you want to give the new data file in the **File name:** field. Here, we have named our data file "Chapter 2 SPSS Beer Data Set.sav."
5. Click **Save** to finish.

▶ **Figure 2.5** Saving Data Files

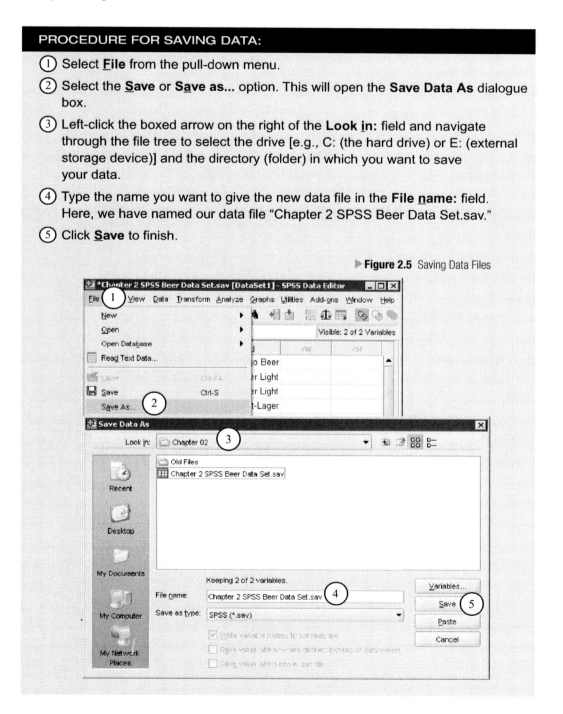

There are three types of files in SPSS: data files, syntax files, and output files. Each file type has a different file extension, which is the string of three letters that appear after the period in a file name. Data files have the file extension ".sav," syntax files have the extension ".sps," and output files have the extension ".spv." It is important to keep this in mind when working with different types of SPSS files. For example, the **Save** and **Save As** windows of SPSS typically only display one type of file even when files of other types may exist within the folder you are searching. The type of file you are shown depends on what window you are currently in (Data Editor, Syntax Editor, or SPSS Viewer).

Be sure to save your work often and save it in multiple places (e.g., on a hard drive or network drive and on removable media: zip disc, floppy disc, CD-R/RW, etc.) so you will not lose anything important. After you have saved your data file once, you can quickly save changes to your file by left-clicking on the save icon (the small black floppy disc) in the Data Editor. To save your file to a different drive, to a new folder, or with a different file name, you will need to use the **Save as...** option from the **File** pull-down menu.

PROCEDURE FOR OPENING DATA FILES:

- Select **File** from the pull-down menu.
- Select **Open** and select **Data...** from the side menu, which will open the **Open File** dialogue box.
- Left-click the boxed arrow on the right of the **Look in:** field and navigate through the file tree to select the drive [e.g., C: (the hard drive), A: (a floppy disc), etc.] and directory (folder) from which you want to retrieve your data.
- Once you select the desired directory, double left-click on the file that you want to open or single left-click on the file and then left-click the **Open** button.

Occasionally, you may not be able to find the file you are looking for even though you know it is supposed to be there. Remember that the SPSS **Open File** dialogue box will only display the files that have the file extension designated in the **Files of type:** field at the bottom of the **Open File** dialogue box. When opening data files ensure that the **SPSS (*.sav)** file type has been selected.

SYNTAX FILES
WHAT IS SYNTAX?

In the "olden days" (12–15 years ago) the Graphical User Interface (GUI) version of SPSS did not exist and all data entry and analysis was done using an SPSS syntax language. Now we have a Windows-based program (a GUI), and we can point-and-click our way through all analyses. The only problem is that when we want to change our analysis procedure we must step through the whole point-and-click process again, which is tiresome and potentially error prone. Fortunately, throughout the base version of SPSS there is the option to **Paste,** which will send our point-and-click commands to a syntax sheet that can be stored as a separate file. This way, we can have all the steps in our analysis recorded and stored. We can also run all of our analysis from the syntax sheet, write syntax for new analyses, or alter the syntax from previous analyses. Saving syntax files for various procedures is great way to build up a library of SPSS tasks and procedures you frequently use. In the beginning, you may want avoid using syntax just to keep things simple, but as you progress and begin to work with real data, you should consider using syntax to help manage your work.

Figure 2.6 illustrates the steps for requesting a frequency analysis for our beer data set example (this will be covered in detail in Chapter 4) and pasting the commands of that analysis into the Syntax Editor. This figure also displays the resulting syntax sheet that is produced. In this example, we have requested frequency analyses for the weekly beer consumption and the brands of beer variables and then have pasted the syntax by left-clicking the **Paste** button [⑥ in Figure 2.6].

▶**Figure 2.6** Example of Pasting Syntax

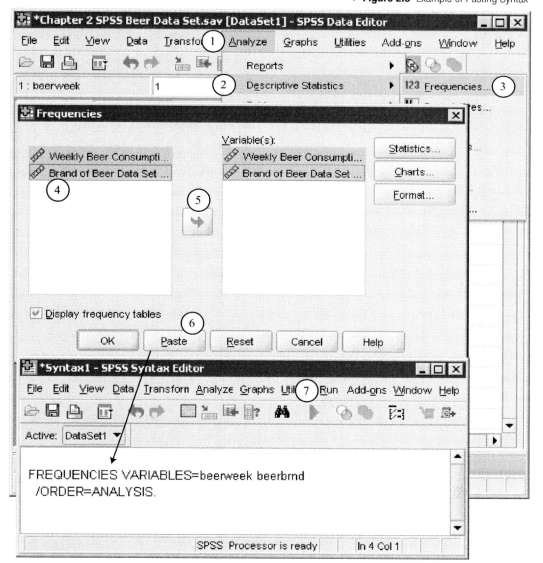

A NOTE ON THE STUDENT VERSION OF SPSS

As we noted previously, the student version of SPSS does not include the Syntax Editor. If you are using the student version, you will not able use the **Paste** options to save a record of your analyses. When using the student version, it is good practice to carefully note the details of the analyses you conduct so that you can accurately reproduce them in the future.

CREATING, SAVING, AND OPENING A SYNTAX SHEET

If no syntax sheet is open when we paste our first procedure, then SPSS automatically opens an untitled sheet. Later we can save the syntax as a syntax file, which has the file extension ".sps" (short for SPSS syntax file). If a syntax sheet is already open, SPSS will paste syntax to the bottom of the currently opened syntax sheet. If multiple syntax sheets are open, SPSS will paste to the sheet that was opened first. To create a new syntax sheet, select **New** from the **File** pull-down menu and then select **Syntax...** from the side menu.

Once you have created a new syntax sheet, you should periodically save your syntax file. The procedures for saving a syntax file are the same as the procedures described for saving data files. Just remember that you must be in the Syntax Editor to save a syntax file.

Existing syntax files can be opened from any of the SPSS windows using the **Open** option from the **File** pull-down menu. Just be sure to select **Syntax...** from the side menu. Otherwise, the desired file may not appear as an option.

EDITING SYNTAX

Syntax can be altered by typing, and it can be moved and removed using the copy, cut, and paste commands identical to those found in most word processors and spreadsheet programs. This becomes quite useful when you are running the same type of analysis many times with only slight alterations. For example, you may want to run the same statistical test multiple times but use a different dependent variable each time. You could point-and-click your way through each desired analysis. Alternatively, you could point-and-click your way through one analysis and Paste the syntax. This syntax can be copied and pasted (using the **Paste** command from the **Edit** pull-down menu), and then the variable names in the syntax can be changed by hand. It may take you some time to become comfortable working with syntax files, but once you do, it will really pay off.

ADDING COMMENTS TO SYNTAX

One way to make syntax a little easier to work with is to add comments that explain what is requested by different parts of the syntax. Your comments will also appear in the output and can help you distinguish between the different analyses you have requested. You can add comments to syntax by typing an asterisk (*) at the beginning of lines containing comments. The asterisk will tell SPSS not to read that line. Without the asterisk, SPSS will create an error message when it tries to read your comment. A comment should end with a period one space after the end of the comment. For example:

　　* This analysis requests the frequencies for the beer data .

SPSS calls this period a *command terminator*.

RUNNING ANALYSES FROM SYNTAX

To run an analysis or multiple analyses from the syntax box, highlight the syntax for the desired analyses and then press the play button on the tool bar. The play button [⑦ in Figure 2.6] resembles the play button on most music or video players (arrow pointing to the right). Analyses can also be run from the **Run** pull-down menu, where there are four options: **All** (runs all analyses on all syntax sheets that are open), **Selection** (runs highlighted area), **Current** (runs all analyses on the currently active syntax sheet), and **To End** (runs analyses on the current syntax sheet that fall below the point where the cursor is currently positioned). Finally, you can run selected syntax by highlighting the desired analyses and right-clicking on the selected syntax. From the list of options that appear in the pop-up menu, select **Run Current**.

OUTPUT FILES

Any time you run an analysis (e.g., Descriptives, Frequencies, or Chi-Square), the results will be presented in a separate window titled SPSS Viewer. Like syntax, this is a separate file that will need to be saved. The extension for these types of files is ".spv" (short for SPSS output viewer).

NAVIGATING THE OUTPUT

Figure 2.7 presents an output file where six different analyses have been requested. The SPSS Viewer is split into two parts: the Outline View [labeled Ⓐ in Figure 2.7] and the Output Display [labeled Ⓑ]. The Outline View allows us to quickly move from one analysis to another by clicking on the part of the analysis you wish to view. For example, in Figure 2.7 the **Frequencies** analysis ① is selected and the first part of the analysis (labeled **Statistics**) is presented in the Output Display field. Similarly, you can move to the first graph you requested by left-clicking on the **Graph** analysis heading ② of the outline.

The Outline View also allows you to collapse and expand parts of analyses or a whole analysis by double-clicking on the desired analysis heading. For example, in Figure 2.7, two of the **Graph** analyses ③ have been collapsed. When analyses or parts of analyses are collapsed, they will not appear in the Output Display field, nor will they appear on printouts of the output. Collapsed parts of the output can be expanded again by double-clicking on the collapsed analysis heading in the Outline View. Analyses can also be deleted from the output file by selecting the desired analysis heading and then using the delete button on the keyboard. You can also copy and paste analyses to different parts of the Outline View in order to change the order in which they appear in the Output Display and in any printouts produced.

The Output Display field can also be used to navigate through the output that you generate. By clicking and dragging the scroll bar Ⓒ to the right of the Output Display, you can move up and down through the output. By left-clicking a part of the output in the Output Display, it becomes active and highlights that part of the analysis in the Outline View. This is a quick way to make sure that you are really looking at the output that you want. It is especially useful when you have conducted several similar analyses with similar variables.

OUTPUT LOGS

In newer versions of SPSS, the syntax associated with an analysis is displayed in a **Log** preceding the analysis output. This syntax can serve as a record of the analysis you have

Figure 2.7 Navigating the Output Viewer

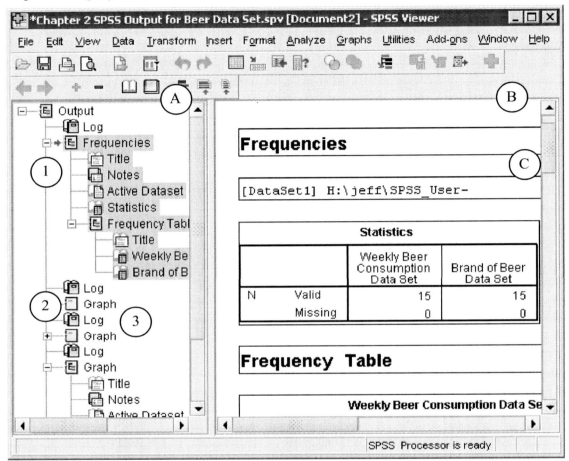

run (including the specific options that were requested), and these analyses can be duplicated by copying the syntax in the Output Display field, pasting it into the Syntax Editor, and running the syntax from there. As with any other part of the output, double-clicking on a **Log** in the Outline View will remove it from the Output Display field, and it will not appear when you print the output file.

PRINTING OUTPUT

To print the output, first ensure that you have all the desired analyses expanded (and all undesired analyses collapsed) in the Outline View. You can use either the printer icon on the Output Navigator toolbar, or you can select the **Print...** option from the **File** pull-down menu. In the **Print** window ensure that the **All visible output** option has been selected. Click **OK** to finish.

Adding a Header to Printouts. Having hard copies of your output is quite useful. However, you will often print multiple versions of your analyses, especially if you find mistakes or add more cases/people to your data set. It is helpful to be able to label your output with identifying information that keeps you from mixing together output pages of other analyses. You can label your output by using a *page header*. In a page header, you can include the time and date the analysis was printed, the filename of the output file, and any custom information you would like to add.

PROCEDURE FOR ADDING A PAGE HEADER:

(1) In the SPSS Viewer, select the **File** pull-down menu.

(2) Select **Page Attributes....** This will open the **Page Attributes** dialogue box.

(3) & (4) Add the Date, Time, and Filename by left-clicking the icons below the Header field.

- You can also choose whether the header will be centered, flush right (right-justified) or flush left (left-justified).
- Custom information can be included by typing in the header field.

(5) Left-click **OK** to finish.

▶**Figure 2.8** Adding Headers to Printed Output

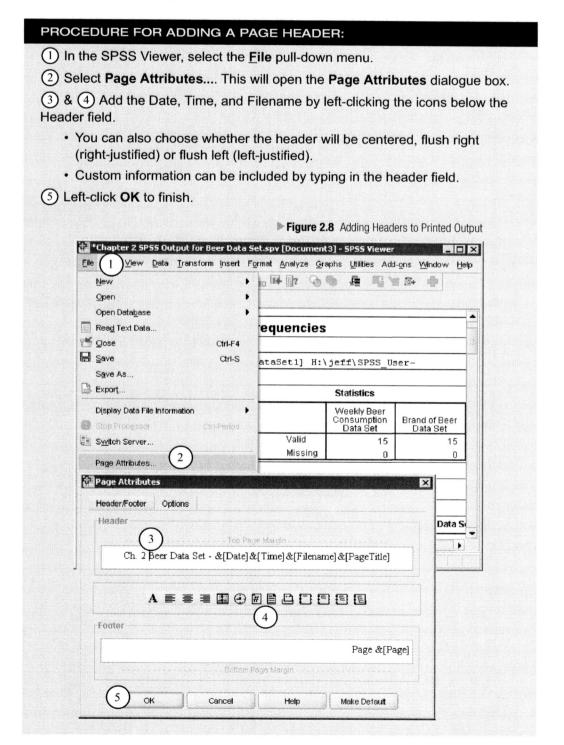

In this example, the custom information (Ch 2. Beer Data Set-), the date, time, and filename have been added to the header. When adding headers, you may notice that the **Page Attributes** default includes the **[Page Title]**. However, you will not have page titles unless you have added them to the Outline View using the option to add a **New Page Title** located in the **Insert** drop down menu. The page titles are the equivalent of the custom information that was added to this example. We recommend adding the information to the header rather than the page title, as it requires fewer steps.

The header you add will now appear at the top of every page of the printed output; however, the header will not appear anywhere in the Outline View or the Output Display field when you are working with the Output Viewer.

SAVING AND OPENING OUTPUT

Once you have generated output and ensured that your analyses were run correctly, you should save the output file.

PROCEDURE FOR SAVING OUTPUT FOR THE FIRST TIME:

- In the SPSS Viewer, select the **File** pull-down menu.
- Select the **Save** or **Save as...** option. This will open the **Save As** dialogue box.
- Left-click the boxed arrow on the right of the **Look in:** field and navigate through the file tree to select the drive [e.g., C: (the hard drive) or E: (an external storage device)] and directory (folder) in which you want to save your output.
- Type the name you want to give the new output file in the **File name:** field.

PROCEDURE FOR OPENING AN EXISTING OUTPUT FILE:

- From any SPSS window, select **Open** from the **File** pull-down menu.
- Select **Output...** from the side menu.
- In the **Open File** dialogue box, ensure that the **Files of type:** option is set to **SPSS (*.spv)**. Otherwise, the desired file may not appear as an option.
- Choose the desired directory from the desired drive and then select the desired file and left-click **Open.**

SUMMARY

This chapter introduced many of the most common operations used in SPSS: creating and retrieving data files, working with syntax files, and working with SPSS output. As you progress to more advanced chapters, you may wish to periodically review the procedures outlined here. You may also discover that there are usually several different ways to accomplish the same objective (some you may like, some you may not). There is no right or wrong way to conduct a procedure as long as it does what you need it to do. There is space here at the end of the chapter to make notes about the procedures you use most often and the ones you discover. It will be helpful for you to keep track of what works for you, what does not, and why.

PRACTICE EXERCISES

1. What are the three windows of SPSS?

2. Within the Data Editor, in which view can data be entered?

3. Each of the following variable names has at least one problem, identify the problem(s) for each:

   2_beer_week

   Cartoon Liking

   Cal&Hobs_Liking.

   beer.brand-2

4. For each of the following descriptions of research variables, which variables should have variable labels and which should have value labels?

   • Participant gender/sex.

   • Number of hours each participant reads cartoons per week.

   • Type of cartoon most frequently read by participants.

   • Participant's rating of how attractive Hagar is on a 7-point numerical scales (1 = very unattractive; 7 = very attractive).

NOTES:

Finding Sums

T his chapter covers procedures for obtaining many of the summed values that form the foundation of most statistical calculations. These procedures will produce values that are identical to the hand calculations typically required in introductory and advanced statistics courses and can be used to check your own hand calculations. Specifically, we demonstrate methods for finding ΣX (sum of X) and ΣY (sum of Y). This chapter also discusses how to use the compute command to generate new variables by changing existing variables and then finding their sums, specifically: ΣX^2, ΣY^2, $\Sigma(X-1)$, $\Sigma(Y-1)^2$, and ΣXY. Even if you have already done so, it may be a good idea for you to review Chapter 2, both before you proceed with this section and as a reference as you progress through this chapter.

SETTING UP THE DATA

For the following examples, we turn to Cartoon 3.1. Assume that a researcher is interested in the degree to which soliciting donations from penguins influences the total amount of contributions (in dollars) collected by Krishna pilgrims. Self-report data from

▷ **Cartoon 3.1**

© Berkeley Breathed, dist. By The Washington Post. Reprinted with Permission.

▶**Table 3.1** Penguin Solicitation Data

Pilgrim	X Independent Variable: Number of Penguins Solicited for Donations	Y Dependent Variable: Total Donations Collected (in Dollars)
1	1	25
2	2	20
3	3	16
4	4	14
5	4	12
6	5	8
7	5	6
8	7	3
9	8	1
10	9	1

▶**Figure 3.1** Variable View for Penguin Solicitation Data

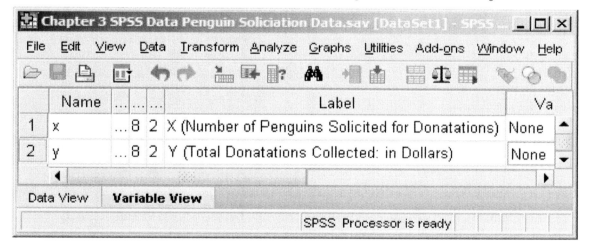

ten spiritual pilgrims are presented in Table 3.1. The first column of data lists the participant numbers used to identify each pilgrim whose performance was measured. The second column, labeled *X*, represents the independent variable, the number of penguins each pilgrim solicited for donations. The third column, labeled *Y*, represents the dependent variable, the total donations collected by each pilgrim. As with all of the SPSS examples in this book, the first step is to set up the data set in the SPSS Data Editor by defining the variables. Figure 3.1 shows the Variable View of the SPSS Data Editor. We have created two new variables named **x** and **y** to correspond with the independent variable (Number of Penguins Solicited for Donations) and the dependent variable (Total Donations Collected: in Dollars), respectively.

Figure 3.2 presents the Data View of the SPSS Data Editor. Here, we have entered the data for all ten of the spiritual pilgrims in our data set for the two variables we are investigating. Remember that columns in the Data View of the Data Editor represent the variables and the rows represent each case (e.g., subject, observation, unit, pilgrim, etc.).

▶ **Figure 3.2** Data View for Penguin Solicitation Data

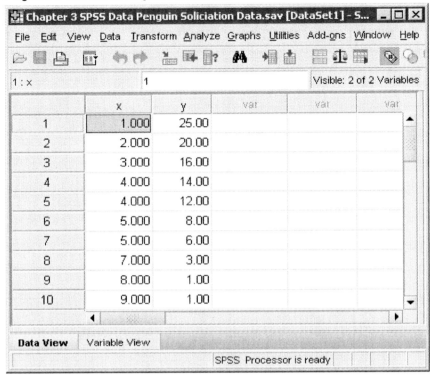

RUNNING THE ANALYSIS

In this first example, we present the steps for obtaining sums using the Descriptives analysis, which is the simplest way to obtain descriptive information about one or more variables. In this example, sums are obtained for variables **x** and **y,** which represent the total number of penguins solicited and the total number of dollars collected by all of the spiritual pilgrims in the sample, respectively. Finding sums represents an important first step in developing an understanding of the data you are working with. It will also be used to generate other statistics, such as averages and measures of variability, which are covered in later chapters. Note that SPSS calls these *Descriptive Statistics*, but remember that whether these values are referred to as parameters or statistics depends on whether your data reflects a population of scores or a sample of scores, respectively.

PROCEDURE FOR RUNNING THE **DESCRIPTIVES...** ANALYSIS:

① Select the **Analyze** pull-down menu.

② Select **Descriptive Statistics**.

③ Select **Descriptives...** from the side menu. This will open the **Descriptives** dialogue box.

④ & ⑤ Enter the variables **x** and **y** in the **Variable(s):** field by either double-clicking on each variable or selecting each variable and left-clicking on the boxed arrow pointing to the right.

⑥ To select the desired descriptive information, select **Options...** .This will open the **Descriptives: Options** dialogue box.

Here, you will need to check the options you want. Notice that the **Mean, Std. Deviation, Minimum, and Maximum** options are automatically selected.

⑦ In our example, we have deselected these options and have checked the **Sum** option. This will simplify the resulting output.

⑧ To return to the **Descriptives** dialogue box, left-click **Continue.**

⑨ Finally, double-check your variables and either select **OK** to run or **Paste** to create syntax to run at a later time.

If you selected the paste option from the procedure above, you should have generated the following syntax:

DESCRIPTIVES
  VARIABLES=x y
  /STATISTICS=SUM .

The procedures for running analyses from the syntax editor are described in Chapter 2.

▶ **Figure 3.3** Running the **Descriptives...** Analysis

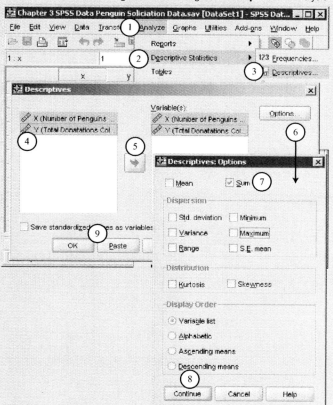

READING THE OUTPUT

As presented in Figure 3.4, the requested descriptive information for each of the variables (in this case the sums of **x** and **y**) is presented within the columns of the Descriptive Statistics table. Each row of data within the table represents a different variable and is labeled with the Variable Label that you gave each variable (if you did not provide variable labels, then the variables will be identified by their less descriptive variable name). In our current example, the first column of data reports the number of cases for each variable (**N**). As you can see in Figure 3.4, we have data for all 10 pilgrims for both variables **x** and **y**. The last row of this column [labeled **Valid N (listwise)**] reports the number of cases (pilgrims) that are not missing any data. This information will be presented every time you run the descriptive analyses, regardless of whether you request it. In this example, we are not missing any data, so Valid N (listwise) is reported as 10. However, if we did not know the total amount of donations collected (**y**) for one pilgrim, then the **Valid N (listwise)** would be 9 instead of 10. Similarly, if we were also missing data for a different pilgrim for variable **x** or **y**, then the **Valid N** would be 8 instead of 10. The second column in the **Descriptives Statistics** table presents the data we requested, the sums of variables **x** and **y**. We obtained the values 48 and 106, respectively.

▶ **Figure 3.4** Output for ΣX and ΣY for Penguin Solicitation Data

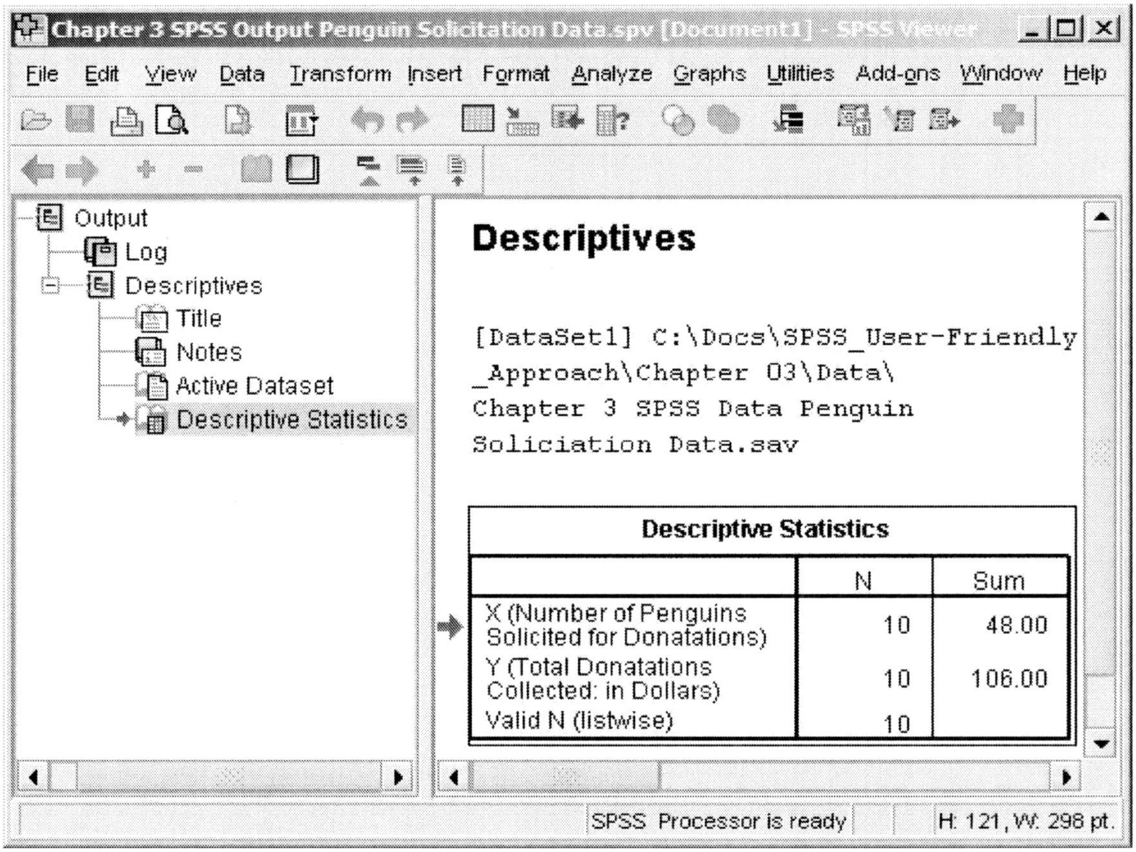

Descriptives

[DataSet1] C:\Docs\SPSS_User-Friendly
_Approach\Chapter 03\Data\
Chapter 3 SPSS Data Penguin
Soliciation Data.sav

Descriptive Statistics

	N	Sum
X (Number of Penguins Solicited for Donatations)	10	48.00
Y (Total Donatations Collected: in Dollars)	10	106.00
Valid N (listwise)	10	

SPSS Processor is ready | H: 121, W: 298 pt.

CHECKING YOUR HAND CALCULATIONS

As you can see, running these analyses can be an accurate way of double-checking the work that you do by hand. If the SPSS output and your hand calculations differ, it means one of them is incorrect. It is probably best first to check the data that you entered in the Data Editor to ensure that it is correct before you start redoing the more time consuming hand calculations. If the SPSS data set seems correct, then check your calculations and see if you can identify where you made your mistake.

FINDING ΣX^2, ΣY^2, AND OTHER COMPLEX SUMMATIONS

Often we are interested in obtaining sums, but the values to be summed are the result of some kind of mathematical operation that is applied to each individual score before we sum them. For example, the expression ΣX^2 tells us to square each score for variable X before we sum it. SPSS allows us to do this by creating a new variable using the **Compute Variable...** procedure. The use of this procedure is illustrated below for ΣX^2.

PROCEDURE FOR COMPUTING VARIABLES:

① Select **Transform** from the pull-down menu.

② Select **Compute Variable...** . This will open the **Compute Variable** dialogue box.

③ Enter the desired variable name for the new variable in the **Target Variable:** field.

- In this case, we have named our new variable **x_sqrd**.

④ To give the new variable a variable label, left-click on the **Type & Label** button. This will open the **Compute Variable: Type and Label** dialogue box.

⑤ Enter the desired variable label [in this case: **X squared (Number of Penguins Solicited: Squared Before Summing)**] into the **Label:** field.

Note that the mathematical equation used to create the variable can be used as the variable label by selecting the **Use expression as label** option.

⑥ Left-click **Continue** to return to the **Compute Variable** dialogue box.

⑦ The final steps involve writing the mathematical equation (the numerical expression) that will compute the value of interest. In this case we want to square variable **x**.

- First, enter the variable name of the variable to be altered in the **Numeric Expression:** field.

- Next, write the desired mathematical equation. In this case, we use the following equation: **x**2**. In SPSS ** is the exponential operator.

- We could also compute our desired X^2 variable using this equation: **x*x**. Like most computer programs, SPSS treats * as the multiplication operator.

⑧ Finally, double-check your variables and equations, and either select **OK** to run or **Paste** to create syntax to run at a later time.

If you selected the paste option from the procedure above, you should have generated the following syntax:

COMPUTE X_sqrd = x ** 2 .
  VARIABLE LABELS X_sqrd 'X squared (Number of Penguins Solicited: Squared Before Summing)'.
  EXECUTE .

▶ **Figure 3.5** Using **Compute Variable...** to Create X^2

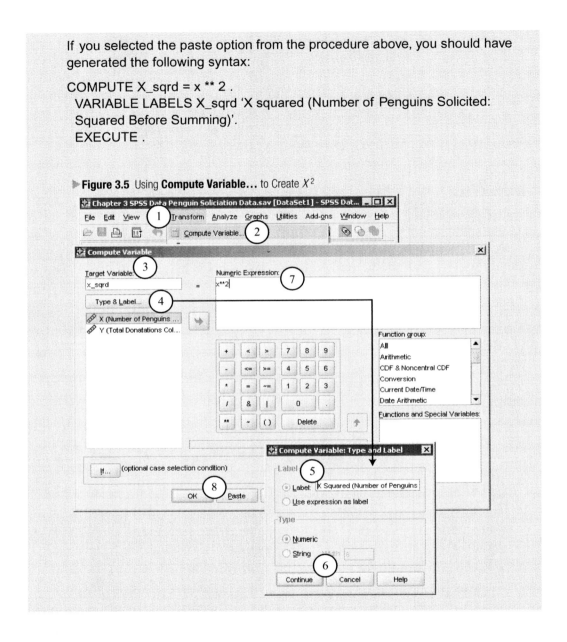

We can create other complex variables using the appropriate numerical expressions, which are presented in Table 3.2. The first column lists the variable names for the newly created variable. The second column presents the new variable labels. The numerical expressions used to create the new variables are presented in the last column.

After running the desired compute statements, the new variables are added to the Data Editor. Figure 3.6 presents the Variable View and Data View of the SPSS Data Editor after running the five compute statements presented in Table 3.2. As each compute statement is run, the newly created variable is inserted into the next available row of the Variable View and the next available column of the Data View. To keep the new variables for future use, you will need to save the data file before closing.

▶ **Table 3.2** More Compute Variable Procedures

New Variable Name	New Variable Label	Numerical Expression
y_sqrd	Y Squared (Total Donations Collected: Squared Before Summing)	y**2
xminus1	1 Subtracted from each X Before Summing	x-1
ymn1sqrd	1 Subtracted from each Y and then Squared Before Summing	(y-1)**2
xy	Each X is Multiplied by its Corresponding Y Value Before Summing	x*y

▶ **Figure 3.6** Variable View and Data View with Newly Computed Variables

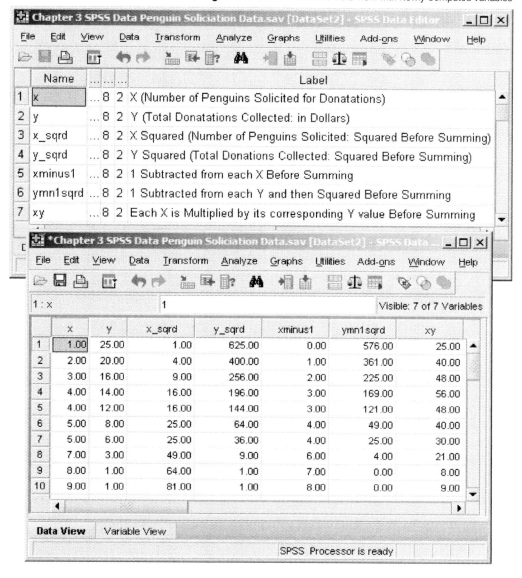

▶**Figure 3.7** ΣX, ΣY, and Newly Created Variables Using Penguin Solicitation Data

Descriptive Statistics

	N	Sum
X (Number of Penguins Solicited for Donatations)	10	48.00
Y (Total Donatations Collected: in Dollars)	10	106.00
X Squared (Number of Penguins Solicited: Squared Before Summing)	10	290.00
Y Squared (Total Donations Collected: Squared Before Summing)	10	1732.00
1 Subtracted from each X Before Summing	10	38.00
1 Subtracted from each Y and then Squared Before Summing	10	1530.00
Each X is Multiplied by its corresponding Y value Before Summing	10	325.00
Valid N (listwise)	10	

FIND THE SUMS AND INTERPRET THE OUTPUT

Once SPSS computes the desired variables, the sums for each new variable can be obtained by repeating the steps for running descriptive statistics presented earlier (illustrated in Figure 3.3) and adding the newly created variables to the **Variable(s):** field. As before, the analyses can be run by selecting **OK** or it can be saved to run later by selecting **Paste.** Selecting **Paste** should provide the following syntax:

```
DESCRIPTIVES
    VARIABLES=x y x_sqrd y_sqrd xminus1 ymn1sqrd xy
    /STATISTICS=SUM .
```

This syntax requests the sums for the original **x** and **y** variables as well as the sums for the newly created variables.

Figure 3.7 presents the output obtained by running the Descriptives analysis. Again, the rows present the data for each variable, which are identified using their respective variable labels.

MORE COMPUTE OPERATORS

Table 3.3 presents other mathematical operators that SPSS uses in compute statements. As you become more familiar with SPSS, you will find many of these operators quite useful. These operators can be used separately or in combination to produce a variety of

▶Table 3.3 Compute Variable Mathematical Operators

Operators		
+ addition	< greater than	~ not
- subtraction	> less than	~= not equal to
* multiplication	<= greater than or equal to	& and
/ division	>= less than or equal to	* or
** exponentiation	= equal to	( ) Grouping operator, e.g., order of operations.

data transformations. The most common use of compute statements by researchers is to combine scores from multiple variables, such as test items or questions on a survey, to form a single score (typically a sum or an average). For example:

var1 + var2 + var3 will produce a new variable that is the sum of three variables.

(var1 + var2 + var3)/3 will produce a new variable that is the average of three variables.

SPSS also provides functions that are operator shortcuts. For example:

var1 + var2 + var3 can also be obtained with the function: *SUM(var1, var2, var3)*.

(var1 + var2 + var3)/3 can also be obtained with the function: *MEAN(var1, var2, var3)*.

SUMMARY

This chapter presented methods for finding the sums of simple variables (e.g., X and Y) and complex variables (obtained by transforming existing simple variables) using the **Compute Variable...** operation. These procedures can be used to check the hand calculations typically required in introductory and advanced statistics courses. This chapter also introduced advanced compute operators that you may find useful as you become a more sophisticated user of SPSS.

PRACTICE EXERCISES

1. For two variables named R and Q, write numeric expressions using SPSS operators that would produce new variables which when summed would produce the following:

a. ΣRQ

b. ΣR^2

c. ΣQ^2

d. $\Sigma(R-1)$

e. $\Sigma(R^2 Q^2)$

f. $\Sigma(RQ)^2$

g. $\Sigma(Q-1)^2$

h. $\Sigma((R-1)^2(R-1)^2)$

Frequency Distributions and Charts

This chapter covers procedures for obtaining frequency distributions and charts using the <u>F</u>requencies... and <u>G</u>raphs options in SPSS. Specifically, we demonstrate methods for summarizing and visually displaying frequency data for variables representing groups and variables representing scores. We also present methods for creating histograms, line charts, and pie charts for variables representing scores, and bar charts and pie charts for group variables. Finally, we present procedures for plotting the average scores of different groups in a single graph.

SETTING UP THE DATA

Cartoon 4.1 presents nine types of college teachers (certainly not an exhaustive list), and it serves as the backdrop for the examples in this chapter. Assume that we have drawn a random sample of 20 students from a medium-sized college and asked each participant to categorize the person that teaches the first class they have during the week. Participants were given six categories to choose from: Steady Droner, Disdainful TA, Genius from Another Dimension, Ol' Doom and Gloom, Single Theory Maniac, and the Beloved Statistics Teacher. Participants were then asked to rate the professor/instructor on a 7-point numerical scale (1 = poor teaching, 7 = exceptional teaching). Figure 4.1 on page 38 presents the Variable View of the SPSS Data Editor where we have defined two variables. The first variable **(prof_type)** represents the different instructor categories, for which value labels have been provided. As you examine this variable, keep in mind that the order in which groups are listed and the numbers used to represent them are arbitrary, and different orders or numbers can be used without affecting the meaning of the data. The second variable **(stu_evals)** represents each student's ratings of the professor/instructor. Figure 4.2 on page 39 presents the Data View of the SPSS Data Editor, where the data is entered for all 20 students. Remember that the columns in the data view represent the variables, and the rows contain the data from particular subjects or cases. In this example, each row contains data collected from a particular student. For example, the first student has an instructor who is a "Steady Droner," and she gave the instructor a rating of 2 out of 7. Similarly, the last student classified their instructor as a "Beloved Statistics Teacher" and gave the instructor a rating of 7 out of 7.

▷ Cartoon 4.1

OBTAINING FREQUENCY TABLES

RUNNING THE ANALYSES

In the procedure box on page 40, we present the steps for running frequency analyses with both score variables (**stu_eval**) and group variables (**prof_type**). Frequency tables

▶ **Figure 4.1** Variable View for College Professor Data Set

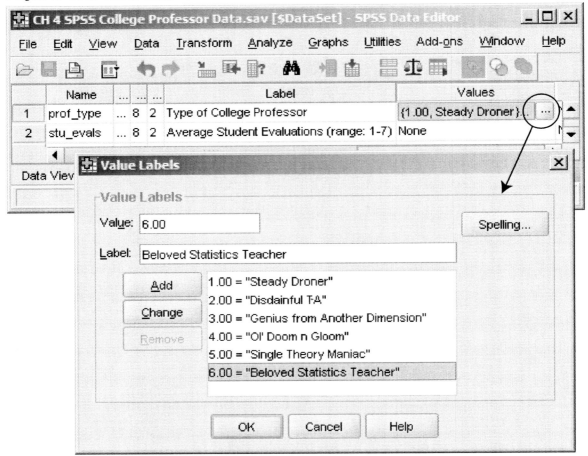

are useful for efficiently summarizing a large amount of data and describing the characteristics of the sample. Frequency tables can also be used for screening data to make sure that it was entered correctly. Specifically, frequency tables will help you see missing data and any scores that are "out of range," like having a 9 on 7-point scale.

It is possible to obtain descriptive statistics (e.g., the sum of X or Y) when running the **Frequencies...** procedure by selecting them from the **Statistics...** options. However, remember that such information is quite meaningless for variables representing groups since the numerical values are arbitrary. For example, the sum of **stu_evals** will indicate the total number of rating points awarded to all of the professors/instructors as a group, but the sum of **prof_type** would not provide any interpretable information.

READING THE FREQUENCIES OUTPUT

The Frequency Analysis Output is presented in Figure 4.4 on page 41. This output consists of two parts. The first part, labeled **Frequencies**, presents any statistics that were requested when running the frequency analysis. If no statistics were requested, then only the sample size will be presented for each variable. The **N Valid**, presented in the first row,

▶**Figure 4.2** Data View for College Professor Data Set

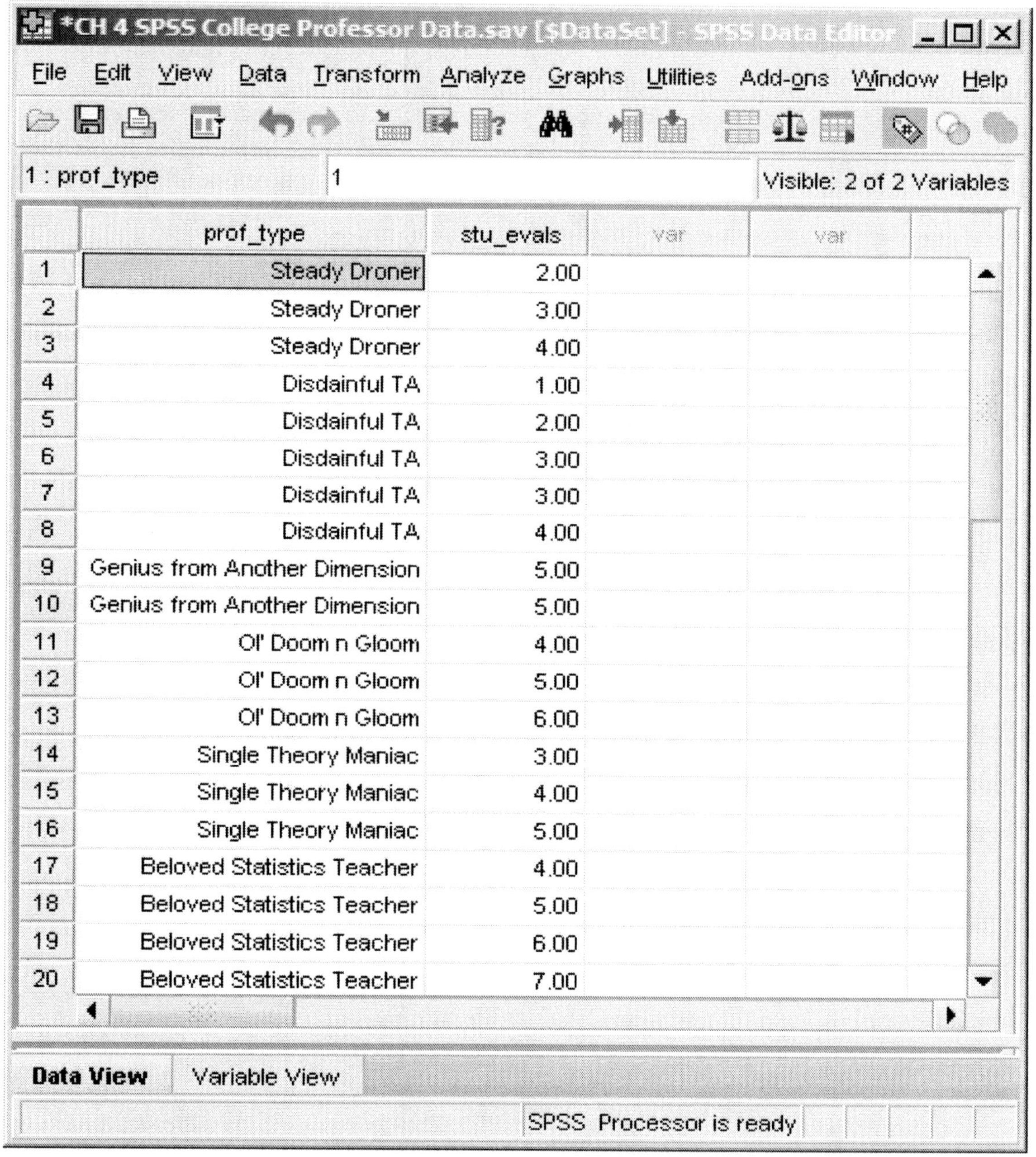

	prof_type	stu_evals	var	var
1	Steady Droner	2.00		
2	Steady Droner	3.00		
3	Steady Droner	4.00		
4	Disdainful TA	1.00		
5	Disdainful TA	2.00		
6	Disdainful TA	3.00		
7	Disdainful TA	3.00		
8	Disdainful TA	4.00		
9	Genius from Another Dimension	5.00		
10	Genius from Another Dimension	5.00		
11	Ol' Doom n Gloom	4.00		
12	Ol' Doom n Gloom	5.00		
13	Ol' Doom n Gloom	6.00		
14	Single Theory Maniac	3.00		
15	Single Theory Maniac	4.00		
16	Single Theory Maniac	5.00		
17	Beloved Statistics Teacher	4.00		
18	Beloved Statistics Teacher	5.00		
19	Beloved Statistics Teacher	6.00		
20	Beloved Statistics Teacher	7.00		

*CH 4 SPSS College Professor Data.sav [$DataSet] - SPSS Data Editor

File   Edit   View   Data   Transform   Analyze   Graphs   Utilities   Add-ons   Window   Help

1 : prof_type   1   Visible: 2 of 2 Variables

Data View   Variable View

SPSS Processor is ready

indicates the number of cases (in this example students) for which you have data. The row labeled **Missing** indicates the number of cases for which no data are available. In our data, we have 20 students reporting data for both variables and no student is missing data for either variable.

The second part of the output, labeled **Frequency Table**, presents frequency information for each variable requested. The first frequency table in Figure 4.4, labeled

PROCEDURE FOR RUNNING FREQUENCY ANALYSES:

1. Select **Analyze** from the pull-down menu.
2. Select **Descriptive Statistics**.
3. Select **Frequencies...** from the side menu. This will open the **Frequencies** dialogue box.
4. & 5. Enter the variables of interest (**prof_type** and **stu_evals**) in the **Variable(s):** field by either double-clicking on each variable or selecting each variable and left-clicking on the boxed arrow.
6. Finally, double-check your variables and either select **OK** to run or **Paste** to create syntax to run at a later time.

If you selected the paste option from the procedure above, you should have generated the following syntax:

FREQUENCIES VARIABLES=prof_type stu_evals
/ORDER= ANALYSIS .

▶**Figure 4.3** Running Frequency Analyses for Quantitative and Qualitative Data

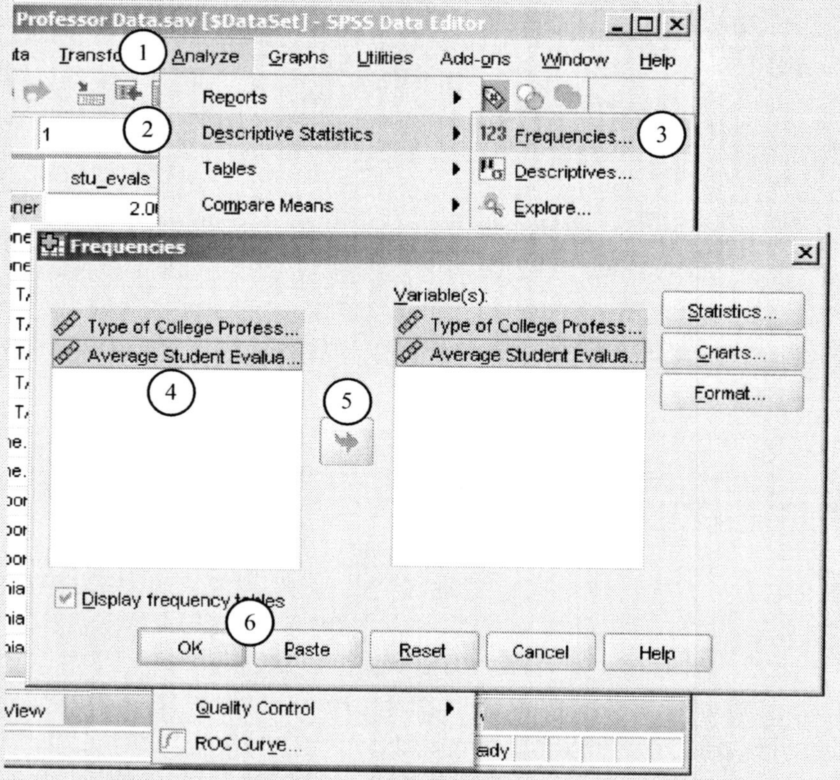

Frequencies

▶▶**Figure 4.4** Output for
College Professor Data

Statistics

		Type of College Professor	Average Student Evaluations (range: 1-7)
N	Valid	20	20
	Missing	0	0

Frequency Table

Type of College Professor

		Frequency	Percent	Valid Percent	Cumulative Percent
Valid	Steady Droner	3	15.0	15.0	15.0
	Disdainful TA	5	25.0	25.0	40.0
	Genius from Another Dimension	2	10.0	10.0	50.0
	Ol' Doom n Gloom	3	15.0	15.0	65.0
	Single Theory Maniac	3	15.0	15.0	80.0
	Beloved Statistics Teacher	4	20.0	20.0	100.0
	Total	20	100.0	100.0	

Average Student Evaluations (range: 1-7)

		Frequency	Percent	Valid Percent	Cumulative Percent
Valid	1	1	5.0	5.0	5.0
	2	2	10.0	10.0	15.0
	3	4	20.0	20.0	35.0
	4	5	25.0	25.0	60.0
	5	5	25.0	25.0	85.0
	6	2	10.0	10.0	95.0
	7	1	5.0	5.0	100.0
	Total	20	100.0	100.0	

Type of College Professor, presents the frequency distribution for the six different types of college professors. The column labeled **Frequency** lists the number of students that reported having each type of professor. The most frequently reported type of professor/instructor was the Disdainful TA (**Frequency** = 5), and the least frequently reported was the Genius from Another Dimension (**Frequency** = 2). The column labeled **Percent** reports the percentage of students who reported having each professor type. These percentages represent the group frequencies relative to the total sample size. They are obtained by dividing each frequency by the total number of cases, regardless of whether any data is missing. In contrast, the third column presents the **Valid Percent**, which reports the frequency relative to the number cases for which no data is missing (the **Valid N**). In this example, the values presented in the **Valid Percent** and the **Percent** columns are the same, because no participants are missing any data. However, when you have variables for which there are missing cases, the two values will differ and you have to think carefully about which percentage is more appropriate to use.

The final column of the SPSS frequency table, labeled **Cumulative Percent**, lists for each group the total of the **Valid Percent** values that have accumulated up through and including the given group. With respect to types of college professors, we see that a little less than one-sixth of the students (15%) has a Steady Droner for the first class of the week; 40% have either the Steady Droner or a Disdainful TA; 50% have either the Droner, the TA, or the Pan-Dimensional Genius; nearly two thirds (65%) have either the Droner, TA, Genius, or Ol' Doom and Gloom; and so forth.

The second frequency table in Figure 4.4, labeled **Average Student Evaluations (range: 1–7)**, presents the frequency distribution for the students' evaluations of their college teachers. Each row presents the **Frequency**, **Percent** (based on total sample size), **Valid Percent** (based on the **N Valid**), and **Cumulative Percent** (based on the **Valid Percent**) for each of the seven possible evaluation scores. Looking at the frequencies and percentages, it appears that the most frequent scores are the ones located toward the middle of the range of scores. The scores 3, 4, and 5 had frequencies of 4, 5, and 5, respectively. Similarly, the cumulative percentage shows that 60% of the sample rated their first instructor of the week as average or lower (scores of 4 or lower).

As a final note on the frequency tables, if you are using SPSS to check frequency tables you have constructed by using hand calculations, your cumulative percentages may not exactly match the SPSS values. This often occurs because SPSS displays only one value after the decimal, rounding the displayed values to the nearest tenth. However, your hand calculations should be relatively close to the SPSS results. Major discrepancies between the two should be cause for concern. If you find a discrepancy, remember to first check your data in the SPSS Data Editor. If the data seem correct, then double-check your hand calculations.

OBTAINING FREQUENCY CHARTS

In the following examples, we present the procedures used to create common charts used to visually display both score and group variables. We will first present procedures for creating histograms and line charts, which are frequency charts for score variables. This is followed by procedures for creating bar and pie charts, which are frequency charts for group variables. Though histograms, pie charts, and bar charts can be obtained from the **Charts…** options of the frequency analyses, we will focus on the use of the **Graphs** options from the main pull-down menu as they offer more options.

HISTOGRAMS

Histograms are useful for displaying frequency information about variables that represent a range of scores. We should note that it is generally considered inappropriate to use histograms to display group data because the bars of the histogram touch, which can imply an uninterrupted continuum of scores. SPSS generally assumes you know what you want and will allow you to request histograms for group variables, but the resulting chart can be difficult to interpret.

PROCEDURE FOR OBTAINING A HISTOGRAM:

① Select the **Graphs** pull-down menu.

② Select **Legacy Dialogs**.

③ Select **Histogram...** from the side menu. This will open the **Histogram** dialogue box.

(Note that the **Panel by** option is not shown in the figure due to space limitations.)

④ Enter the variable representing the scores of interest **(stu_evals)** in the **Variable:** field by selecting the variable and left-clicking on the boxed arrow pointing to the **Variable:** field.

⑤ To include the normal curve in your histogram, check the **Display normal curve** option.

⑥ To add titles to the chart, left-click the **Titles...** button, which will open the **Titles** dialogue box.

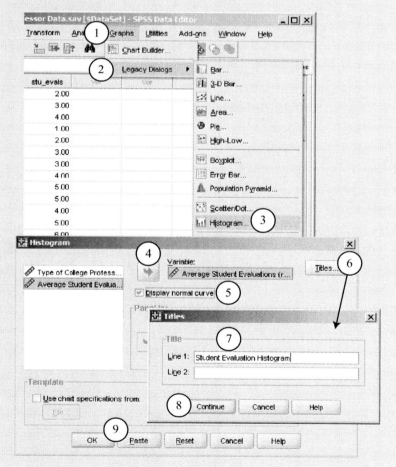

▶ **Figure 4.5**
Obtaining
Histograms

⑦ Type the text of the title in the **Line 1:** field. (Note that the **Subtitle** and **Footnote** fields from the **Titles** dialogue box are not shown in the figure due to space limitations.)

⑧ Left-click **Continue** to return to the **Histogram** dialogue box.

⑨ Double-check your variables and either select **OK** to run or **Paste** to create syntax to run at a later time.

If you selected the paste option from the procedure above, you should have generated the following syntax:

```
GRAPH
  /HISTOGRAM(NORMAL)=stu_evals .
  /TITLE='Student Evaluation Histogram' .
```

Figure 4.6 presents the resulting histogram for the students' ratings of the professor/instructor who teaches their first class of the week. In this histogram, each bar represents a score for which the labels appear on the horizontal axis *(X)*. The frequency or number of cases with a given score is represented by the vertical axis *(Y)*.

▶**Figure 4.6**
Histogram for
College Professor
Data

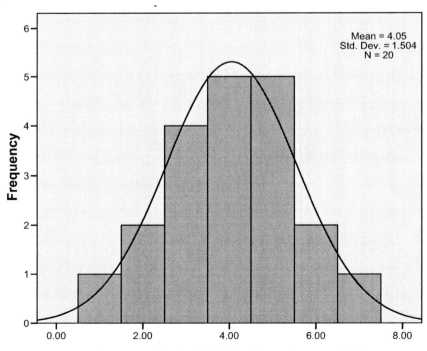

Student Evaluation Histogram

Mean = 4.05
Std. Dev. = 1.504
N = 20

Average Student Evaluations (range: 1-7)

Like the frequency table, the student evaluation histogram shows that the most frequently occurring scores are the middle scores (3, 4, and 5), with frequencies of 4, 5, and 5. The histogram also provides some of the most frequently used statistics: the mean, the standard deviation, and the total sample size. Further, the histogram displays an overlay of the normal curve, so the obtained distribution of scores can be compared visually to an ideal distribution. From the overlay of the normal curve, you can get a rough idea of whether your distribution is skewed (not-symmetrical) or kurtotic (overly flat or peaked). In this case, the distribution seems to fit well with the normal curve.

When the variable of interest represents a broad range of scores, the bars of the histogram will represent groups of scores called class intervals. For example, if the teacher ratings had ranged from 1 to 40, SPSS would have grouped them into 20 groups of 2 scores: 1-2, 3-4, 5-6, etc. The class intervals are labeled using a value that falls within the range of that group of scores.

LINE CHARTS

Here, we present the steps for producing a line chart using a variable representing scores. These same steps can also be used to create line charts for group variables.

PROCEDURE FOR OBTAINING A LINE CHART:

① Select **Graphs** from the pull-down menu.

② Select **Legacy Dialogs**.

③ Select **Line...** from the side menu. This will open the **Line Charts** dialogue box.

④ & ⑤ Ensure that the **Simple** option is selected and then left-click **Define**, which will open the **Define Simple Line: Summaries for Groups of Cases** dialogue box.

(Note that the **Panel by** option is not shown in this figure due to space limitations.)

⑥ Enter the variable of interest **(stu_evals)** in the **Category Axis:** field by selecting the variable and left-clicking on the boxed arrow pointing to the field.

⑦ Ensure that the **N of cases** is selected in the **Line Represents** options.

⑧ To include a title for this chart, left-click on the **Titles...** button, which will open the **Titles** dialogue box.

(Note that the **Subtitle** and **Footnote** fields are not shown in this figure due to space limitations.)

⑨ Type your title in the **Line 1:** field. In this case, we have given our chart the title "College Professor Line Chart."

⑩ Left-click **Continue** to return to the previous box.

⑪ Finally, double-check your variables and options and either select **OK** to run or **Paste** to create syntax to run at a later time.

If you selected the paste option from the procedure above, you should have generated the following syntax:

GRAPH
  /Line (Simple)=COUNT BY stu_evals
  /TITLE= 'College Professor Data Line Chart' .

▶ **Figure 4.7** Obtaining Line Charts

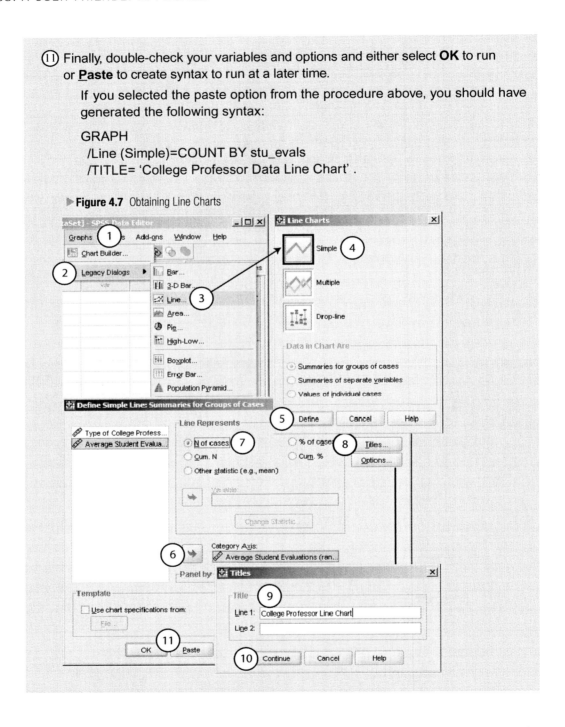

Figure 4.8 presents the line chart for the student evaluation data. Each point on the X-Axis corresponds to a rating value. As with the histogram, the Y-Axis represents the frequency counts for each score. For example, one professor got a rating of 1, two got a rating of 2, and four got a rating of 3. Again, we can see that the most frequently occurring scores are located in the middle of the range of scores.

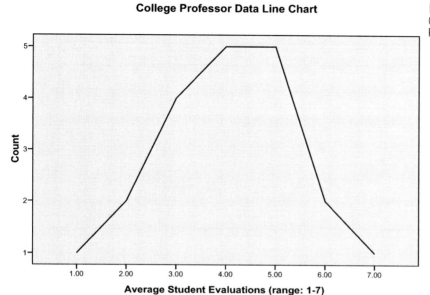

BAR CHARTS

Bar charts are often used to display frequency data for group variables. Bar charts look a lot like histograms, but the bars do not touch in bar charts because the X-Axis represents separate groups and not a continuous range of scores. Also unlike histograms, bar charts are not compared to the normal curve. This is because frequency distributions of group data can have different shapes based on the way you have chosen to order the groups.

PROCEDURE FOR OBTAINING A BAR CHART:

1. Select **Graphs** from the pull-down menu.
2. Select **Legacy Dialogs**.
3. Select **Bar...** from the side menu. This will open the **Bar Charts** dialogue box.
4. Ensure that the **Simple** and **Summaries for groups of cases** options are selected.
5. Left-click the **Define** button, which will open the **Define Simple Bar: Summaries for Groups of Cases** dialogue box.
   - (Note that the **Panel by** option is not shown in this figure due to space limitations.)
6. Enter the group variable of interest **(prof_type)** in the **Category Axis:** field by selecting the variable and left-clicking on the boxed arrow pointing to the field.
7. Ensure that the **N of cases** is selected in the **Bars Represent** options.
   - To include a title for this chart, left-click on the **Titles...** option. We have not included a title in this example.

⑧ Finally, double-check your variables and options and either select **OK** to run or **Paste** to create syntax to run at a later time.

If you selected the paste option from the procedure above, you should have generated the following syntax:

```
GRAPH
  /BAR(SIMPLE)=COUNT BY prof_type
```

▶ **Figure 4.9** Obtaining Bar Charts

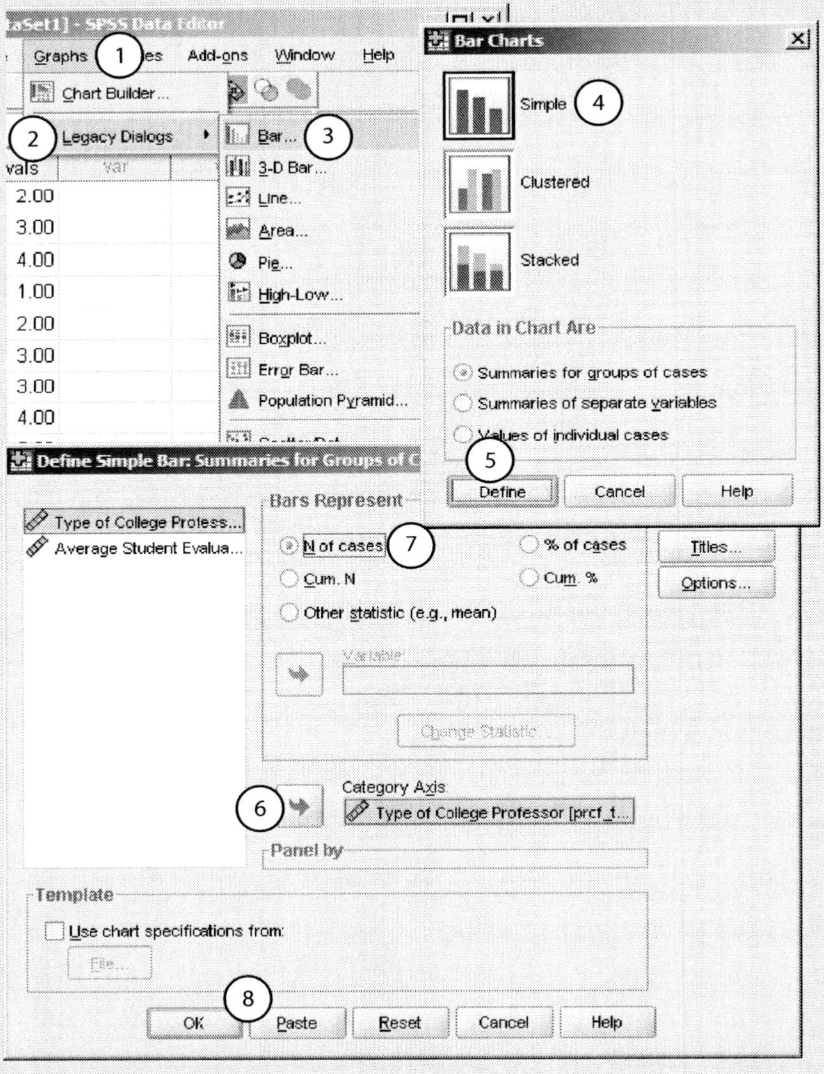

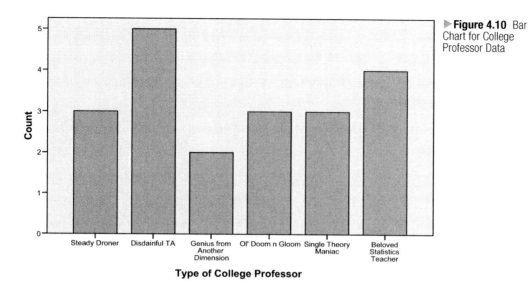

undefined▶**Figure 4.10** Bar Chart for College Professor Data

Figure 4.10 presents the bar chart for the six different types of college professors/ instructors. Each bar on the *X*-Axis represents a different type of professor/instructor. The values on *Y*-axis represent the frequency counts for each type of professor/ instructor. Like the frequency table, the bar chart shows us that the most common type of instructor teaching the students' first class of the week is a Disdainful TA and the least common is the Genius from Another Dimension.

PIE CHART

Like bar charts, pie charts are used to display frequency data for group variables. However, pie charts show the percentage of the whole sample that each group represents. These relative frequencies are represented as "slices" of the pie. For a particular group, the larger the slice the larger the percentage of the sample that group comprises.

PROCEDURE FOR OBTAINING A PIE CHART:

① Select **Graphs** from the pull-down menu.

② Select **Legacy Dialogs**.

③ Select **Pie...** from the side menu. This will open the **Pie Charts** dialogue box.

④ & ⑤ Ensure that the **Summaries for groups of cases** option is selected and then left-click **Define**, which will open the **Define Pie: Summaries for Groups of Cases** dialogue box.

(Note that the **Panel by** option is not shown in this figure due to space limitations.)

⑥ Enter the group variable of interest **(prof_type)** in the **Define Slices by:** field by selecting the variable and left-clicking on the boxed arrow pointing to the field.

⑦ Ensure that the **N of cases** is selected in the **Slices Represent** options.

⑧ To include a title for this chart, left-click on the **Titles...** button, which will open the **Titles** dialogue box.

(Note that the **Subtitle** and **Footnote** fields are not shown in this figure due to space limitations.)

⑨ Type your title in the **Line 1:** field. In this case, we have given our chart the title "College Professor Data Pie Chart."

⑩ Left-click **Continue** to return to the previous box.

⑪ Finally, double-check your variables and options and either select **OK** to run or **Paste** to create syntax to run at a later time.

If you selected the paste option from the procedure above, you should have generated the following syntax:

```
GRAPH
 /PIE=COUNT BY prof_type
 /TITLE='College Professor Data Pie Chart' .
```

▶ **Figure 4.11** Obtaining Pie Charts

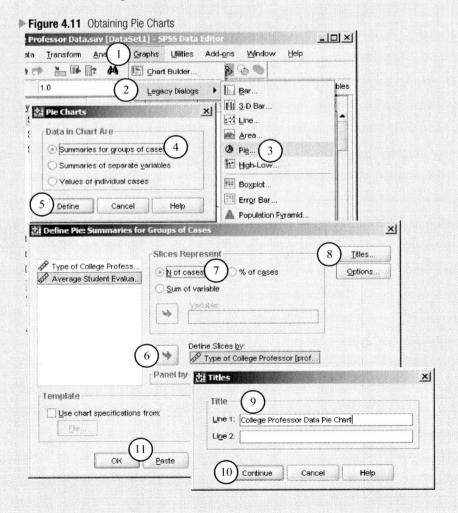

College Professor Data Pie Chart

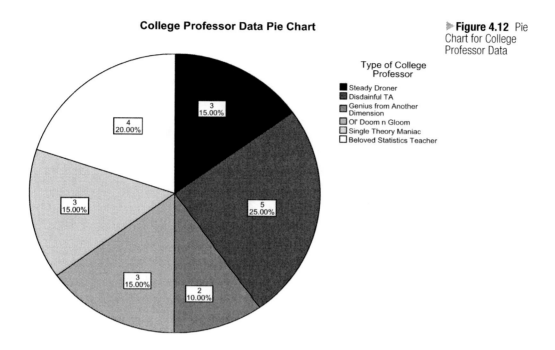

Figure 4.12 Pie Chart for College Professor Data

Figure 4.12 presents the pie chart for the student evaluation data. Each slice is labeled with the type of college professor it represents (identified in the legend to the right of the chart) and contains both the frequency count and percentage for that type of professor. Though this chart was created using the procedure presented above, the frequency counts and percentages must be added in the output navigator. This is accomplished by double-clicking on the chart in the Output Display field of the SPSS Output Viewer. The **Chart Editor** dialogue box will appear with several pull-down menu options. From the **Elements** pull-down menu, select **Show Data Labels**. This will open the **Properties** dialogue box. In the **Data Value Labels** tab, **count** (i.e., frequencies) will be listed in the **Displayed:** field. We have added the **percent** (listed in the **Not Displayed:** field) to the **Displayed:** field. You can also include the value labels within each slice by adding the variable name to the **Displayed:** field.

OBTAINING CHARTS OF MEANS

Frequency tables and charts summarize the data and help to describe the characteristics of variables. However, as social and behavioral scientists, we are often interested in describing the relationships between variables. Plotting group means can visually represent the relationship between a group variable and a variable representing a set of scores. Subsequent chapters will demonstrate several statistical tests that can be used to formally test the size and meaningfulness of these relationships (e.g., *t*-Tests and One-Way Analysis of Variance). Another type of graph, called a scatterplot, shows the relationship between two variables representing scores. The procedures for obtaining scatterplots are presented in the chapter on Correlation and Regression analyses (Chapter 11).

BAR CHART OF MEANS

Like a bar chart, a bar chart of means represents each group of interest with its own bar. However, instead of frequency information, the length of each bar represents the average score for a given group. In this example, the bar chart of means will display the average ratings each type of professor received from their students.

PROCEDURE FOR OBTAINING A BAR CHART OF MEANS:

Follow steps 1 through 5 of the procedure for obtaining bar charts presented on page 47, which will open the **Define Simple Bar: Summaries for Groups of Cases** dialogue box, as shown in Figure 4.13 below.

(Note that the **Panel by** option is not shown in this figure due to space limitations.)

▶ **Figure 4.13** Obtaining a Bar Chart of Means

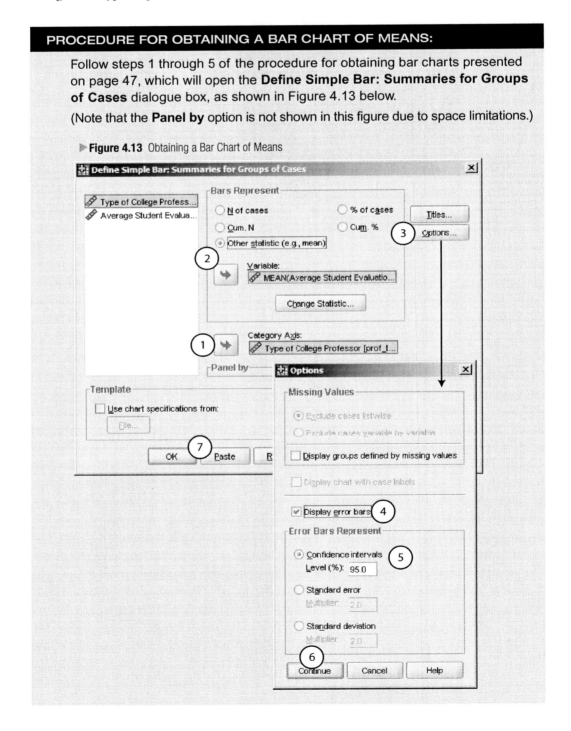

① Enter the group variable of interest **(prof_type)** in the **Category Axis:** field by selecting the variable and left-clicking on the boxed arrow pointing to the field.

② Select **Other statistic (e.g., mean)** from the **Bars Represent** options, and enter the variable representing the scores of interest **(stu_evals)** in the **Variable:** field of the **Bars Represent** options.

③ To add error bars representing confidence intervals, left-click the **Options...** button. This will open the **Options** dialogue box.

④ Select the **Display error bars** option.

⑤ Select the **Confidence intervals** option and set the **Level (%):** to 95.0 (95% is the default so you should not have to do anything unless you want to change the level.)

⑥ To return to the **Define Simple Bar: Summaries for Groups of Cases** dialogue box, left-click the **Continue** button.

⑦ Finally, double-check your variables and options and either select **OK** to run or **Paste** to create syntax to run at a later time.

If you selected the paste option from the procedure above, you should have generated the following syntax:

```
GRAPH
  /BAR(SIMPLE)=MEAN(stu_evals) BY prof_type
  /INTERVAL CI(95.0)
```

Figure 4.14 presents the bar chart of means representing the average student evaluations for each type of college professor/instructor. Like other bar charts, the X-Axis represents the six different types of college professors. However, the Y-axis no longer represents the frequency counts. It now represents the student evaluation scores. Looking at the chart, it appears Disdainful TAs have the lowest average evaluation (about 2.5) and Beloved Statistics Instructors have the highest average evaluation (about 5.5).

The bars for each category also have little lines of varying lengths extending above and below the upper-most point. These are the error bars for the 95% confidence interval we requested when generating the chart, and they represent potential sampling error. Any time a score from a sample is measured, there is always some chance that it differs from the score of the population. (As you may recall from Chapter 2, William Gossett from Guinness Brewery demonstrated this.) The 95% confidence interval shows us the range of scores within which we can be 95% sure that the true population score will fall. In more practical terms, when the error bars of two groups overlap, it means that they do not meaningfully differ; they are not significantly different. In Figure 4.14, all of the error bars overlap, so we cannot say there are any interpretable group differences with respect to the professors' student evaluations. Also notice that the error bars are missing for the Genius from Another Dimension group. This occurred because all the members of the group have the same score, so meaningful confidence intervals cannot be generated for that group.

Figure 4.14 Bar Chart of Means for College Professor Data

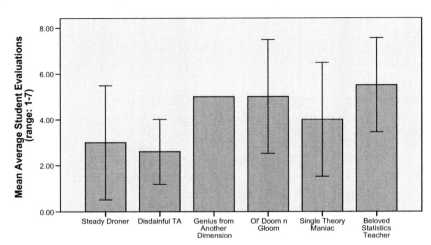

Average Student Evalation for College Professors

Error bars: 95% CI

Figure 4.15 Line Chart of Means for College Professor Data

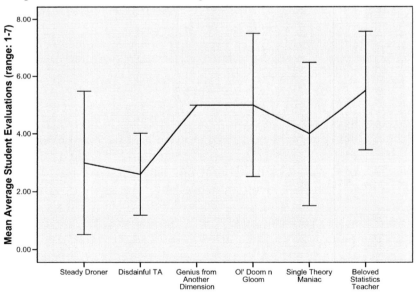

Error bars: 95% CI

LINE CHART OF MEANS

A line chart of means can be generated by following the same steps used to generate a bar chart of means within the **Define Simple Line: Summaries for Groups of Cases** dialogue box. Figure 4.15 displays the line chart of means for the college professor data. The interpretation of this chart is identical to the bar chart of means.

SUMMARY

This chapter introduced some basic procedures for generating frequency tables and frequency charts which organize and summarize data for variables representing groups or scores. This chapter also introduced procedures for generating plots of means that display the relationship between a group variable and a variable representing a set of scores. When working with the charts presented here, you should keep in mind that SPSS will produce whatever you ask for, even if it is completely meaningless. For example, if you request a histogram of a qualitative variable or a bar chart for a quantitative variable, you will get what you ask for, but the results will be difficult if not impossible to meaningfully interpret.

PRACTICE EXERCISES

Assume that researchers have drawn a different sample of 24 college sophomores and asked participants to report their current GPA and classify their favorite professor/instructor as one of the six types of professors: Steady Droner, Disdainful TA, Genius from Another Planet, Ol' Doom and Gloom, Single Theory Maniac, or Beloved Statistics Instructor. The data collected are presented in Table 4.1.

▶**Table 4.1** Practice Exercise Data

Participant	Favorite College Professor	Current GPA
1	Steady Droner	2.6
2	Steady Droner	2.8
3	Steady Droner	3.0
4	Steady Droner	3.2
5	Steady Droner	3.4
6	Disdainful TA	2.0
7	Disdainful TA	2.2
8	Disdainful TA	2.4
9	Disdainful TA	2.6
10	Genius from Another Dimension	3.2
11	Genius from Another Dimension	3.4
12	Genius from Another Dimension	3.6
13	Ol' Doom n Gloom	2.8
14	Ol' Doom n Gloom	3.0
15	Ol' Doom n Gloom	3.2
16	Single Theory Maniac	3.0
17	Single Theory Maniac	3.2
18	Single Theory Maniac	3.4
19	Single Theory Maniac	3.6
20	Beloved Statistics Instructor	3.2
21	Beloved Statistics Instructor	3.4
22	Beloved Statistics Instructor	3.6
23	Beloved Statistics Instructor	3.8
24	Beloved Statistics Instructor	4.0

1. Generate frequency tables for these two variables.

   a. Which group(s) and which scores have the highest frequency?

   b. Which group(s) and which scores have the lowest frequency?

   c. Which set of groups and which range of scores include the first half of the sample (based on the cumulative percent)?

2. For the group variable, generate a bar chart, line chart, and pie chart.

3. For the score variable, generate a histogram and a line chart.

   a. How does this distribution compare to the normal distribution?

4. For the group variable and score variable, generate a bar chart of means with error bars representing the 95% confidence intervals.

   a. Are there any meaningful (statistically significant) differences in GPA between groups?

Describing Distributions

This chapter introduces procedures for obtaining descriptive data using two different SPSS analysis options: Frequencies and Descriptives. Specifically, it covers procedures for generating measures of central tendency (*Mean, Median,* and *Mode*), measures of variability (*Range, Variance,* and *Standard Deviation*), and measures of normality (*Skewness* and *Kurtosis*). Similar to the frequency distributions presented in the previous chapter, these statistics allow us to summarize large amounts of data and efficiently communicate crucial characteristics of our data to others.

The examples in this chapter focus on techniques for describing score variables. With the exception of the mode, none of the statistics presented in this chapter are appropriate for describing group variables. Because we generally use numbers to represent groups in SPSS, if you ask SPSS to produce the mean, median, standard deviation, variance, etc., for a group variable, it will do so. However, the obtained results would be meaningless in most cases.

SETTING UP THE DATA

For the following examples, we have created a data set based on Cartoon 5.1. To investigate the impact different media have on the thought processes of children, researchers gathered a sample of 20 eight-year-olds. The researchers recorded the number of thoughts each child generated while watching TV and while reading a book during a 30-minute lab session. The complexity of each thought was rated by independent judges. For each child, scores were recorded for the most complex thought generated while watching TV and while reading. Figure 5.1 presents the Variable View of the SPSS Data Editor, where we have defined four variables. The first variable, named **book_tpm,** represents the

▶ Cartoon 5.1

▶ **Figure 5.1** Variable View for TV Thought Data

number of thoughts per minute each child had while reading a book. The second variable, named **tv_tpm,** represents the number of thoughts per minute each child had while watching TV. The third and fourth variables, respectively named **book_tcplx** and **tv_tcplx,** represent the rating of the most complex thought generated by each child while reading a book and while watching television. The thought complexity scores can range between 0 (least complex) and 9 (most complex). Figure 5.2 presents the Data View of the SPSS Data Editor where the scores for all 20 children have been entered.

▶ **Figure 5.2** Data View for TV Thought Data

	book_tpm	tv_tpm	book_tcplx	tv_tcplx
1	1.00	2.00	0.00	0.00
2	2.00	3.00	1.00	1.00
3	3.00	4.00	2.00	1.00
4	4.00	4.00	3.00	1.00
5	4.00	5.00	5.00	1.00
6	5.00	5.00	6.00	1.00
7	5.00	5.00	6.00	1.00
8	5.00	6.00	6.00	2.00
9	6.00	6.00	6.00	2.00
10	6.00	6.00	7.00	2.00
11	6.00	6.00	7.00	2.00
12	6.00	6.00	7.00	3.00
13	7.00	6.00	7.00	3.00
14	7.00	7.00	8.00	3.00
15	7.00	7.00	8.00	3.00
16	8.00	7.00	8.00	4.00
17	8.00	8.00	8.00	6.00
18	9.00	8.00	8.00	7.00
19	10.00	9.00	8.00	8.00
20	11.00	10.00	9.00	9.00

MEASURES OF CENTRAL TENDENCY: MEAN, MEDIAN, AND MODE

Measures of central tendency summarize data sets by providing values that can serve as the best representative of all the scores in the data set. The *Mean*, *Median*, and *Mode* are each based on different definitions of what it means to best represent a set of scores. The mean is the average of all the scores (each score is summed and the sum is divided by the number of scores). The median is the score for which half of the sample has a score of this magnitude or greater and half has a score of this magnitude or less. The mode is the most frequently occurring score or scores; some distributions have more than one mode. When the scores in a data set are normally distributed and therefore completely symmetrical, the mean, median, and mode will have the same value (or close to it). In this example, we present the steps for using the **Frequencies...** option to find the Mean, Median, and Mode for the television-watching and book-reading data. It is possible to obtain the mean for a variable using the **Descriptives...** option, but it does not provide the median or the mode.

PROCEDURE FOR OBTAINING MEASURES OF CENTRAL TENDENCY USING THE **FREQUENCIES...** OPTION:

1. Select **Analyze** from the pull-down menu.

2. Select **Descriptive Statistics**.

3. Select **Frequencies...** from the side menu. This will open the **Frequencies** dialogue box.

4. Enter the variables of interest (**book_tpm, tv_tpm, book_tcplx,** and **tv_tcplx**) in the **Variable(s):** field by either double-clicking on each variable or selecting each variable and left-clicking on the boxed arrow pointing to the right.

5. To request the measures of central tendency, left-click the **Statistics...** button. This will open the **Frequencies Statistics** dialogue box.

6. Check the desired statistics/parameters. In this case, we have selected the **Mean, Median,** and **Mode**.

7. Left-click **Continue** to return to the **Frequencies** dialogue box.

8. Finally, double-check your variables and either select **OK** to run or **Paste** to create syntax to run at a later time.

   If you selected the paste option from the procedure above, you should have generated the following syntax:

   ```
   FREQUENCIES VARIABLES=book_tpm tv_tpm book_tcplx tv_tcplx
     /STATISTICS=MEAN MEDIAN MODE
     /ORDER=ANALYSIS .
   ```

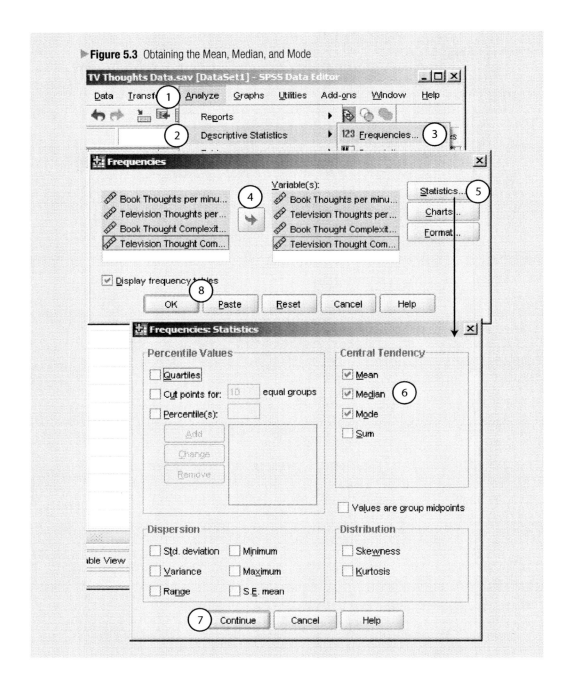

▶**Figure 5.3** Obtaining the Mean, Median, and Mode

READING THE OUTPUT

The Frequency Analysis Output is presented in Figure 5.4. This output consists of two parts: **Statistics** and **Frequency Table**. Figure 5.4 only displays the **Statistics** table which shows the statistics that were requested from among the **Statistics...** options. The **N Valid**, presented in the first row, indicates the number of cases with data for each variable. In this example, we have data for 20 eight-year-olds for each variable. The row labeled **Missing** indicates the number of cases for which no data is available. In this example, no child is missing data for any variable.

▶ Figure 5.4 Measure of Central Tendency for TV Thought Data

Statistics

		Book Thoughts per Minute	Television Thoughts per Minute	Book Thought Complexity	Television Thought Complexity
N	Valid	20	20	20	20
	Missing	0	0	0	0
Mean		6.0000	6.0000	6.0000	3.0000
Median		6.0000	6.0000	7.0000	2.0000
Mode		6.00	6.00	8.00	1.00

The remaining rows of this table present the mean, median, and mode for each variable. The variables **book_tpm** and **tv_tpm** both have means, medians, and modes with values of 6. This indicates that eight-year-olds in our sample have an average of 6 thoughts per minute whether they are reading a book or watching TV. This also means that half the children had 6 thoughts or fewer and half had 6 thoughts or more. Further, it appears that 6 thoughts per minute is the most frequently occurring number of thoughts generated when children read books and when they watched TV. Finally, for both variables, the fact that the mean, median, and mode all have the same value suggests that the data is symmetrically distributed.

With respect to thought complexity when reading a book, the mean was 6, the median was 7, and the mode was 8. This pattern of data indicates that a majority of the sample had quite complex thoughts when reading books, and comparatively few children had simple thoughts. Alternatively, when watching TV, the mean, median, and mode for thought complexity were 3, 2, and 1 respectively. This indicates that a majority of the sample had quite simple thoughts when watching TV and comparatively few children had complex thoughts. Further, these patterns suggest that data for thought complexity are not normally distributed. It appears that the complexity of thoughts while reading a book is negatively skewed and thought complexity while watching TV is positively skewed. (Skewness will be described in more detail later in the chapter.)

MEASURES OF VARIABILITY: RANGE, VARIANCE, AND STANDARD DEVIATION

Like measures of central tendency, measures of variability summarize an entire data set. Rather than reflecting the most representative scores, measures of variability represent the degree to which scores differ from one another, or how much they vary. The *Range* of scores reflects the numerical distance between the highest and lowest scores in the data set. *Variance* is the average of the squared distance each score is from the mean. *Standard Deviation*, calculated by taking the square root of the variance, represents the average distance of each score from the mean. The greater the value of the range, variance, and standard deviation, the more spread out the scores are across the distribution.

In this example, we present the steps for using the **Descriptives...** option to find the minimum score, maximum score, range, variance, and standard deviation for a score variable. As illustrated earlier, it is also possible to obtain these statistics for a variable using the **Frequencies...** option.

PROCEDURE FOR OBTAINING MEASURES OF VARIABILITY USING THE **DESCRIPTIVES...** OPTION:

① Select **Analyze** from the pull-down menu.

② Select **Descriptive Statistics**.

③ Select **Descriptives...** from the side menu. This will open the **Descriptives** dialogue box.

④ Enter the desired variables (**book_tpm, tv_tpm, book_tcplx,** and **tv_tcplx**) in the **Variable(s):** field by either double-clicking on each variable or selecting the variable and left-clicking on the boxed arrow pointing to the right.

▶ **Figure 5.5** Obtaining Measures of Variability

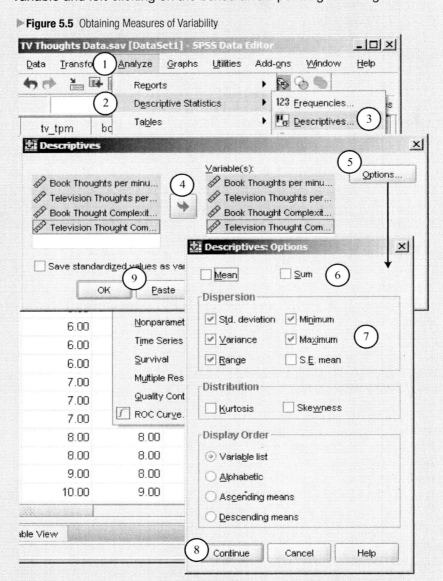

⑤ To request measures of variability, left-click the **Options...** button. This will open the **Descriptives: Options** dialogue box.

⑥ The default options include the mean, standard deviation (std. deviation), minimum, and maximum. In this example, we have deselected the **Mean** option.

⑦ Select the desired statistics. In this case, we have selected the **Std. deviation**, **Variance**, **Range**, **Minimum**, and **Maximum**.

⑧ Left-click **Continue** to return to the **Descriptives** dialogue box.

⑨ Finally, double-check your variables and either select **OK** to run or **Paste** to create syntax to run at a later time.

If you selected the paste option from the procedure above, you should have generated the following syntax:

```
DESCRIPTIVES VARIABLES=book_tpm tv_tpm book_tcplx tv_tcplx
    /STATISTICS=STDDEV VARIANCE RANGE MIN MAX .
```

▶ **Figure 5.6** Measure of Variability for TV Thought Data

Descriptive Statistics

	N	Range	Minimum	Maximum	Std. Deviation	Variance
Book Thoughts per minute	20	10.00	1.00	11.00	2.53398	6.421
Television Thoughts per minute	20	8.00	2.00	10.00	1.94666	3.789
Book Thought Complexity	20	9.00	.00	9.00	2.55467	6.526
Television Thought Complexity	20	9.00	.00	9.00	2.55467	6.526
Valid N (listwise)	20					

READING THE OUTPUT

The Descriptives Analysis Output is presented in Figure 5.6. The **Descriptive Statistics** table presents the statistics that were requested from among the **Descriptives: Options**. The **N**, presented in the first column, indicates the number of cases with data for each variable. In this example, we have data from all 20 children for all four variables. The last row, labeled **Valid N (listwise)**, indicates the number of cases that have data for all four variables (i.e., cases that are not missing data for any variable). In this example, no children are missing data for any of the variables of interest.

The remaining columns of this table present the **Range**, **Minimum**, **Maximum**, **Standard Deviation**, and **Variance**. It is important to remember that SPSS provides the sample standard deviation and the sample variance, which use N-1 as the denominator of the variance formula. It does not provide the Population Parameter for these measures of variability, which uses N as the denominator of the variance formula. Keep this in mind if you are trying to check your own hand calculations with population data. In this case, to check the numerator of your hand calculation for variance, you can multiply the variance reported in SPSS by N-1, and the resulting value (often referred to as the sum of squares) should match the numerator for your hand calculations.

Examining the output for our descriptives analysis, it appears that there is more variability in the number of thoughts generated when reading a book than when watching

TV. Though the average number of thoughts generated is the same when reading or watching TV (based on the means presented earlier), it appears that TV inspires a more uniform number of thoughts (influencing people in the same way), compared to reading. With respect to the complexity of thoughts generated while reading a book or watching TV, it appears that the scores are equally spread out within this distribution, as the values of the measures of variability for both variables are the same. However, we do not know whether the scores are dispersed in the same way. We should be cautious about inferring that the two sets of scores are spread out in the same manner, given that inspection of the means presented earlier in the chapter suggests that thought complexity data for TV watching and book reading may be skewed in opposite directions.

MEASURES OF NORMALITY: SKEWNESS AND KURTOSIS

Measures of normality indicate the degree to which data conforms to the Normal Distribution (also referred to as the Normal Curve, Bell Curve, or Gaussian Curve). *Skewness* indicates the degree to which distributions of data are symmetrical. When distributions are positively skewed, a substantial majority of the scores are bunched toward the bottom of the range of scores, and significantly fewer scores extend toward the top of the range. The thin tail (or skew) extends toward the larger positive numbers. With negatively skewed distributions, a majority of the scores are bunched toward the top of the scale, and few scores extend toward the bottom. Figure 5.7 on the next page shows positively and negatively skewed distributions. Typically less familiar to students is the concept of *Kurtosis*, which refers to the degree to which the distribution is more peaked (*leptokurtic*) or flatter (*platykurtic*) than the normal distribution. Figure 5.7 shows examples of leptokurtic and platykurtic distributions. Measures of normality allow us to make more informed interpretations of other descriptive statistics. For example, when distributions are substantially skewed, we know that the means are typically not the most representative score and that a majority of the variability between scores is limited to one end of the distribution.

Estimates of skewness and kurtosis can be obtained using either the **Frequencies...** or **Descriptives...** options described in this chapter. Figure 5.8 on page 65 presents the skew and kurtosis scores obtained using the **Frequencies...** procedure by selecting the **Skewness** and **Kurtosis** options from within the **Frequencies: Statistics** dialogue box. This figure also presents histograms for book thoughts per minute, television thoughts per minute, book thought complexity, and television thought complexity, with the normal curve superimposed on each. The statistics table presents the by now familiar information regarding the number of cases and missing values along with the following: **Skewness**, **Standard Error of Skewness**, **Kurtosis**, and **Standard Error of Kurtosis**. With respect to skewness, the closer the value is to 0, the more symmetrical the distribution of the data. Larger positive values for skewness indicate a more positively skewed distribution. Larger negative values for skewness indicate a more negatively skewed distribution. Regarding the number of thoughts per minute, the skewness statistic is 0 for book reading and TV watching, indicating a symmetrical distribution of scores. Alternatively, thought complexity while reading books is negatively skewed (-1.242), and thought complexity while watching TV is positively skewed (1.242). You can see these patterns reflected in the corresponding histograms.

With respect to Kurtosis, the closer the value is to 0, the more normally clustered the scores. Larger positive values for kurtosis indicate a more *leptokurtic* (peaked or overly-clustered) distribution. Larger negative values for kurtosis indicate a *platykurtic* (flat or under–clustered) distribution. For all the variables in our example data set, the values are either close to 0 or only mildly leptokurtic.

For most of the statistical tests commonly used, it is assumed that the data are normally distributed, so it is important to determine whether the data conform to the normal distribution. In general, the data is considered to be different from the normal distribution (peaked, flat, or asymmetrical) when the ratio of the skewness or kurtosis statistic to its standard error is greater than 2 or less than -2. For thought complexity while reading, the skewness is -1.242, the standard error of skewness is .512, and the ratio of skewness to its standard error is -2.426. This suggests that this variable meaningfully differs from the normal distribution. For thought complexity while reading a book, the kurtosis is .599, the standard error of kurtosis is .992, and the ratio of kurtosis to its standard error is .604. Though this variable is skewed, it does not appear to be significantly more peaked than the normal distribution. When a variable differs from the normal distribution, either with respect to skewness or kurtosis, we should be cautious when interpreting any statistical procedures we undertake with it. Though many statistics can still be validly interpreted when the assumptions of normality are not met, they typically require other types of conditions to be met. You may want to consult more advanced books when working with skewed or kurtotic data.

▶**Figure 5.8** Measures of Normality for TV Thought Data

Statistics

		Book Thoughts per Minute	Television Thoughts per Minute	Book Thought Complexity	Television Thought Complexity
N	Valid	20	20	20	20
	Missing	0	0	0	0
	Skewness	.000	.000	−1.242	1.242
	Std. Error of Skewness	.512	.512	.512	.512
	Kurtosis	−.046	.204	.599	.599
	Std. Error of Kurtosis	.992	.992	.992	.992

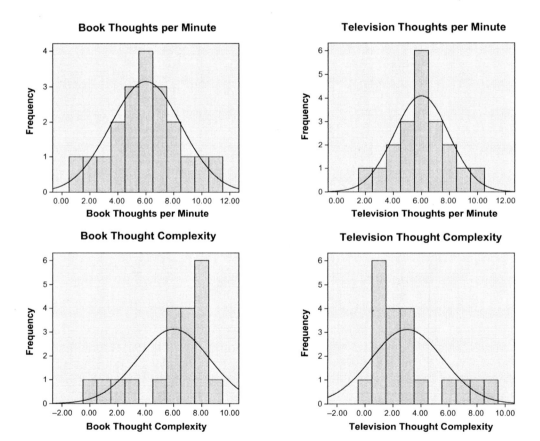

SUMMARY

This chapter presented procedures for obtaining basic descriptive information about variables representing scores, including measures of central tendency, measures of variability, and measures of normalcy. The example study focused on the number and complexity of thoughts eight-year-olds had while either watching TV or reading a book. It was demonstrated that two sets of scores can have the same means but still have quite different values for measures of variability. Along the same lines, two variables can have the same variance, standard deviation, and range, but have distributions of scores that are radically different (e.g., they could be skewed in opposite directions). Finally, when a variable is skewed, the measures of central tendency can differ from one another. Examining measures of central tendency, variability, and normality allow you to meaningfully summarize large amounts of data. These summaries allow you communicate the characteristics of your data to others and help you get to know your data before proceeding with more complex statistical operations.

PRACTICE EXERCISES

Assume that researchers are interested in determining whether different forms of TV watching are equivalent. To this end, they measured the thoughts generated by eight-year-olds while watching ten randomly picked television shows: five from the Discovery Channel and five reality shows. For both types of shows, the number of thoughts was tabulated. The complexity of each thought was rated by independent judges, and the score for the most complex thought was recorded. The data are presented in Table 5.1. For each variable, find the mean, median, mode, range, variance, standard deviation, skewness, and kurtosis. What do these statistics tell us about the thoughts of eight-year-olds while watching these two different types of shows?

▶ **Table 5.1** Practice Exercise Data

Case	Reality TV Thoughts per Min.	Discovery Channel Thoughts per Min.	Reality TV Thought Complexity	Discovery Channel Thought Complexity
1	4	1	0	3
2	5	1	1	5
3	6	1	2	6
4	6	2	2	6
5	7	2	2	7
6	7	2	2	7
7	7	2	2	7
8	8	3	2	7
9	8	3	2	7
10	8	3	2	7
11	8	3	2	7
12	8	3	2	7
13	8	3	2	7
14	9	4	2	7
15	9	4	2	7
16	9	4	2	7
17	10	4	2	8
18	10	5	2	8
19	11	5	3	9
20	12	6	4	9

Compute Statements: Reversing Scores, Combining Scores, and Creating Z-Scores

This chapter covers some compute statements that are commonly used with measures consisting of multiple items—like questionnaires, personality scales, or classroom tests. Remember that compute statements allow us to create new variables by changing existing variables in some way. First, we will demonstrate how score variables can be numerically reflected or reversed so that they can be interpreted in the same way as other variables that have been worded in an opposite direction. Second, we will demonstrate how to combine scores from multiple variables into a single score using the **SUM** and **MEAN** functions. Finally, we will demonstrate how to convert data into Z-scores, which you can use to check some hand calculations that are typically encountered in introductory statistics courses.

SETTING UP THE DATA

The examples in this chapter are based on Cartoon 6.1, which implies that lions have quite positive attitudes toward the zebras' "repestenatives." In order to investigate these

▶ **Cartoon 6.1**

PEARLS BEFORE SWINE   *BY STEPHAN PASTIS*

attitudes, our researchers developed a four item self-report questionnaire titled Zebra Eating Attitudes for Lions (ZEAL). This questionnaire asks lions to rate the degree to which they agree with the following statements using a 7-point numerical rating scale (1 = strongly disagree and 7 = strongly agree):

1. I find zebras quite irresistible.
2. I would definitely invite a zebra to my home for dinner.
3. I would walk a mile for a zebra.
4. I would never eat a zebra.

Figure 6.1 shows the Variable View of the Data Editor where four variables have been created to represent the four items of the ZEAL. Figure 6.2 presents the Data View of the Data Editor where the 10 lions' responses have been entered.

REVERSE SCORING VARIABLES

When writing questionnaires, it is a common practice to write some of the questions (often referred to as items) so that the meaning of the answer is in the opposite direction of other items in the questionnaire. For example, question four of the ZEAL currently represents a variable where a high score indicates a negative attitude toward eating zebras and a low score indicates a positive attitude. Responses to the other items in the questionnaire have the opposite meaning: a high score represents a positive attitude

▶**Figure 6.1** Variable View of Lion Zebra Attitudes Data

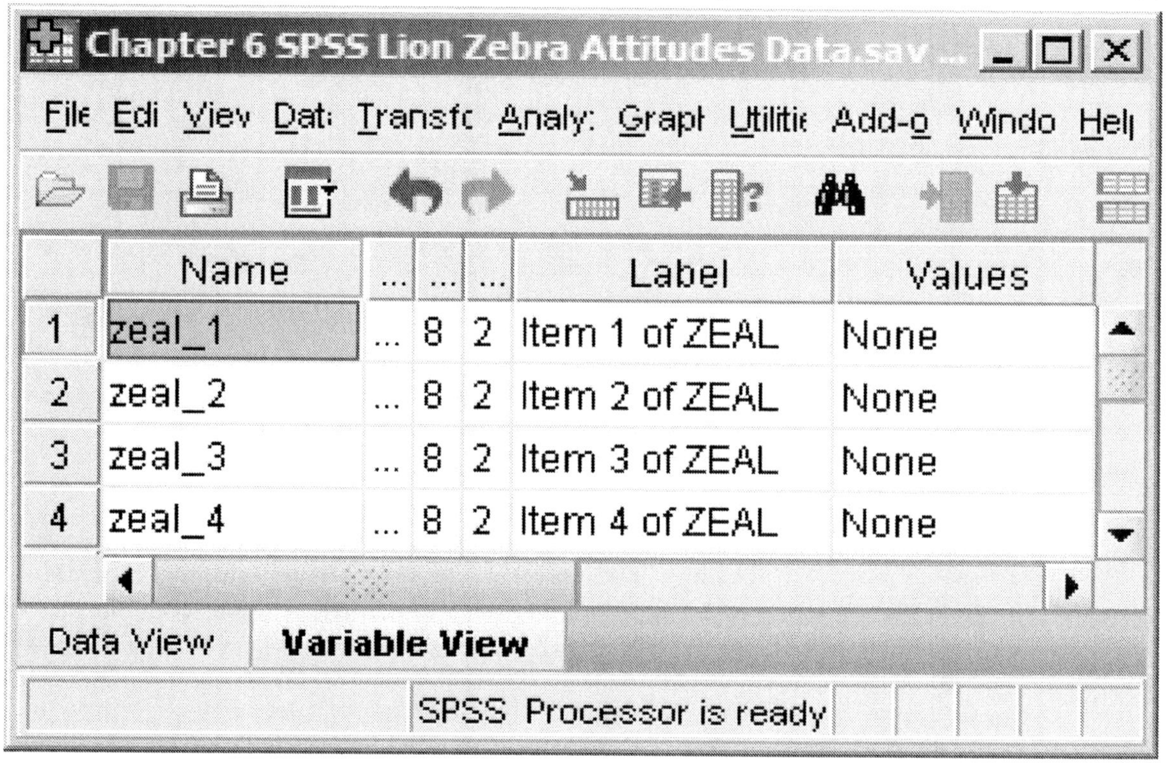

▶ **Figure 6.2** Data View of Lion Zebra Attitudes Data

	zeal_1	zeal_2	zeal_3	zeal_4
1	1.00	2.00	1.00	7.00
2	2.00	2.00	1.00	7.00
3	3.00	4.00	3.00	6.00
4	3.00	2.00	4.00	5.00
5	4.00	5.00	5.00	4.00
6	4.00	3.00	2.00	3.00
7	5.00	5.00	6.00	4.00
8	5.00	7.00	7.00	2.00
9	6.00	5.00	6.00	2.00
10	7.00	6.00	6.00	1.00

*Chapter 6 SPSS Lion Zebra Attitudes Data.sav [Dat...

File Edit View Data Transfor Analyz Graph Utilitie Add-or Window Help

1 : zeal_1   1.0   Visible: 10 of 10 Variables

Data View   Variable View

SPSS Processor is ready

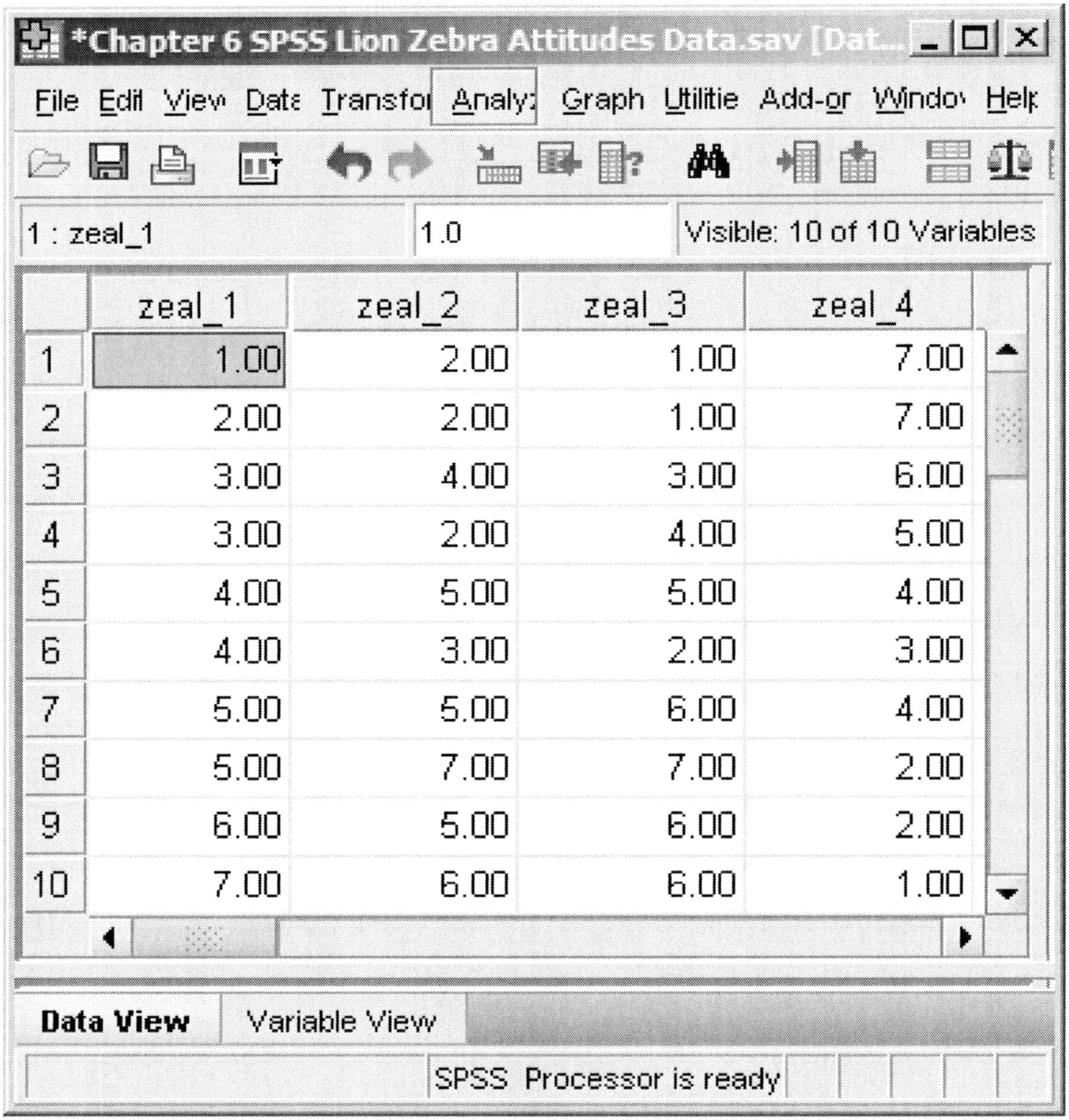

and a low score represents a negative attitude. Typically, negatively worded items are included to ensure that participants think carefully about each question.

In order to combine negatively worded items with the other items in a questionnaire, we have to reverse the scoring of the responses to the negative items so that their meaning corresponds to the meaning of the responses to the other items. The responses to item 4 on the ZEAL need to be reversed before they can be combined with the responses to the other items. The 1s become 7s, 2s become 6s, 3s become 5s, 4s remain 4s, 5s become 3s, 6s become 2s, and 7s become 1s. Compute statements can make this quite easy. If we subtract every score from 8, we will achieve the desired effect.

PROCEDURE FOR REVERSING SCORES OF A 7-POINT SCALE ITEM

(1) Select **Transform** from the pull-down menu.

(2) Select **Compute Variable….** This will open the **Compute Variable** dialogue box.

(3) Enter the desired name for the new variable in the **Target Variable:** field. In this example, we used the name **zeal_4r** to indicate its reversed status.

(4) Add a Variable Label by left-clicking the **Type & Label...** button. This will open the **Compute Variable: Type and Label** dialogue box.

(5) Enter the desired label for the new variable in the **Label:** field. In this example, we have used "Item 4 of ZEAL Reversed (8 - score)," which includes a description of how the new variable was computed.

(6) Left-click **Continue** to return to the **Compute Variable** dialogue box.

(7) Enter the formula for computing the new variable in the **Numeric Expression:** field. Because we have a 1–7 scale, we have used **8 - zeal_4** as the formula.

(8) Finally, double-check your variables and either select **OK** to run or **Paste** to create syntax to run at a later time.

If you selected the paste option from the procedure above, you should have generated the following syntax:

COMPUTE zeal_4r=8-zeal_4 .
VARIABLE LABELS zeal_4r 'Item 4 of ZEAL Reversed (8-score)' .
EXECUTE .

▶ **Figure 6.3** Reverse Scoring a 7-point Scale Item

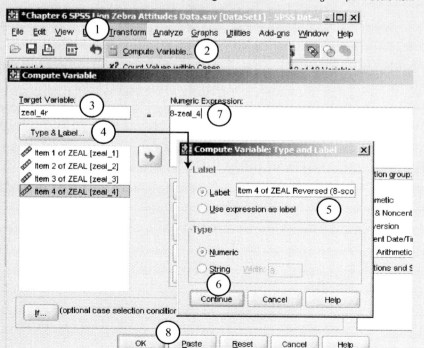

▶**Figure 6.4** Data View with Reversed Item

	zeal_1	zeal_2	zeal_3	zeal_4	zeal_4r	var
1	1.00	2.00	1.00	7.00	1.00	
2	2.00	2.00	1.00	7.00	1.00	
3	3.00	4.00	3.00	6.00	2.00	
4	3.00	2.00	4.00	5.00	3.00	
5	4.00	5.00	5.00	4.00	4.00	
6	4.00	3.00	2.00	3.00	5.00	
7	5.00	5.00	6.00	4.00	4.00	
8	5.00	7.00	7.00	2.00	6.00	
9	6.00	5.00	6.00	2.00	6.00	
10	7.00	6.00	6.00	1.00	7.00	

Item 4 of ZEAL Reversed (8-score)

Figure 6.4 shows part of the Data View of the Data Editor where the new reversed version of item 4 (**zeal_4r**) has been created. The 7s have been changed to 1s, 6s to 2s, 5s to 3s, etc., so that a higher score now indicates a more positive attitude toward eating zebras. Notice that we have left the variable **zeal_4** in its unaltered form, which makes it easier to check the SPSS data against the responses to the completed questionnaires if necessary.

In this example, we used a 1–7 scale and subtracted each score from the constant 8 to create the reverse score variable. However, if you have a different scale, then you will have to use a different constant. For example, a 1–5 scale would use 6 as the constant; a 1–9 scale would use 10 as the constant. Alternatively, if the scale was a 0–7, then the constant would be 7. This would turn the 7s into 0s and the 0s into 7s. Further, if you are using a scale with positive and negative values (e.g., $-3, -2, -1, 0, 1, 2, 3$), then multiplying the scores by -1 would be an easy way to reverse the scores.

GENERATING MULTI-ITEM SCALE SCORES

Often when researchers use measures that have multiple items, they can combine the items to form a single score. Typically, the items are either summed to form a single score or they are averaged. The following examples demonstrate how to use compute statements to create sums and averages of multiple items.

SUMMING RESPONSES

The basic steps for summing responses are the same as those in the procedure for reverse scoring an item. Figure 6.5 only shows the steps unique to obtaining sums of multiple items.

PROCEDURE FOR SUMMING MULTIPLE ITEMS

Follow steps 1 and 2 of the procedures for reverse scoring an item presented earlier in this chapter, which will open the **Compute Variable** dialogue box as shown in Figure 6.5.

(1) Enter the desired name for the new variable in the **Target Variable:** field. In this example, we used the name **zeal_tot**, to indicate that it is a total/summed score.

(2) Add a Variable Label by left-clicking the **Type & Label…** button. This will open the **Compute Variable: Type and Label** dialogue box.

(3) Enter the desired label for the new variable in the **Label:** field. In this example, we have used "ZEAL Total Score (sum of four items)."

(4) Left-click **Continue** to return to the **Compute Variable** dialogue box.

(5) Select **Statistical** from the **Function group:** list.

(6) & (7) Double-click **Sum** from the resulting options in the **Functions and Special Variables:** list, or left-click **Sum** from the list and then left-click the boxed arrow to the left of the list. This will add the following text to the **Numeric Expression:** field: **SUM(?, ?)**. This function will generate a sum for the variables that we place inside the parentheses.

▶ **Figure 6.5** Summing Multiple Items

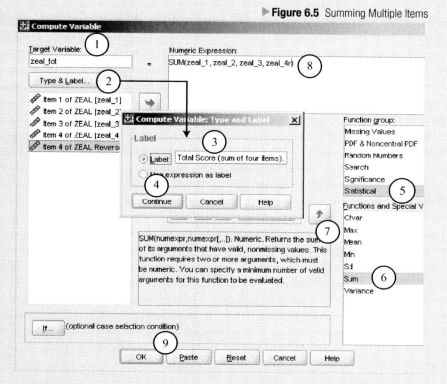

⑧ Replace the question marks with the variables names of interest.

- Variable names can be typed by hand, added by double-clicking each variable from the list, or added by left-clicking each variable and left-clicking the boxed arrow pointing toward the **Numeric Expression: field**.

- Be sure to separate each variable with a comma and a space.

- In this example, we request of the sum of **zeal_1, zeal_2, zeal_3,** and **zeal_4r** with the following numerical expression: **SUM (zeal_1, zeal_2, zeal_3, zeal_4r).**

⑨ Finally, double-check your variables and either select **OK** to run or **Paste** to create syntax to run at a later time.

If you selected the paste option from the procedure above, you should have generated the following syntax:

```
COMPUTE zeal_tot=SUM(zeal_1, zeal_2, zeal_3, zeal_4r) .
  VARIABLE LABELS zeal_tot 'ZEAL Total Score (sum of four items).' .
  EXECUTE .
```

AVERAGING RESPONSES

To obtain the mean of the responses to multiple items, the same basic procedures for obtaining sums can be used. However, instead of selecting **Sum** from the **Functions and Special Variables:** list, select the **Mean** option. This will add the following function to the **Numeric Expression:** field: **MEAN(?, ?)**. This function will return the mean for any variables added within the parentheses. For this example, we created a new variable, named **zeal_mean**, with the label "ZEAL Mean Score (mean of four items)." To generate the new variable, we wrote the following numeric expression: **MEAN(zeal_1, zeal_2, zeal_3, zeal_4r).** Pasting this procedure results in the following syntax:

```
COMPUTE zeal_mean=MEAN(zeal_1, zeal_2, zeal_3, zeal_4r) .
  VARIABLE LABELS zeal_mean 'ZEAL Mean Score (mean of four items)' .
  EXECUTE .
```

Figure 6.6 on the next page shows part of the Data View of the Data Editor where the sum and mean variables (**zeal_tot** and **zeal_mean**) are included. These variables were added by the **Compute Variable** procedures we conducted. For the total (summed) score, the first lion had a score of 5, which is the sum of the lion's scores for item 1, item 2, item 3, and item 4 reversed (i.e., $1 + 2 + 1 + 1 = 5$). Similarly, for the mean (averaged) score, the first lion had a score of 1.25, which is the sum of items 1, 2, 3, and 4 (reversed) divided by 4 $[(1 + 2 + 1 + 1)/4 = 1.25]$.

As you work with SPSS, you will likely discover different procedures for generating the same scores demonstrated here. For example, instead of using the **SUM** function, we could have written an equation that would have added together the variables of interest (e.g., **zeal_1 + zeal_2 + zeal_3 + zeal_4r**). Similarly, the **MEAN** function could be

▶**Figure 6.6** Data View of Summed and Averaged Scores

	zeal_1	zeal_2	zeal_3	zeal_4	zeal_4r	zeal_tot	zeal_mean
1	1.00	2.00	1.00	7.00	1.00	5.00	1.25
2	2.00	2.00	1.00	7.00	1.00	6.00	1.50
3	3.00	4.00	3.00	6.00	2.00	12.00	3.00
4	3.00	2.00	4.00	5.00	3.00	12.00	3.00
5	4.00	5.00	5.00	4.00	4.00	18.00	4.50
6	4.00	3.00	2.00	3.00	5.00	14.00	3.50
7	5.00	5.00	6.00	4.00	4.00	20.00	5.00
8	5.00	7.00	7.00	2.00	6.00	25.00	6.25
9	6.00	5.00	6.00	2.00	6.00	23.00	5.75
10	7.00	6.00	6.00	1.00	7.00	26.00	6.50

replaced with [(**zeal_1** + **zeal_2** + **zeal_3** + **zeal_4r**)/4]. For the most part, these user-defined expressions are just as effective as the functions generated by SPSS. A notable exception occurs when means are obtained for variables that have missing data. The **MEAN** function will uniquely adjust the denominator for each participant based on the number of variables for which the participant has data. If a participant only has data for three variables, then the sum of the three items will be divided by three, even if everyone else had data for four items. The user-defined formula [(**zeal_1** + **zeal_2** + **zeal_3** + **zeal_4r**)/4] will not make this adjustment. Each of these approaches may be more or less appropriate depending on how the scores are going to be used and what they are presumed to mean.

GENERATING Z-SCORES

Often, researchers are interested in evaluating individual scores relative to known or theoretical population distributions (e.g., the Normal Curve). These distributions are typically represented using a range of standardized scores called Z-scores. Converting your data to Z-scores allows a variety of comparisons to be made. For example, when a score is converted to a Z-score, we can estimate the likelihood that a score of that magnitude would be expected to occur in a given population. Further, once converted to Z-scores, data from different measures can be compared, even when their units of measurement differ.

Most introductory statistics textbooks offer rather extensive coverage of Z-scores. However, different textbooks take different approaches to calculating Z-scores. Some texts assume that the data you are working with represents population data, other texts assume that the data represents sample data, and still others may describe both approaches. As shown in Formulas 6.1 and 6.2, Z–scores are a ratio of the difference between a given score and the mean (either a population mean: μ, or a sample mean: $\overline{X}$) divided by the standard deviation (from either a population: σ, or a sample: s).

Formula 6.1 Z–Score based on Population Parameters

$$Z = \frac{X - \mu}{\sigma}$$

Formula 6.2 Z–Score based on Sample Statistics

$$Z = \frac{X - \overline{X}}{s}$$

Because population standard deviations and sample standard deviations each use different denominators in their calculation (See Formulas 6.3 and 6.4), each produces different values when calculated from the same data. This will result in different Z–scores for data assumed to represent a sample and data assumed to represent a population.

Formula 6.3 Population Standard Deviation

$$\sigma = \sqrt{\frac{\sum(X - \overline{X})^2}{n}} \text{ or } \sigma = \sqrt{\frac{\sum X^2 - \frac{(\sum X)^2}{n}}{n}}$$

Formula 6.4 Sample Standard Deviation

$$s = \sqrt{\frac{\sum(X - \overline{X})^2}{n-1}} \text{ or } s = \sqrt{\frac{\sum X^2 - \frac{(\sum X)^2}{n}}{n-1}}$$

When using SPSS to check the hand calculated Z–score that your textbook most likely requires, it is important to be clear about whether the data you are working with represents a sample or a population. Depending on whether you have sample or population data, you will have to use different procedures within SPSS to obtain Z–scores that match your hand calculations.

Z-SCORES FOR SAMPLE DATA: USING THE **DESCRIPTIVES...** OPTION

If you are asked to generate Z–scores for a data set and it is assumed that you working with sample data (and therefore the sample standard deviation), then SPSS offers a very easy way to generate Z–Scores for the entire data set using the **Descriptives...** option.

PROCEDURE FOR OBTAINING SAMPLE Z-SCORES USING THE <u>D</u>ESCRIPTIVES... OPTION

The first three steps for opening the **Descriptives...** dialogue box are not shown in Figure 6.7.

- Select <u>A</u>nalyses from the pull-down menu.
- Select **D<u>e</u>scriptive Statistics**.
- Select **<u>D</u>escriptives...** from the side menu. This will open the **Descriptives** dialogue box.

① Enter the variable(s) of interest in the **<u>V</u>ariable(s):** field. In this example, we have entered **zeal_tot** and **zeal_mean**.

② Select the **Save standardi<u>z</u>ed values as variables** option.

③ Finally, double-check the variables of interest and either select **OK** to run or **<u>P</u>aste** to create syntax to run at a later time.

If you selected the paste option from the procedure above, you should have generated the following syntax:

```
DESCRIPTIVES VARIABLES=zeal_tot zeal_mean
   /SAVE
   /STATISTICS=MEAN STDDEV MIN MAX .
```

▶**Figure 6.7** Obtaining Sample Z-Scores

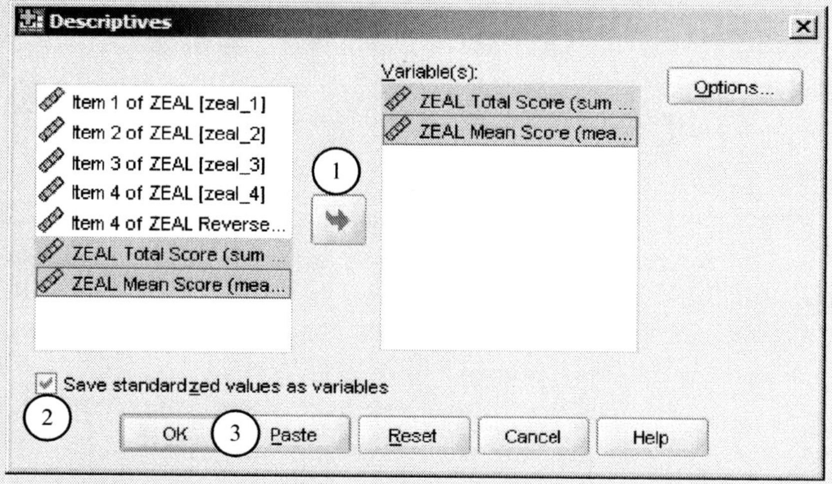

New variables representing the sample Z-Scores for the variables requested will be added automatically to the Data Editor. They will have the name of the old variable with a Z in front of it. See figure 6.8 on page 79 for an example.

Z-SCORES FOR POPULATION DATA: USING THE COMPUTE VARIABLE... OPTION

If you are asked to find Z-Scores based on the population mean and standard deviation, then the **Compute Variable...** option can be used. If you have been provided with the population mean and standard deviation, then follow the steps described in the procedure below. Alternatively, if you have not been given the population mean and standard deviation, you will have to calculate these values from your data set. In this example, the mean for **zeal_tot** is 16.100. Though SPSS will not calculate population variances or standard deviations, you can have SPSS generate the sample variance and convert it to a population variance by multiplying the sample variance by n−1, and then dividing the result by n. In the present example, the sample variance for **zeal_tot** is 56.322. If we multiply it by n−1 (56.322 × 9 = 506.898) and then divide the product by n (506.898/10 = 50.6898), we now have the population variance (σ^2). Taking the square root of the population variance leaves you with the population standard deviation. (σ = 7.1197).

PROCEDURE FOR OBTAINING THE POPULATION Z-SCORE USING THE COMPUTE VARIABLE... OPTION

- Select **Transform** from the pull-down menu.
- Select **Compute Variable....** This will open the **Compute Variable** dialogue box.
- Enter the desired name of the new variable in the **Target Variable:** field. In this example, we used "zeal_totz."
- Create a variable label if desired (left-click the **Type & Label...** button). In this example, we use the label "Zeal Total Score Z-Scored."
- Enter the Z-Score equation in the **Numeric Expression:** field.

  For this example, we used the following expression: **(zeal_tot − 16.100)/7.1197.**
- Finally, double-check your variables and either select **OK** to run or **Paste** to create syntax to run at a later time.

  If you selected the paste option from the procedure above, you should have generated the following syntax:

  ```
  COMPUTE zeal_totz=(zeal_tot-16.1)/7.1197 .
      VARIABLE LABELS zeal_totz 'ZEAL Total Score Z-Scored.' .
      EXECUTE .
  ```

Figure 6.8 shows part of the Data View of the Data Editor where three new variables have been created. **Zzeal_tot** and **Zzeal_mean** represent the sample Z-scores for the summed and averaged scores of the Zebra Eating Attitudes for Lions measure. Notice that each lion has the same score for both of the sample Z-score variables. Again, Z-scores are useful for making comparisons between different measures that utilize different scales of measurement. In this example, the sample Z-scores are identical because they came

▶ **Figure 6.8** Data View: Including New Z-Score Variables

	zeal_tot	zeal_mean	Zzeal_tot	Zzeal_mean	zeal_totz
1	5.00	1.25	-1.47905	-1.47905	-1.5591
2	6.00	1.50	-1.34580	-1.34580	-1.4186
3	12.00	3.00	-0.54632	-0.54632	-0.5759
4	12.00	3.00	-0.54632	-0.54632	-0.5759
5	18.00	4.50	0.25317	0.25317	0.2669
6	14.00	3.50	-0.27982	-0.27982	-0.2950
7	20.00	5.00	0.51967	0.51967	0.5478
8	25.00	6.25	1.18591	1.18591	1.2501
9	23.00	5.75	0.91941	0.91941	0.9691
10	26.00	6.50	1.31915	1.31915	1.3905

from the same measures scored with two different scales of measurement (sums versus averages).

The variable named **zeal_totz** represents the population Z-scores for the summed scores of the Zebra Eating Attitudes for Lions measure. Notice that these values differ from the sample Z-score values. This reflects the smaller value of the population standard deviation in comparison to the sample standard deviation, resulting in larger Z-score values. Further, you should note that we have increased the number of decimal places shown for the data points by adjusting values in the **Decimals** column of the Variable View of the Data Editor. You may need to adjust this so that the values displayed by SPSS match your hand calculations, depending on how many decimal places your instructor wants you to work with. (Four decimal places is fairly common.)

SUMMARY

This chapter covered some of the more common uses of the Compute Variable option. First, this chapter introduced a method for reversing the scoring of items so they can be interpreted in the same manner as other items in a measure. Second, methods for summing and averaging multiple items into a single score were presented. Finally, we covered methods for generating Z-scores. As you work more with these procedures, you will find that there are many different ways you can complete some of the tasks presented in this chapter. However, when you discover new techniques, it is generally a good idea to go back and check the results against procedures that you are more familiar with to ensure the new technique actually does what you think it should.

PRACTICE EXERCISES

Assume that a research team plans to initiate a cultural sensitivity training program to help improve Lion-Zebra relations. To assess the effectiveness of the program, researchers have developed a measure titled Lion's Openness to the Value of Embracing Zebras (LOVEZ). The measure consists of the following items, which are rated on 5-point scale of agreement (1 = strongly disagree; 5 = strongly agree):

1. Zebras should be hugged and not eaten.

2. Herd life is immoral.

3. Pride life is the only acceptable way to live.

4. Zebra culture offers an important contribution to life on the savanna.

Note that items 2 and 3 should be reversed when scoring. Table 6.1 presents the data for eight lions collected prior to their participation in the sensitivity training. For this data set, complete the following exercises:

1) Reverse score the appropriate items by subtracting each score from the appropriate constant. (Hint: you will not be able to use 8 as the constant.)

2) Create a variable representing the sum of the LOVEZ items. Be sure to use the appropriate reverse-scored items.

▶ **Table 6.1** Practice Exercise Data

Lion	Item 1	Item 2	Item 3	Item 4
1	5	1	2	4
2	5	2	1	5
3	4	2	2	4
4	4	3	1	3
5	3	3	3	4
6	3	2	4	3
7	2	4	5	2
8	1	5	5	1

3) Create a variable representing the mean of the LOVEZ items.

4) Create a variable representing the sample Z-scores of the sum of the LOVEZ items.

5) Create a variable representing the population Z-score of the sum of the LOVEZ items.

Comparing Means in SPSS (*t*-Tests)

This chapter covers procedures for testing the differences between two means using the SPSS **Compare Means** analyses. Specifically, we demonstrate procedures for running One-Sample *t*-tests, Independent-Samples *t*-tests, and Paired-Samples *t*-tests (also called Matched-Samples, Difference-Samples, or Repeated-Measures *t*-tests). Many textbooks include *Z*-tests in the comparing means chapter, but SPSS does not provide procedures for running *Z*-tests. This is mostly because situations where the population variance is known are typically rare. Further, when working with large samples, *t*-values approximate *Z*.

▶ **Cartoon 7.1**

THE FAR SIDE® By GARY LARSON

Cow poetry

This chapter is the first in the text to cover the topic of hypothesis testing, and it assumes that you have some familiarity with the logic and purpose of such analyses. It is also assumed that you have a basic understanding of the concept of statistical significance and of alpha as a representation of the level of statistical significance. If you are not familiar with these concepts, we recommend that you consult a text that offers a comprehensive introduction to hypothesis testing.

The examples used in this chapter are based on Cartoon 7.1. Assume that we are interested in measuring cow intelligence by counting the number of times different cows touch the electric fence. Presumably, more intelligent cows will touch the fence less frequently. For the following examples, we have created a data set by randomly drawing a sample of 30 cows from the population of cows owned by Farmer Perry. With the measurements we take from this sample, we are going to ask three research questions. First, does the average number of times the cows in our sample touch the electric fence differ from that of the larger population of Farmer Perry's cows? We will use the One-Sample *t*-test to answer this question. Second, do different types of cows in our sample (Holstein vs. Jersey) differ with respect to the average number of times they touch the fence? We will use the Independent-Samples *t*-test to answer this question. Finally, is the fence-touching behavior of our sample of cows affected by completing Cow School? To answer this question, we will ask two more specific questions. a) Does the sample of cows differ from the population of cows after the sample completes school? We will use the One-Sample *t*-test to answer this question. b) Does the frequency with which cows touch the fence after attending Cow School differ from the number times they touched the fence before attending school? We will use the Paired-Samples *t*-test to answer this question.

SETTING UP THE DATA

Figure 7.1 presents the Variable View of the SPSS Data Editor, where we have defined three new variables: two variables represent score data and one represents group data. The first variable (a score variable) represents the frequency with which the cows in our sample touch the electric fence. We have given it the variable name **fencetch** and given it the variable label "Number of Times Cows Touch the Electric Fence."

The second variable (a group variable) represents the breed of cow for each of our subjects: Holstein vs. Jersey. We have given it the variable name **breed** and the variable label "Cow Breed (Holstein vs. Jersey)." Because it is a group variable, we provided value labels for the two groups of breeds. The value of 1 was assigned to the Holstein group, and the value of 2 was assigned to the Jersey group.

The third variable (a score variable) represents the frequency with which the cows in our sample touch the electric fence after the sample had completed three weeks of Cow School. We have given it the variable name **fenctch2** and the variable label "Time 2 Fence Touch: Post–Cow School."

Figure 7.2 presents the Data View of the SPSS Data Editor. Here, we have entered the data from our sample of 30 cows for each of our three variables. Note that there are two windows presented in the figure. The left-hand window (labeled Ⓐ) presents the data for the first half of the sample (cows 1 to 15). Window Ⓑ represents the same SPSS window where we have scrolled down to show the data for the remaining cows (subjects 16 to 30). Remember that the columns represent each of the different variables and the rows represent each observation, which in this case is each cow. For example,

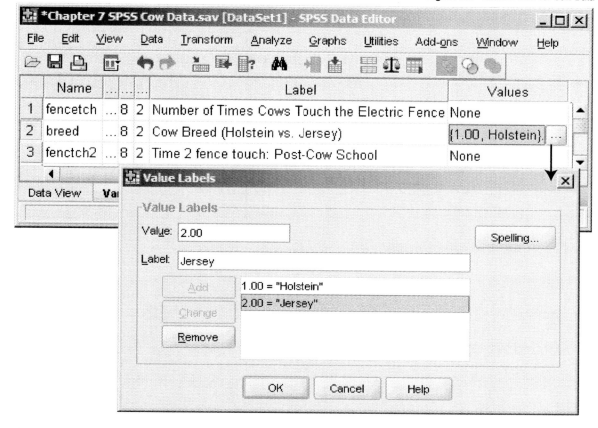

the first cow, a Holstein, touched the fence two times before attending Cow School and two times after. Similarly, the 30th cow, a Jersey, touched the fence 25 times before attending Cow School and 21 times after.

ONE-SAMPLE *t*-TEST

The One-Sample *t*-test allows us to test whether a sample mean ($\overline{X}$) is significantly different from a population mean (μ) when only the sample Standard Deviation (*s*) is known. You should consider using the One-Sample *t*-test when you have scores collected from a single group (a single sample) and you want to compare the group's average score to some known comparison value (typically a population mean).

RUNNING THE ONE SAMPLE *t*-TEST

In this example, we present the steps for using the **One–Sample T Test...** procedure to determine whether a sample mean is significantly different from a criterion value, in this case the population mean. Before you can run this type of analysis, you will need to know the value with which you want to compare your sample mean. SPSS calls this value a test value. In this case, our test value is 10 and was obtained by finding the average number of times every one of Farmer Perry's cows touched the electric fence (i.e., the population mean for fence touching).

▶ Figure 7.2 Data View for Cow Data

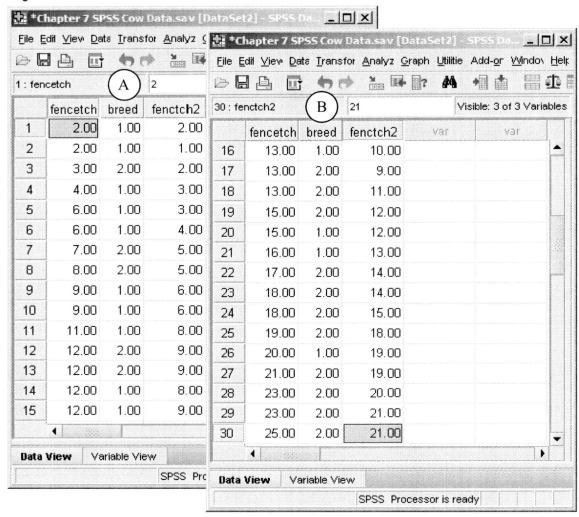

In the procedure presented below, we are going to perform two tests at the same time. The first test will compare the mean of the **fencetch** variable, the frequency of touching the electric fence prior to attending Cow School, with the population mean for touching the electric fence. The second test will compare the mean of the **fenctch2** variable, the frequency of touching the electric fence after attending Cow School, with the population mean for touching the electric fence.

PROCEDURE FOR RUNNING THE ONE-SAMPLE T TEST

① Select the **Analyze** pull-down menu.

② Select **Compare Means**.

③ Select **One-Sample T Test...** from the side menu. This will open the **One-Sample T Test** dialogue box.

④ Enter the variables **fencetch** and **fenctch2** in the <u>Test Variable(s):</u> field by either double-clicking on each variable or selecting the variables and left-clicking on the boxed arrow pointing to the right.

⑤ Enter the population mean in the **Test <u>V</u>alue:** field. In this case, our test value is 10.

⑥ Finally, double-check your variables and the test value, and either select **OK** to run or **<u>Paste</u>** to create syntax to run at a later time.

If you selected the paste option from the procedure above, you should have generated the following syntax:

T-TEST
 /TESTVAL=10
 /MISSING=ANALYSIS
 /VARIABLES=fencetch fenctch2
 /CRITERIA=CIN (.95) .

▶**Figure 7.3** Running One-Sample T Test for Cow Data

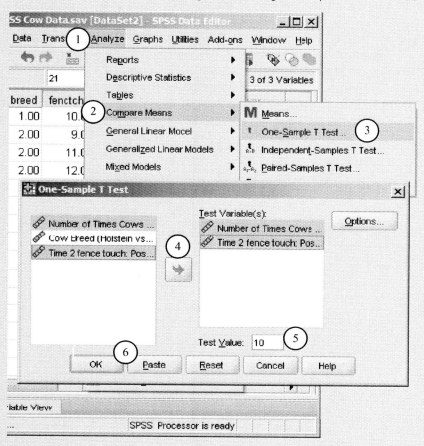

READING THE ONE-SAMPLE *t*-TEST OUTPUT

The One-Sample *t*-test output is presented in Figure 7.4. This output consists of two tables: **One-Sample Statistics** and **One-Sample Test.** For each variable being tested, the **One-Sample Statistics** table presents the sample size (**N**), mean, standard deviation, and the standard error of the mean (calculated by dividing the standard deviation by the square root of N).

The One-Sample Test table reports the *t* values obtained, the degrees of freedom (**df**), the two-tailed alpha level or level of significance (**Sig.**), and the difference between the sample mean and the test value (**Mean Difference**). In this example, the mean difference equals the difference between the sample mean and the population mean. This part of the output also reports a confidence interval for the mean difference. These confidence intervals indicate the range of possible mean difference values that would be expected to occur simply due to chance alone. If the sample mean and the test value (in this case the population mean) were different only due to chance, the value of the mean difference would fall between the lower and upper limit of the confidence interval 95% of the time. When the actual mean difference falls outside of this confidence interval, it is generally considered to be a significant difference, one that is meaningful and non-random.

With respect to the first hypothesis regarding the cows' fence-touching behavior prior to attending Cow School, we have obtained a *t*-value of 2.387, with 29 degrees of freedom, which is the sample size (n = 30) minus 1. Unlike the table of critical *t*-values typically used to evaluate hand-calculated statistics, SPSS reports the exact level of significance. In this example, the *t* is significant at the .024 alpha level, indicating that there is a 2.4% probability that the difference between the sample mean and population mean occurred due to chance alone. Typically, when the likelihood that a test statistic, in this case *t*, might have occurred due to chance alone is 5% or less (alpha $\leq$ .05), we can conclude that the effect is significant. With respect to our example, we can conclude that the difference between the sample mean and the expected population mean is meaningful. The average number of times the cows in our sample touch the electric fence is significantly

Figure 7.4 Output for One-Sample *t*-Test

T-Test

One-Sample Statistics

	N	Mean	Std. Deviation	Std. Error Mean
Number of Times Cows Touch the Electric Fence	30	12.8000	6.42409	1.17287
Time 2 fence touch: Post-Cow School	30	10.2667	6.09654	1.11307

One-Sample Test

	Test Value = 10					
					95% Confidence Interval of the Difference	
	t	df	Sig. (2-tailed)	Mean Difference	Lower	Upper
Number of Times Cows Touch the Electric Fence	2.387	29	.024	2.80000	.4012	5.1988
Time 2 fence touch: Post-Cow School	.240	29	.812	.26667	-2.0098	2.5432

different from the average number of times the entire population of Farmer Perry's cows touch the electric fence. We can be more specific by looking at the Mean Difference statistic and say that our sample of cows touched the electric fence an average of 2.8 more times than the general population of cows.

With respect to the fence-touching behavior of our sample after attending Cow School, we have obtained a *t*-value of .24, which is not significant. The alpha level associated with this *t* value for 29 degrees of freedom is .812, indicating that there is an 81.2% chance that a mean difference of this size would occur by chance alone. Because the alpha value of .812 is much larger than the .05 alpha level, we should conclude that after attending Cow School, our sample no longer differs significantly from the entire population of Farmer Perry's cows. The mean difference of .2661 is likely due to sampling error.

INDEPENDENT-SAMPLES *t*-TEST

RUNNING THE INDEPENDENT-SAMPLES *t*-TEST

The Independent-Samples *t*-test allows us to test whether two sample means are significantly different from each other. You should consider using the Independent-Samples *t*-test when you have one independent variable consisting of two groups and one dependent variable consisting of scores. In our current example, the independent variable, **breed**, consists of the Holstein and Jersey groups. For the dependent variable, we will use the score variable **fencetch**, representing the number of times each cow touched the electric fence prior to attending Cow School. With this data, we can test the hypothesis that the average number of times that unschooled Holstein cows touch the electric fence significantly differs from the average number of times that unschooled Jersey cows touch the electric fence.

PROCEDURE FOR RUNNING THE INDEPENDENT-SAMPLES T TEST

① Select the **Analyze** pull-down menu.

② Select **Compare Means**.

③ Select **Independent-Samples T Test...** from the side menu. This will open the **Independent-Samples T Test** dialogue box.

④ Enter the score variable **fencetch** in the **Test Variable(s):** field by left-clicking the variable and left-clicking on the boxed arrow pointing to the **Test Variable(s):** field.

⑤ Enter the group variable **breed** in the **Grouping Variable:** field.

⑥ Left-click the **Define Groups...** button. This will open the **Define Groups** dialogue box, where we can indicate what values have been paired with each group in our data set.

⑦ Enter the numerical values that have been used to represent the groups of interest into the **Group 1:** and **Group 2:** fields.

• In this case, we have used the numerical values of 1 and 2 to represent our groups and have entered those values in the **Group 1:** and **Group 2:** fields, respectively.

⑧ Left-click **Continue** to return to **Independent-Samples T Test** dialogue box.

⑨ Finally, double-check your variables and either select **OK** to run or **Paste** to create syntax to run at a later time.

If you selected the paste option from the procedure above, you should have generated the following syntax:

```
T-TEST
GROUPS=breed(1 2)
  /MISSING=ANALYSIS
  /VARIABLES=fencetch
  /CRITERIA=CIN(.95) .
```

▶ **Figure 7.5** Running Independent-Samples T Test

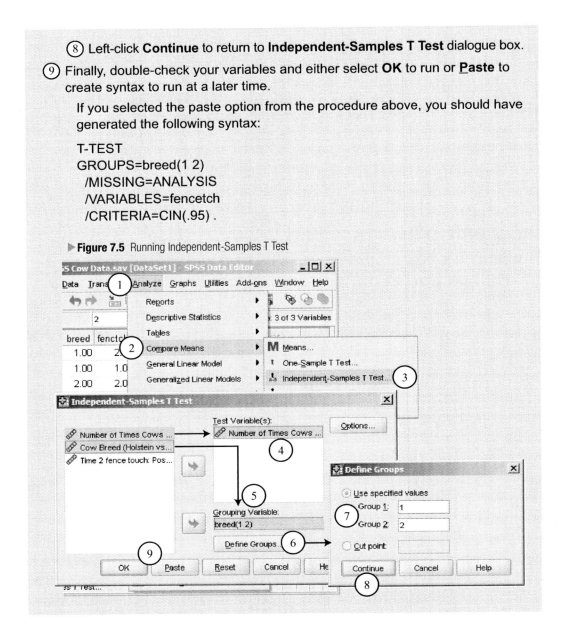

READING THE INDEPENDENT-SAMPLES *t*-TEST OUTPUT

Figure 7.6 on the next page presents the output for the Independent–Samples T Test. The output consists of two major parts, **Group Statistics** and **Independent Samples Test**. The **Group Statistics** table provides the sample sizes (**N**), means, standard deviations, and the standard error of the mean for the score variable for each group. With respect to our current example, there were 14 Holsteins in our sample, and they touched the electric fence an average of 9.7857 times with a standard deviation of 5.38057 and a standard error of the mean of 1.43802. Similarly, there were 16 Jerseys, and they touched the electric fence an average of 15.4375 times with a standard deviation of 6.22863 and a standard error of the mean of 1.55716.

▶**Figure 7.6** Output for Independent Samples *t*-Test

T-Test

Group Statistics

	Cow Breed...	N	Mean	Std. Deviation	Std. Error Mean
Number of Times Cows Touch the Electric Fence	Holstein	14	9.7857	5.38057	1.43802
	Jersey	16	15.4375	6.22863	1.55716

Independent Samples Test

		Levene's Test for Equality of Variances (A)		t-test for Equality of Means (B)	
		F	Sig.	t	df
Number of Times Cows Touch the Electric Fence	Equal variances assumed	.368	.549	-2.640	28
	Equal variances not assumed			-2.666	27.998

Independent Samples Test

		t-test for Equality of Means (B)		
		Sig. (2-tailed)	Mean Difference	Std. Error Difference
Number of Times Cows Touch the Electric Fence	Equal variances assumed	.013	-5.65179	2.14095
	Equal variances not assumed	.013	-5.65179	2.11958

Independent Samples Test

		t-test for Equality of Means (C) 95% Confidence Interval of the Difference	
		Lower	Upper
Number of Times Cows Touch the Electric Fence	Equal variances assumed	-10.03733	-1.26624
	Equal variances not assumed	-9.99357	-1.31000

The Independent-Samples Test output contains the results of two distinct tests. The first are for Leven's Test for Equality of Variances (which we have labeled Ⓐ), which tests the assumption that the variability within each group is equal. This assumption must be met in order to properly use independent-samples *t*-tests. If the amount of variability in each group is equal, then the standard *t*-test procedures covered in most textbooks can be used. However, if the variance of the two groups is not equal, then you need to use a modified test that corrects for this. The results of both the standard *t*-test and the modified *t*-test are presented in the output in the rows labeled "Equal variances assumed" and "Equal variances not assumed," respectively. To decide which *t*-test results to use, you must look at the alpha level (**Sig.**) of Levene's Test for Equality of Variances, which we have circled in Figure 7.6. If the alpha level is greater than .05, then you can assume that group variances are equal and you will use the upper row of *t*-test results. If the alpha level is .05 or less, then you should assume that the group variances are not equal and use the lower row of *t*-test results. In this case, the alpha level is .549 (larger than .05), so the first row of *t*-test results is appropriate, which is circled and labeled Ⓑ in Figure 7.6.

The **Independent Samples Test** table also provides us with the t obtained, degrees of freedom (**df**), the two–tailed level of significance (**Sig.**), and the mean difference (the difference between the two group means). In this example, we have obtained a t-value of -2.64 and, with 28 degrees of freedom ($df = n-2$), it is significant at the .013 alpha level. It appears that Holstein and Jersey cows are significantly different with respect to the frequency with which they touch the electric fence. More specifically, by examining the group means and the mean difference (Group 1 mean $-$ Group 2 mean), we see that the Holsteins touched the electric fence an average of 5.6518 fewer times than the Jersey cows.

Part Ⓒ of the Independent Samples Test table provides confidence intervals for the difference between the group means. This interval allows us to estimate the actual mean difference between groups found in the population based on potential sampling error. In this case, we can be 95% confident that the actual difference in fence-touching frequency found between all Holsteins and all Jersey cows in the population is somewhere between -1.26624 and -10.03733.

PAIRED-SAMPLES *t*-TEST

RUNNING THE PAIRED-SAMPLE *t*-TEST

Like other t-tests, the Paired–Samples t-test allows us to test whether two sample means are significantly different from each other. The Paired–Samples t is appropriate when the means are collected from the same group on two separate occasions (typically called repeated-measures or within-groups designs). Also, the Paired–Samples t may be used when means are collected from two different groups where each member of one group has been paired or matched with a member of the other group based on one or more characteristics (e.g., age, IQ, economic status, etc.). In our current example, we have measured fence-touching behavior twice: once before our cows attended Cow School (**fencetch**) and once after (**fenctch2**). With this data, we can test the hypothesis that the average number of times that unschooled cows touch the electric fence differs significantly from the average number of times that the same cows touch the electric fence after attending three weeks of Cow School.

PROCEDURE FOR RUNNING THE PAIRED-SAMPLES T TEST

① Select the **Analyze** pull-down menu.

② Select **Compare Means**.

③ Select **Paired-Sample T Test...** from the side menu. This will open the **Paired-Sample T Test** dialogue box.

④ Select the first score variable (**fencetch**) by left-clicking on the variable and then left-clicking the boxed arrow. Repeat these steps for the second score variable (**fenctch2**). The two variables will now appear as Pair 1 in the **Paired Variables:** field.

⑤ The order of the variables (which is treated as variable 1 and which is treated as variable 2) can be switched by clicking on the double-headed boxed arrow. If you have requested multiple analyses, you can change the order in which they will appear by using the up and down boxed arrows.

⑥ Finally, double-check your variables and either select **OK** to run or **Paste** to create syntax to run at a later time.

If you selected the paste option from the procedure above, you should have generated the following syntax:

T-TEST
PAIRS= fencetch WITH fenctch2 (PAIRED)
    /CRITERIA=CIN(.95)
    /MISSING=ANALYSIS .

▶**Figure 7.7** Running the Paired-Samples T Test

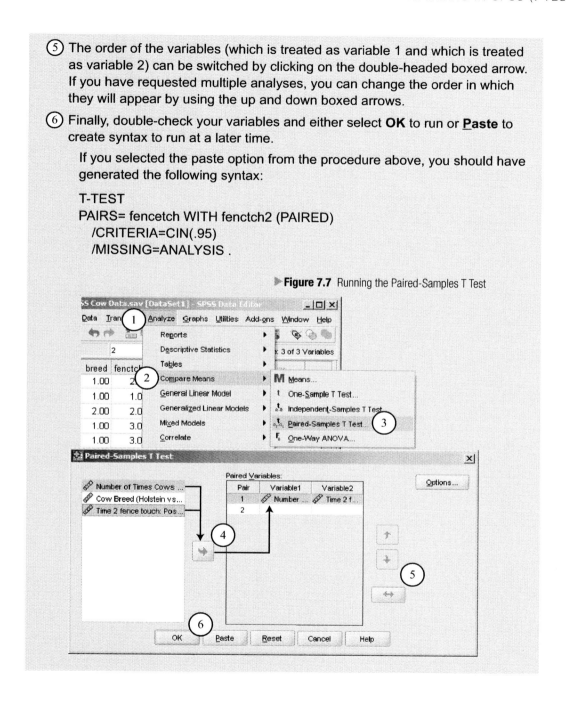

READING THE PAIRED-SAMPLES *t*-TEST OUTPUT

Figure 7.8 presents the output for the Paired–Samples *t*-test. This output consists of three major parts: **Paired Samples Statistics**, **Paired Samples Correlations**, and **Paired Samples Test.** The **Paired Samples Statistics** table provides the mean, sample sizes (**N**), standard deviations, and the standard error of the mean for each score variable.

▶ **Figure 7.8** Output for Paired Samples *t*-Test

T-Test

Paired Samples Statistics

		Mean	N	Std. Deviation	Std. Error Mean
Pair 1	Number of Times Cows Touch the Electric Fence	12.8000	30	6.42409	1.17287
	Time 2 fence touch: Post-Cow School	10.2667	30	6.09654	1.11307

Paired Samples Correlations

		N	Correlation	Sig.
Pair 1	Number of Times Cows Touch the Electric Fence & Time 2 fence touch: Post-Cow School	30	.988	.000

Paired Samples Test

		Paired Differences				
	(A)				95% Confidence Interval of the Difference	
		Mean	Std. Deviation	Std. Error Mean	Lower	Upper
Pair 1	Number of Times Cows Touch the Electric Fence - Time 2 fence touch: Post-Cow School	2.53333	1.04166	.19018	2.14437	2.92230

Paired Samples Test

		Paired Differences		
	(B)	t	df	Sig. (2-tailed)
Pair 1	Number of Times Cows Touch the Electric Fence - Time 2 fence touch: Post-Cow School	13.321	29	.000

The **Paired Samples Correlations** table presents a hypothesis testing statistic that will be covered in a later chapter on Correlation and Regression. Essentially, this statistic tells us how strongly related our two variables are. The closer the correlation value gets to 1 or –1 the more related our two variables are.

The **Paired Samples Test** table is split into two parts, which we have labeled (A) and (B). Part (A) presents the basic parts of the formula to obtain the *t* value for a paired sample test. First, the mean difference is reported in the column labeled **Mean.** The mean difference is the numerator of the Paired-Samples *t* formula and is obtained by subtracting the mean for the first measurement from the mean for the second measurement. In this case, the mean for the post-Cow School fence-touching variable (10.2667) is subtracted from the mean for the pre-Cow School fence-touching variable (12.8000), which produces a value of 2.5333. The second column, labeled "Std. Deviation," reports the standard deviation of the difference, which is part of the denominator of the Paired-Samples *t* formula. The third column, labeled "Std. Error Mean," reports the standard error of the mean difference, which is obtained by dividing the standard deviation of the difference by the square root of *n*. The standard error of the mean difference is the complete numerator of the Paired-Samples *t* formula. The last two columns of this table present the boundaries of the 95% confidence interval, within which the true mean difference for the population is expected to fall.

Part Ⓑ of the Paired Samples Test table presents the *t* obtained, degrees of freedom, and the two-tailed level of significance (alpha). In this case, the *t* obtained is 13.321, there are 29 degrees of freedom ($df = n - 1$), and it is significant at least at the .001 alpha level. Though SPSS reports a significance level of .000, it is generally inappropriate to report this level since we can never be 100% sure our results did not occur by chance alone. Reporting .001 is the preferred method.

With respect to the hypotheses of our current example, we can conclude that the pre–Cow School fence-touching behavior for our sample of cows differed from their post–Cow School fence-touching behavior. More specifically, based on an examination of the difference between the pre– and post–Cow School fence-touching behavior means, our sample of cows touched the electric fence an average of 2.5333 times more often before attending Cow School compared to their post–Cow School fence-touching frequency.

SUMMARY

In this chapter, we covered the use of several tests that compare group means. Specifically, we demonstrated how to conduct a Single Sample *t*-test within SPSS to compare a sample mean with a population mean, how to conduct an Independent-Samples *t*-test to compare two sample means, and how to conduct a Paired-Samples *t*-test to compare the means obtained from a single group at two different points in time (or two groups that have been matched). Subsequent chapters will introduce methods for comparing means when you have more than two groups (ANOVA) or when you want to consider more than one group variable at a time (Factorial ANOVA). However, these procedures will include follow-up tests that are conceptually identical to the *t*-tests we have just introduced.

PRACTICE EXERCISES

Assume a researcher is interested in measuring the attitudes a particular population of cows hold about poetry. The researcher draws a random sample of 20 cows from the herd. Each cow is asked to rate the degree to which they like poetry using a single item 7-point numerical scale ranging from 1 (Strongly Dislike Poetry) to 7 (Strongly Like Poetry). The cows' attitudes were measured at two time points: once prior to the administration of a poetry appreciation intervention and once after. With respect to the intervention, cows were randomly assigned to one of two groups. One group attended a two hour poetry appreciation class and the other group served as a control group. The results of the study are presented in Table 7.1. Use this data to conduct the analyses that would answer the research questions below. For each analysis, report the appropriate group means, group standard deviations, *t*-values, degrees of freedom, sample size (N), level of significance, and describe the results obtained (e.g., did the groups significantly differ with respect to the attitude of interest).

1. Are the cows' pre-intervention and post-intervention poetry attitudes different from the poetry attitudes of the entire herd, estimated to be 4.00?

2. Are the cow's pre-intervention poetry attitudes different from the post-intervention attitudes, regardless of which intervention group they belong to?

3. Are the post-intervention attitudes toward poetry of the group that attended the poetry appreciation class significantly different from the post-intervention attitudes held by the control group?

4. Are the pre-intervention attitudes toward poetry of the group that attended the poetry appreciation class significantly different from the pre-intervention attitudes held by the control group?

▶**Table 7.1** Practice Exercise Data

Cow	Pre-Intervention Poetry Attitude	Post-Intervention Poetry Attitude	Intervention Group: Poetry Appreciation Class vs. No Class
1	1	1	Class
2	1	1	No Class
3	2	1	Class
4	2	2	No Class
5	3	1	Class
6	3	3	No Class
7	3	1	Class
8	3	3	No Class
9	4	1	Class
10	4	4	No Class
11	4	2	Class
12	4	4	No Class
13	5	3	Class
14	5	5	No Class
15	5	3	Class
16	5	5	No Class
17	6	4	Class
18	6	6	No Class
19	7	4	Class
20	7	7	No Class

One-Way ANOVA: Means Comparison with Two or More Groups

The previous chapter demonstrated methods for testing differences between the means of two groups. This chapter presents steps for testing differences between the means of two or more groups using the SPSS **ANOVA** procedures. Procedures are presented for running a One-Way Analysis of Variance (ANOVA), generating Fisher's LSD Post Hoc Tests, and creating a chart that plots the group means. You should consider using the one-way ANOVA when you have one independent variable consisting of two or more groups and one dependent variable consisting of scores for all the members of each group.

SETTING UP THE DATA

Assume that researchers are testing eight-year-olds' tolerance for spicy foods (See Cartoon 8.1). Thirty children have been randomly assigned to one of three groups. Each group receives one of three types of chili sauce, each made with a different type of chili pepper: poblano *(capsicum annuum c.)*, jalapeno *(capsicum annuum c.)*, and habanero *(capsicum chinense)*. The level of spicy heat for each of the three chili peppers is measured in Scoville Units and is found to be 1,000–1,500 Scoville Units for the poblano peppers, 2,500–8,000 Scoville Units for the jalapeno peppers, and 100,000–350,000 Scoville Units for the habanero peppers. The researchers measured the time in seconds it took before each of the thirty children had a "volcanic eruption" (i.e., spewed) after tasting the sauce. The data obtained by our scientists is presented in Table 8.1.

Figure 8.1 presents the Variable View of the SPSS Data Editor where we have defined two variables. The first variable corresponds to the three different groups of children that

▶ Cartoon 8.1

▶ **Table 8.1** Volcanic Eruption Data

Number of Seconds before Eight-Year-Olds Volcanically Erupt after Tasting Chili Sauce		
Poblano Peppers 1,000–1,500 su	Jalapeno Peppers 2,500–8,000 su	Habanero Peppers 100,000–300,000 su
10	8	5
11	9	6
12	10	7
13	11	8
14	12	9
14	12	9
15	13	10
16	14	11
17	15	12
18	16	13

▶ **Figure 8.1** Variable View for Volcanic Eruption Data

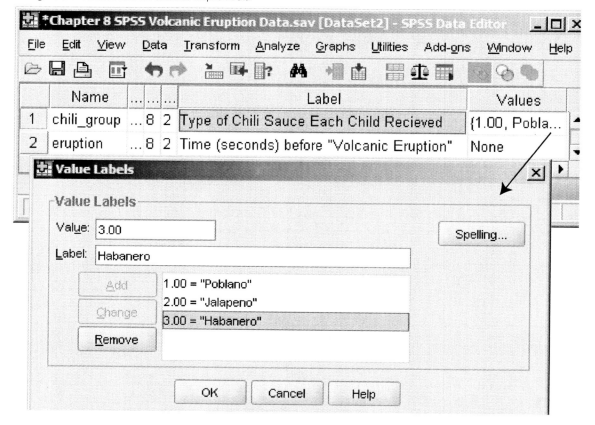

received the three different types of chili sauce. This variable is named **chili_group** and is labeled "Type of Chili Sauce Each Child Received." We have assigned numerical values to each group and supplied value labels. We have paired 1 with the label "Poblano," 2 with "Jalapeno," and 3 with "Habanero." The second variable represents the latency (amount of time) between the child tasting the chili sauce and spewing it. We have given it the variable name **eruption** and the label "Time (seconds) before 'Volcanic Eruption'."

Figure 8.2 presents the Data View of the SPSS Data Editor. Here we have entered the volcanic eruption data for the 30 children in our sample. Remember that the columns represent each variable and the rows represent each observation, which in this case is

Figure 8.2 Data View for Volcanic Eruption Data

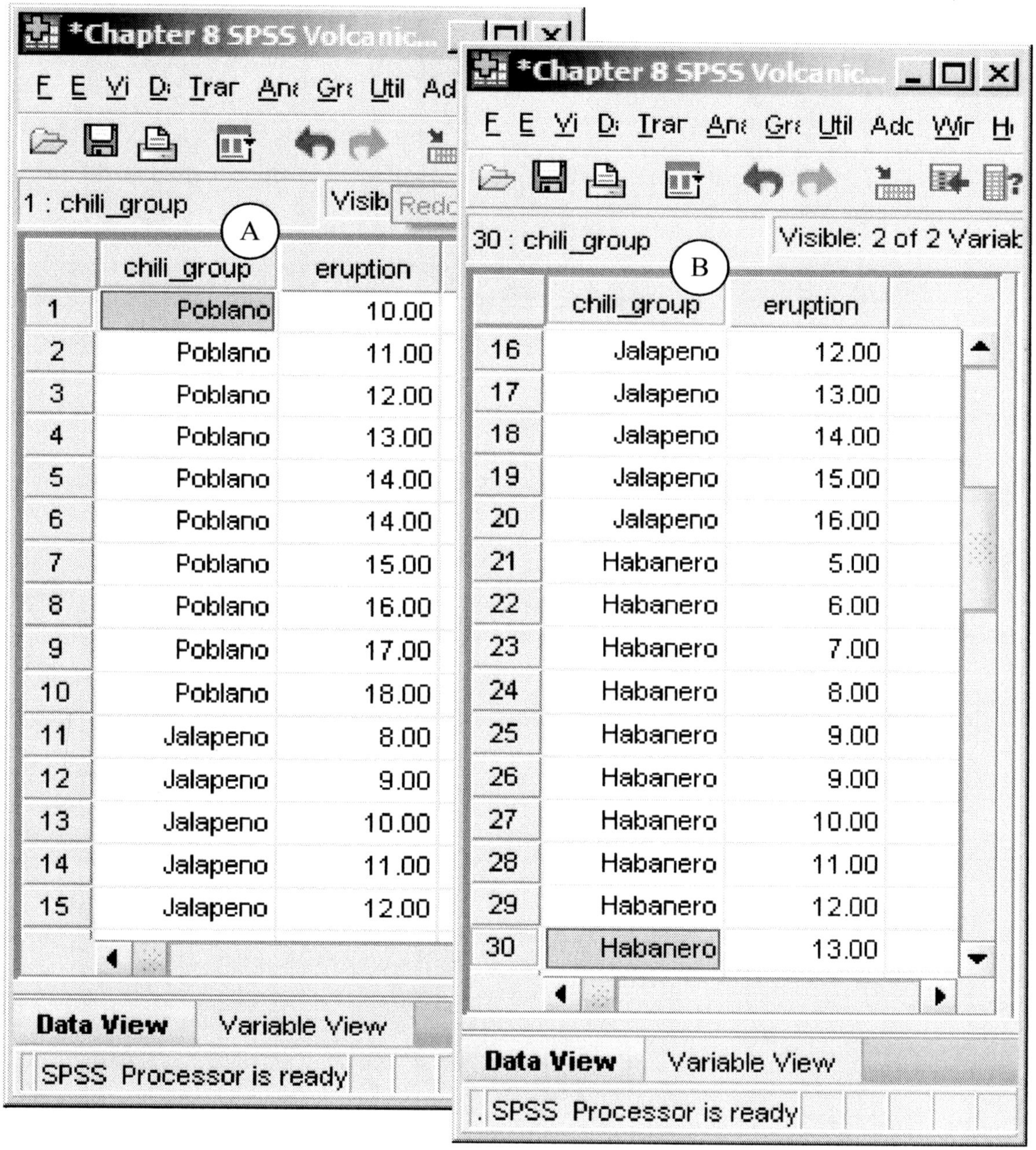

	chili_group	eruption
1	Poblano	10.00
2	Poblano	11.00
3	Poblano	12.00
4	Poblano	13.00
5	Poblano	14.00
6	Poblano	14.00
7	Poblano	15.00
8	Poblano	16.00
9	Poblano	17.00
10	Poblano	18.00
11	Jalapeno	8.00
12	Jalapeno	9.00
13	Jalapeno	10.00
14	Jalapeno	11.00
15	Jalapeno	12.00
16	Jalapeno	12.00
17	Jalapeno	13.00
18	Jalapeno	14.00
19	Jalapeno	15.00
20	Jalapeno	16.00
21	Habanero	5.00
22	Habanero	6.00
23	Habanero	7.00
24	Habanero	8.00
25	Habanero	9.00
26	Habanero	9.00
27	Habanero	10.00
28	Habanero	11.00
29	Habanero	12.00
30	Habanero	13.00

each eight-year-old. For example, the first child (found in part Ⓐ of the figure) tasted poblano chili sauce and spewed after 10 seconds. Similarly, the 30th child (found in part Ⓑ of the figure) tasted the habanero chili sauce and spewed after 13 seconds.

RUNNING THE ANALYSES

To assess eight-year-olds' tolerance for spicy food, the researchers have designed a study that will determine whether hotter chili sauces will cause children to erupt faster than milder chili sauces. The one-way ANOVA will determine whether the mean eruption time for each group differs from any of the other groups. If the results of the ANOVA are significant, then meaningful group differences exist. However, when you have more than two groups, a statistically significant one-way ANOVA result alone does not indicate which groups differ. In order to determine which groups significantly differ follow-up tests are required. In this chapter we use the Fisher's LSD *t*-tests to probe a significant one-way ANOVA result.

PROCEDURE FOR RUNNING A ONE-WAY ANOVA

① Select **Analyze** from the pull-down menu.

② Select **Compare Means**.

③ Select **One-Way ANOVA...** from the side menu. This will open the **One-Way ANOVA** dialogue box.

④ Enter the variable representing scores (**eruption**) in the **Dependent List:** field by left-clicking on the variable and left-clicking on the boxed arrow pointing to the **Dependent List:** field.

⑤ Enter the variable representing groups (**chili_group**) in the **Factor:** field by left-clicking on the variable and left-clicking on the boxed arrow pointing to the **Factor:** field.

⑥ Request the LSD *t*-tests by left-clicking the **Post Hoc...** button. Figure 8.4 presents the **One-Way ANOVA: Post Hoc Multiple Comparisons** dialogue box.

⑦ Select **LSD** under the **Equal Variances Assumed** options.

⑧ Left-click **Continue** to return to the **One-Way ANOVA** dialogue box.

⑨ Left-click the **Options...** button (shown in Figure 8.3 on the next page) to request descriptive statistics for each of the groups and a line chart that will plot the group means. This will open the **One-Way ANOVA: Options** dialogue box (shown in Figure 8.4 on the next page).

⑩ Select **Descriptive** from the **Statistics** options. This will provide you with the sample size, mean, standard deviation, standard error of the mean, and range for each group.

⑪ Select the **Means plot** option. This will provide you with a line chart that graphs the group means.

⑫ Left-click **Continue** to return to the **One-Way ANOVA** dialogue box.

▶**Figure 8.3** Procedure for Running the One-Way ANOVA

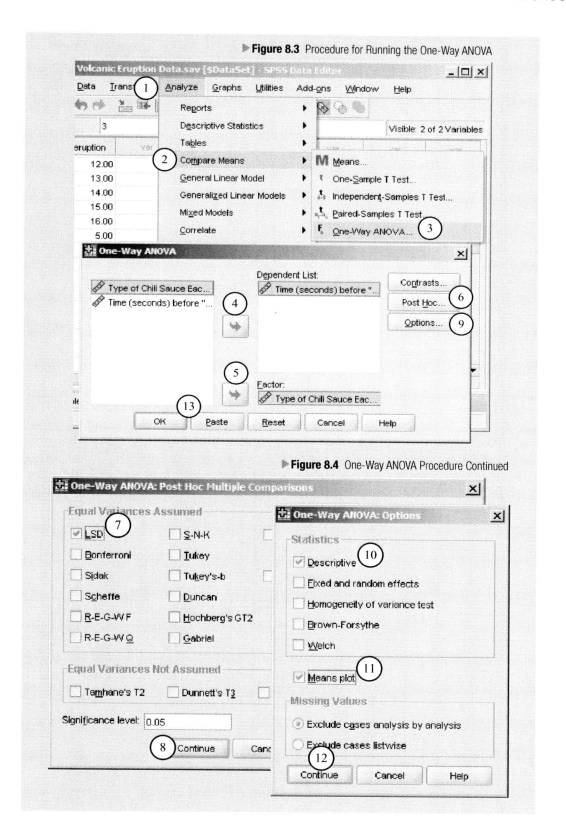

▶**Figure 8.4** One-Way ANOVA Procedure Continued

⑬ Finally, double-check your variables and options and either select **OK** to run or **Paste** to create syntax to run at a later time.

If you selected the paste option from the procedure above, you should have generated the following syntax:

```
ONEWAY
    eruption BY chili_group
        /STATISTICS DESCRIPTIVES
        /PLOT MEANS
        /MISSING ANALYSIS
        /POSTHOC = LSD ALPHA(.05) .
```

READING THE ONE-WAY ANOVA OUTPUT

The One-Way Anova Output is presented in Figures 8.5, 8.6, and 8.7. This output consists of four major parts: **Descriptives** (in Figure 8.5), **ANOVA** (in Figure 8.5), **Post Hoc Tests** (in Figure 8.6), and the **Means Plots** (in Figure 8.7).

READING THE DESCRIPTIVES OUTPUT

The **Descriptives** table (part Ⓐ of Figure 8.5) provides each groups' sample size (**N**), mean, standard deviation, standard error of the mean (the standard deviation divided by the square root of N, which estimates the potential for sampling error), and minimum and maximum scores. This part of the output also presents the confidence intervals within which we are 95% confident that the true population mean of time before eruption for each group will fall. We usually only need to concern ourselves with the means and standard deviations for each group. In this case, the means and standard deviations

▶ **Figure 8.5** ANOVA Output for Volcanic Eruption Data

Oneway

Descriptives Ⓐ

Time (seconds) before "Volcanic Eruption"

	N	Mean	Std. Deviation	Std. Error	95% Confidence Interval for Mean		Minimum	Maximum
					Lower Bound	Upper Bound		
Poblano	10	14.0000	2.58199	.81650	12.1530	15.8470	10.00	18.00
Jalapeno	10	12.0000	2.58199	.81650	10.1530	13.8470	8.00	16.00
Habanero	10	9.0000	2.58199	.81650	7.1530	10.8470	5.00	13.00
Total	30	11.6667	3.25188	.59371	10.4524	12.8809	5.00	18.00

ANOVA Ⓑ

Time (seconds) before "Volcanic Eruption"

	Sum of Squares	df	Mean Square	F	Sig.
Between Groups	126.667	2	63.333	9.500	.001
Within Groups	180.000	27	6.667		
Total	306.667	29			

(presented in parentheses) for the poblano group, the jalapeno group, and the habanero group are 14.00 (2.58199), 12.00 (2.58199), and 9.00 (2.58199), respectively. Eyeballing our data, we begin to suspect that the habanero group erupted more quickly than the other two groups.

READING THE ANOVA OUTPUT

Like ANOVA Summary Tables presented in most textbooks, the three rows of the **ANOVA** table for our example (part Ⓑ of Figure 8.5) present the different components of an ANOVA: Between Groups information, Within Groups information, and information regarding the Total sample. The first column shows that the **Sums of Squares** between groups ($SS_{between}$) is 126.667, the Sums of Squares within (SS_{within}) is 180.00, and the Sums of Squares for the total sample (SS_{total}) is 306.667.

The second column presents the degrees of freedom (**df**) between groups (number of groups minus 1), degrees of freedom within groups (n minus number of groups), and total degrees of freedom (n minus 1). In this case, the $df_{between}$ is 2 because there are 3 groups, the df_{within} is 27 because there are 30 children in the sample and 3 groups, and the df_{total} is 29 because there are 30 children in the sample.

The third column presents the **Mean Square** (MS) between groups and within groups, respectively. $MS_{between}$ is obtained by dividing the $SS_{between}$ by the $df_{between}$. In this case $MS_{between} = 63.333$. Similarly, MS_{within} is obtained by dividing the SS_{within} by the df_{within}. In this case $MS_{within} = 6.667$.

The fourth and fifth columns present the final **F** statistic and its associated level of significance (alpha level), respectively. The F is obtained by dividing the $MS_{between}$ by MS_{within} and results in an $F_{obtained}$ of 9.500. Looking at the value given in the **Sig.** column, we can see that the $F_{obtained}$ is significant at the .001 alpha level. This falls well below the .05 alpha level, which is generally accepted as the upper limit for establishing statistical significance, so we can conclude that significant differences exist between the group means. Also, the alpha level .001 tells us the odds are 1 in 1000 that the differences we found occurred by chance alone. However, even though we know that at least one of our group means is significantly different from another group mean, the F statistic does not indicate which groups differ significantly and which do not. To obtain this information, we must turn to the Multiple Comparisons output presented in Figure 8.6.

READING THE MULTIPLE COMPARISONS OUTPUT

The Multiple Comparisons output presents the results of Fisher's LSD (Least Significant Difference) t-tests that were requested from the Post Hoc options. Before discussing the output, it may be helpful to review the formula for the LSD t-test (Formula 8.1)

Formula 8.1 $$t_{LSD} = \frac{\overline{X}_1 - \overline{X}_2}{\sqrt{MS_{Within}\left(\frac{1}{n_1} + \frac{1}{n_2}\right)}}$$

Like other t-tests, the LSD t is a ratio of the mean difference (calculated in the numerator) and the standard error of the mean (calculated in the denominator). The LSD t is different from other t-tests because the standard error of the mean is based on the value of the Mean Square Within (MS_{Within}) obtained from the ANOVA table.

▶**Figure 8.6** ANOVA Output for Volcanic Eruption Data Continued

Multiple Comparisons

Time (seconds) before "Volcanic Eruption"
LSD

(I) Type of Chili Sauce	(J) Type of Chili Sauce	Mean Difference (I-J)	Std. Error	Sig.	95% Confidence Interval	
					Lower Bound	Upper Bound
Poblano	Jalapeno	2.00000	1.15470	.095	−.3692	4.3692
	Habanero	5.00000*	1.15470	.000	2.6308	7.3692
Jalapeno	Poblano	−2.00000	1.15470	.095	−4.3692	.3692
	Habanero	3.00000*	1.15470	.015	.6308	5.3692
Habanero	Poblano	−5.00000*	1.15470	.000	−7.3692	−2.6308
	Jalapeno	−3.00000*	1.15470	.015	−5.3692	−.6308

* The mean difference is significant at the 0.05 level.

The **Multiple Comparisons** table is divided into three major rows, one for each group tested. Each row is labeled Poblano, Jalapeno, and Habanero, accordingly. Within each major row, the remaining two groups comprise minor rows of their own. For example, major row 1, Poblano, contains the minor rows labeled Jalapeno and Habanero, respectively. Each minor row represents a Post Hoc LSD *t*-test, which tests whether the means of the two groups in that row are significantly different. In the first minor row of major row 1, we are assessing whether the average amount of time it took children to erupt after eating poblano chili sauce is significantly different from the amount of time it took children who ate jalapeno chili sauce to erupt. Similarly, the second minor row of major row 1 compares the eruption times of children who ate poblano chili sauce with the times of children who ate habanero chili sauce.

The first column of data, labeled **Mean Difference (I-J),** presents the result of subtracting the minor row mean from the major row mean. The mean for the major row group is treated as $\overline{X}_1$, the first score in the numerator of Formula 8.1, and the mean for the minor row group is treated as $\overline{X}_2$, the second score in the numerator of Formula 8.1. For major row 1: minor row 1, the mean difference (2.00) is found by subtracting the mean time to erupt for the group tasting the jalapeno chili sauce (12.00) from the mean time to erupt for the group tasting the poblano chili sauce (14.00).

The second column of data, labeled **Std. Error,** presents the denominator of the LSD *t*-test. All of the comparisons in this example have the same standard error of the mean (1.15470), because they all use the same MS Within (6.667) and because all the groups have 10 children (See Formula 8.2).

Formula 8.2
LSD Standard Error of the Mean

$$= \sqrt{MS_{within}\left(\frac{1}{n_1} + \frac{1}{n_2}\right)} = \sqrt{6.667\left(\frac{1}{10} + \frac{1}{10}\right)}$$

$$= \sqrt{6.667(.20)} = \sqrt{1.3334} = 1.1547$$

SPSS does not display the resulting LSD *t*-value, but dividing the mean difference (column 1) by the standard error (column 2) will provide the LSD *t*-value. The third column of data, labeled **Sig.**, is the last column of concern. It presents the exact level of significance, or alpha level, associated with the obtained LSD *t*-value. As you can see, the difference between the means of the poblano and jalapeno groups is not significant. The value .095 falls well above the .05 alpha level cutoff that most researchers require to establish significance. We can conclude that the speed with which children volcanically erupted did not meaningfully differ among children who tasted the poblano chili sauce or the jalapeno chili sauce.

In the second minor row of the poblano major row, the habanero group mean (9.00) is subtracted from the poblano group mean (14.00). In this case, we have a mean difference, standard error, and significance level of 5.00, 1.15470, and .000, respectively. Thus, we can conclude that the children who tasted the poblano chili sauce waited significantly longer to erupt than the children who tasted the habanero chili sauce. This difference is significant at least at the .001 alpha level, meaning that fewer than 1 in 1000 samples would be expected to show group differences of this magnitude as a result of chance alone.

In the second major row, two comparisons are being made. The jalapeno group is being compared with the poblano group (minor row 1) and with the habanero group (minor row 2). The first comparison (Jalapeno–Poblano) is redundant with the comparison made between poblano and jalapeno present in the Poblano major row. You may notice that the mean difference of Jalapeno–Poblano has a different sign than the mean difference of Poblano–Jalapeno (−2 instead of +2), as the mean time before eruption for children tasting the poblano chili sauce is now being subtracted from the mean time for children tasting jalapeno chili sauce. Regardless, this comparison answers the same question asked previously: are the poblano and jalapeno means significantly different? Looking at the exact significance level for the Jalapeno–Poblano comparison, we see that the significance level is the same as what was obtained for the Poblano–Jalapeno comparison.

Conversely, the Poblano–Habanero comparison has not yet been evaluated. Here, the habanero group mean (9.00) is subtracted from the jalapeno group mean (12.00). The mean difference, standard error, and significance level are 3.00, 1.15470, and .015, respectively. Since the significance level is smaller than the required .05 alpha level, we can conclude that children who tasted the jalapeno chili sauce waited significantly longer to volcanically erupt than did children who tasted the habanero chili sauce.

The final major row in this output, labeled Habanero, presents the Habanero–Poblano and Habanero–Jalapeno comparisons. These comparisons are redundant with the Poblano–Habanero and the Jalapeno–Habanero comparisons presented above. There is no need to interpret these results.

In summary, the LSD multiple comparisons output indicates that the children who tasted the habanero chili sauce volcanically erupted significantly faster than the children who tasted either the poblano chili sauce or the jalapeno chili sauce. Further, the children who tasted the jalapeno sauce and the children who tasted the poblano chili sauce did not differ significantly with respect to how quickly they erupted.

READING THE MEANS PLOTS

Figure 8.7 graphically displays the average time in seconds it took before the three different groups of children erupted after tasting the different types of chili sauce. The X-axis represents each of the three different groups: poblano, jalapeno, and habanero. The

Figure 8.7 ANOVA Output for Volcanic Eruption Data Continued

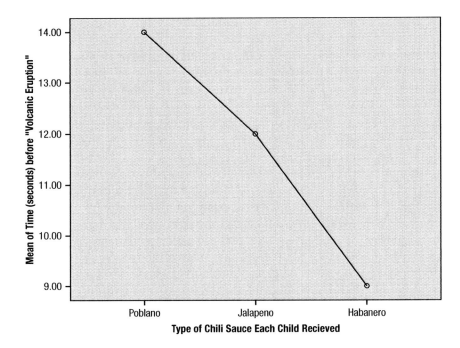

Y-axis represents spewing latency or the time it took for each child to erupt after tasting. In this case, the habanero group had the shortest latency (9.00) compared to the jalapeno group (12.00) and the poblano group (14.00).

SUMMARY

This chapter reviewed the basic procedures for conducting ANOVA with three groups. An example experiment tested eight-year-olds' reactions to tasting three different types of chili sauce (poblano, jalapeno, and habanero). The ANOVA compared the average amount of time that passed between tasting chili sauce and erupting volcanically among the three experiment groups. It was found that the groups did in fact differ. Post Hoc tests (Fisher's LSD) showed exactly which groups were different. Specifically and not surprisingly given its measured level of spiciness, the children who tasted habanero chili sauce erupted more quickly than the children who tasted one of the other two sauces. So what can we conclude? Though giving any type of chili sauce to an eight-year-old will result in rather negative consequences for all involved, the reaction will be noticeably faster if the sauce is made from habaneros.

When working with your own data, you may want to keep a few things in mind. First, for data with more groups, the procedures will be identical but the Descriptives, Multiple Comparisons, and Means Plots sections of the output will reflect the increased level of complexity. Further, it should be noted that this chapter focused on the use of Post Hoc tests (specifically, the Fisher's LSD *t*-test), and this test is offered as a simple introduction to testing specific mean differences in an ANOVA framework. Though the LSD *t*-test is appropriate for probing the result of a one-way ANOVA comparing three groups, this test is considered less appropriate when working with more than three groups. For these situations, other t-test-based approaches should be considered.

PRACTICE EXERCISES

Assume that the same researchers who conducted the chili sauce experiment also collected data regarding the amount of water (measured in milliliters) each child consumed after tasting one of the three chili sauces. This data is presented in Table 8.2. Use the One-Way ANOVA and LSD Post Hoc Tests to determine what effect, if any, tasting the different sauces had on the amount of water the eight-year-olds drank. For the ANOVA, report the F, N, between-subjects degrees of freedom, within-subjects degrees of freedom, and alpha level (level of significance). Then indicate whether the analysis was significant. For each group, report the means, standard deviations, and the sample sizes. If the results of the ANOVA are significant, interpret the Post Hoc LSD t-tests and indicate which group means, if any, are significantly different. What can you conclude from these results?

▶ **Table 8.2** Practice Exercise Data

Water Consumed (ml) after Tasting Chili Sauce		
Group 1 Poblano	Group 2 Jalapeno	Group 3 Habanero
0	100	150
50	150	200
100	200	250
150	250	300
200	300	350
200	350	400
250	400	450
250	450	500
300	500	550
300	550	600

chapter nine

Factorial ANOVA

This chapter covers the procedures for conducting a Factorial ANOVA. Similar to the one-way ANOVA and *t*-tests covered in previous chapters, factorial ANOVA is used to determine whether group means significantly differ from one another. Factorial ANOVA differs from these other tests in that it includes more than one independent variable in its design. Because multiple independent variables are included in the factorial ANOVA, multiple effects must be tested. For example, in a design with two independent variables, we need to test the *main effect* of each independent variable and the *interaction* between the two independent variables. For a given variable, the test of the main effects is analogous to a one-way ANOVA and will determine whether the average of the differences between the group means of a given variable is significant. Testing for interaction effects addresses a more complex question: determining whether the relationship between one independent variable and the dependent variable is altered by the influence of the second independent variable. For example, an interaction may show that the independent variable is significantly associated with the dependent variable when looking only at participants in group A of a second independent variable, but no significant effect is found when looking only at participants in group B. This chapter will show you how to use the factorial ANOVA procedure to test the significance of the *main effects* and the *interaction effect* when working with two independent variables. In addition, this chapter covers procedures for testing *simple effects*, which are steps a researcher would need to take in order to fully interpret a significant interaction between two independent variables.

Cartoon 9.1 provides an example of a situation that might lend itself to a study with two independent variables. To investigate the effects of subliminal messages on behavior, an investigator designs a study where the two independent variables are group variables. The researcher is interested in whether the method by which a subliminal message is presented makes a difference in the effectiveness of the message. She decides she will expose half the subjects in her study to *pictures* containing a subliminal message and half the subjects to *words* containing a subliminal message. The type of stimulus used to present the subliminal message is the first independent variable. We will refer to this variable as Stimulus Type.

Disturbingly, the subliminal message presented to subjects in this study is always related to "sticking cucumbers in your nose and Spam on your head." In order to accurately describe the effects of the first independent variable, Stimulus Type, the researcher decides she will need to take the effects of a second variable into account. The researcher believes that the subliminal message will be equally effective when presented through words or pictures, *but only for subjects who have positive attitudes* about wearing Spam on their heads and putting a cucumber in their noses. The researcher also believes people

Cartoon 9.1 Bloom County by Berkley Breathed

with negative attitudes about wearing Spam and cucumbers as fashion accessories will be influenced by the subliminal message if it is presented using words, but not if the message is presented using pictures. Consequently, she decides that half the subjects will be recruited for the study because they have positive attitudes about wearing Spam and cucumbers as fashion accessories. The other half of the subjects will be recruited because they have negative attitudes about Spam and cucumbers as fashion accessories. The researcher names this second independent variable Food as a Fashion Accessory.

▶ **Figure 9.1** 2×2 Design for Spam and Cucumbers Subliminal Message Study

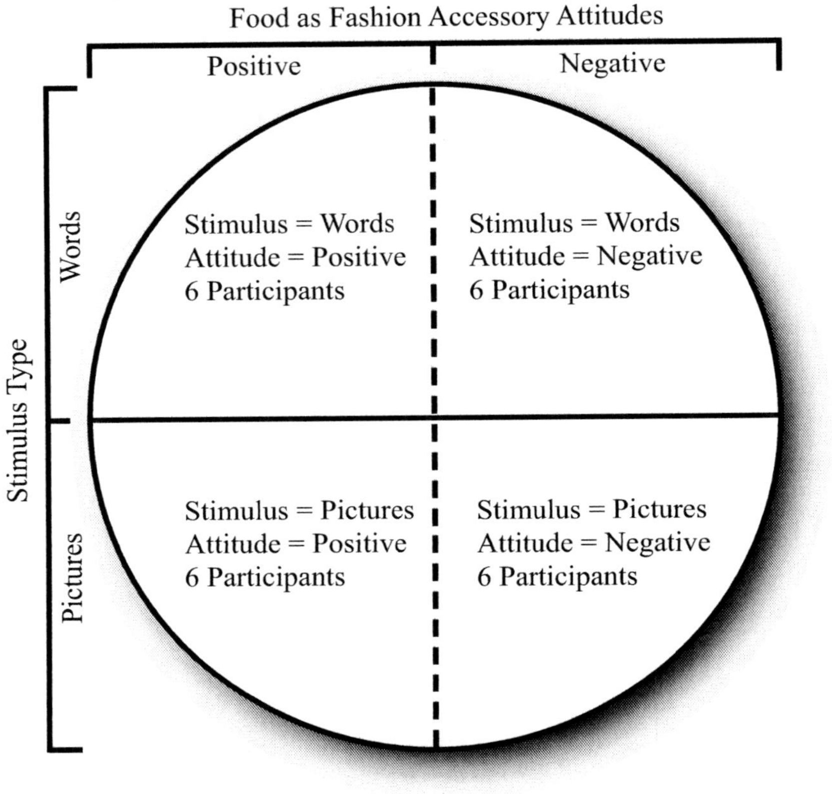

Food as Fashion Accessory Attitudes

	Positive	Negative
Words	Stimulus = Words Attitude = Positive 6 Participants	Stimulus = Words Attitude = Negative 6 Participants
Pictures	Stimulus = Pictures Attitude = Positive 6 Participants	Stimulus = Pictures Attitude = Negative 6 Participants

Stimulus Type

The researcher collects data from twelve subjects who think positively about food as a fashion accessory (what we call the "positive" condition for this variable) and 12 subjects who think negatively about food as a fashion accessory (what we call the "negative" condition), for a total of 24 subjects. She exposes half of those who think negatively about food as a fashion accessory to words containing the subliminal message and the other half to pictures containing the subliminal message. She does the same with those who think positively of food as a fashion accessory. The researcher now has data from subjects in every combination of the two levels of the Stimulus Type variable and the two levels of Food as a Fashion Accessory variable. This type of grouping forms what is known as a 2 × 2 (read two-by-two) design and results in four separate groups of subjects. Figure 9.1 illustrates the groupings.

The dependent variable in this study is the Spam- and cucumber-wearing behavior of the participants. The researcher decides to measure the effectiveness of the subliminal messages by recording the number of times during the seven days after exposure to the subliminal message that subjects obey the message by wearing Spam on their heads and putting a cucumber in their noses.

SETTING UP THE DATA

The first step in setting up the data file for the Spam and cucumbers example is to define the three variables of interest described above. Figure 9.2 shows the Variable View of the

Figure 9.2 Variable View for Spam and Cucumber Data

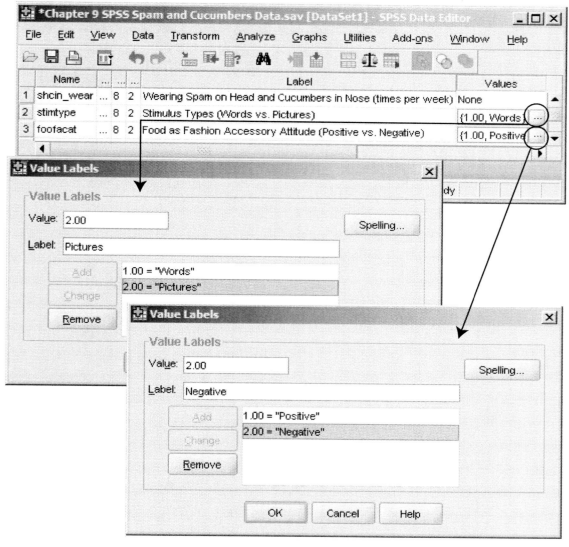

SPSS Data Editor for the data set where we have given variable names and variable labels to each variable. We gave the dependent variable in this study the variable name **shcin_wear** and the variable label "Wearing Spam on Head and Cucumbers in Nose (times per week)." We gave the first independent variable the variable name **stimtype** and the variable label "Stimulus Types (Words vs. Pictures)." The value labels of "Pictures" and "Words" were assigned to the data values of 1 and 2, respectively. We gave the second independent variable the variable name **foofacat** and the variable label "Food as Fashion Accessory Attitude (Positive vs. Negative)." The value labels of "Positive" and "Negative" were assigned to the data values of 1 and 2, respectively.

After entering the three desired variables in the Variable View, the data will need to be entered for each participant (See Figure 9.3). Scores for **shcin_wear** (the frequency

▶ **Figure 9.3** Data View for Spam and Cucumber Data

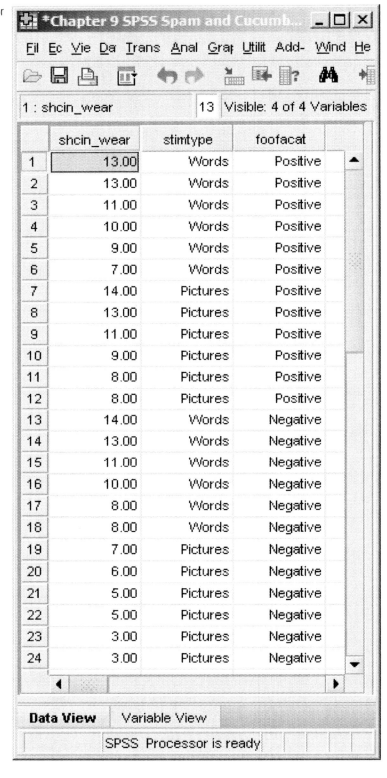

with which they put Spam on their head and cucumbers in their nose) are entered in Column 1. Scores for **stimtype** are entered in column 2. Values of 1 are entered for subjects exposed to subliminal messages through pictures, and values of 2 are entered for subjects exposed to subliminal messages through words. Scores for **foofacat** are entered in column 3. Values of 1 are entered for subjects with positive attitudes and values of 2 are entered for subjects with negative attitudes.

We can see in Figure 9.3 that Participant 1 wore Spam and cucumbers a total of 13 times in one week after being exposed to a subliminal message consisting of words. Participant 1 also reported having a positive attitude toward using food as a fashion accessory. In contrast, Participant 24 wore Spam and cucumbers 3 times after receiving the subliminal message in picture form, and reported having negative attitudes toward using food to accessorize.

RUNNING THE ANALYSIS

With respect to the Spam and cucumbers example, the factorial ANOVA procedure below will first test the main effect of the stimulus type, determining whether the average frequency of wearing Spam and cucumbers for participants who were exposed to the subliminal message in words is significantly different from participants who were exposed to the subliminal message in pictures. Second, it will test the main effect of the different attitudes toward food as fashion accessory, determining whether the average frequency of wearing Spam and cucumbers for participants with negative attitudes is significantly different from the average for participants with positive attitudes. Finally, this analysis will test for an interaction between the stimulus type variable and the food-as–fashion-accessory variable, determining whether the effectiveness of the different subliminal stimulus types depends upon whether participants have positive or negative attitudes toward wearing food as a fashion accessory. However, significant interactions can reflect a variety of patterns of data, so the pattern of group means will need to be subjected to further tests, which are described in the simple effects testing section presented later in the chapter.

PROCEDURE FOR RUNNING A FACTORIAL ANOVA

1. Select **Analyze** from the pull-down menu.
2. Select **General Linear Model**.
3. Select **Univariate...** from the side menu. This will open the **Univariate** dialogue box.
4. Enter the dependent variable, **shcin_wear**, into the **Dependent Variable:** field by selecting it from the list and then left-clicking on the boxed arrow next to the **Dependent Variable:** field.
5. Enter the two independent variables, **stimtype** and **foofacat**, into the **Fixed Factor(s):** field by highlighting both variables and left-clicking the appropriate boxed arrow.

⑥ To obtain graphs of the main effects and interactions, left-click on **Plots....** This will open the **Univariate: Profile Plots** dialogue box, labeled Ⓐ in Figure 9.5 on the next page.

⑦ Enter **stimtype** from the **Factors:** list into the **Horizontal Axis:** field.

⑧ Click the **Add** button. This will give you the graph of the main effect for stimulus type.

  • Repeat steps 7 and 8 with the second independent variable, **foofacat**.

⑨ To obtain the graph of the interaction: first enter **stimtype** in the **Horizantal Axis:** field, then enter **foofacat** into the **Separate Lines:** field, and finally left-click the **Add** button.

⑩ To finalize the selections and return to the **Univariate** dialogue box (shown in Figure 9.4), left-click **Continue**.

⑪ To obtain the means, standard deviations, effect sizes, and other descriptive information for each of the research groups, left click on the **Options...** button (shown in Figure 9.4). This will open the **Univariate: Options** dialogue box [Labeled Ⓑ in Figure 9.5].

▶ **Figure 9.4** Running a Factorial ANOVA

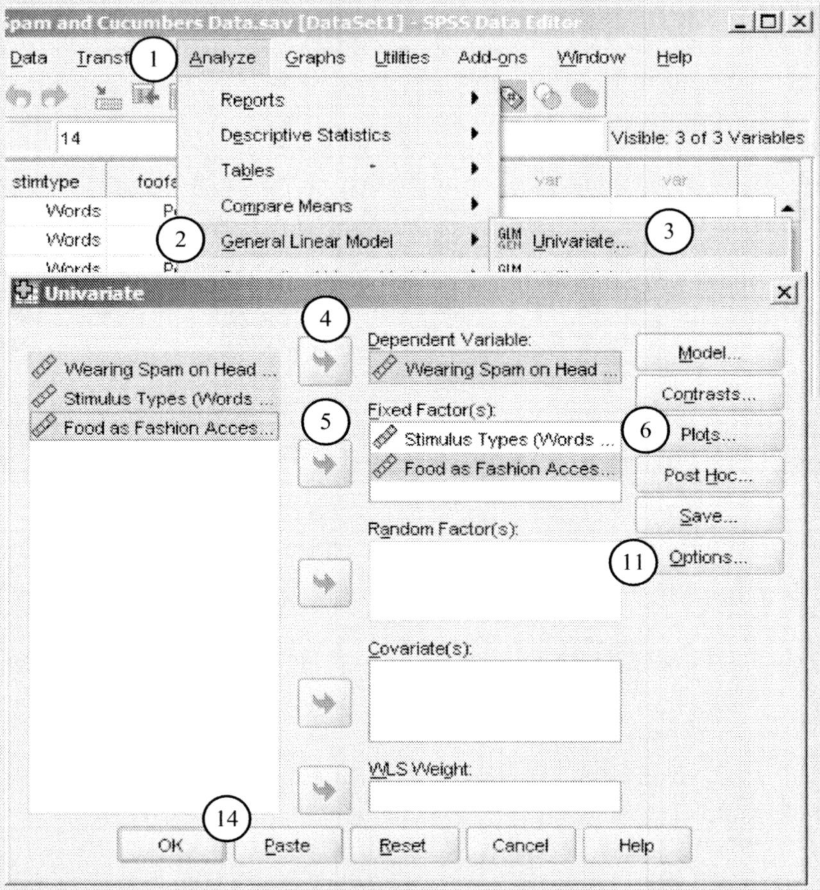

12. Check the **Descriptive statistics** option and **Estimates of effect size** in the **Display** section of the dialogue box.

13. Finalize your selection and return to the **Univariate** dialogue box by left-clicking **Continue**.

14. Finally, double-check your variables and all selected options and either select **OK** to run or **Paste** to create syntax to run at a later time.

If you chose the paste option, you should have the following syntax:

```
UNIANOVA shcin_wear BY stimtype foofacat
  /METHOD=SSTYPE(3)
  /INTERCEPT=INCLUDE
  /PLOT=PROFILE(stimtype foofacat stimtype*foofacat)
  /PRINT=ETASQ DESCRIPTIVE
  /CRITERIA=ALPHA(.05)
  /DESIGN=stimtype foofacat stimtype*foofacat .
```

▶**Figure 9.5** Running a Factorial ANOVA Continued

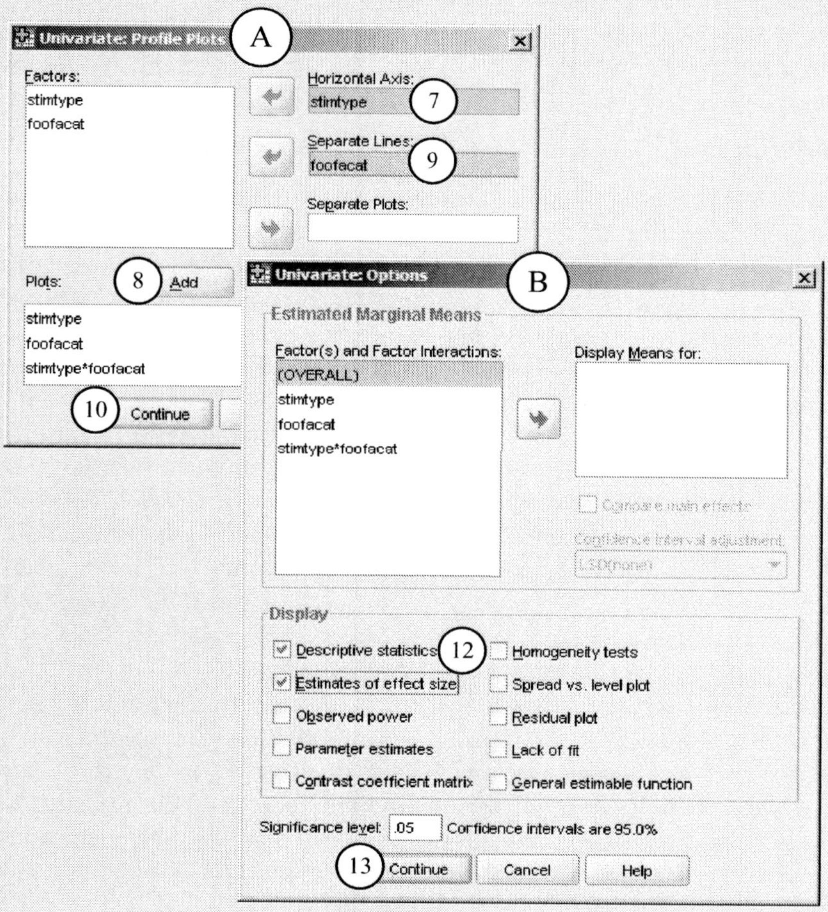

When conducting a factorial ANOVA, keep in mind that if you have at least one independent variable that has three or more groups, the Post Hoc tests should be requested. Just like one-way ANOVA, when you have three or more groups, a significant main effect will not tell you which groups differ, so Post Hoc tests (like the Fischer LSD *t*-test) are useful for interpreting a significant main effect. To request Post Hoc tests, left-click on the **Post Hoc...** button (shown in Figure 9.4). This will open the **Univariate: Post Hoc Multiple Comparisons for Observed Means** dialogue box (not shown in these figures). Enter the variables with three or more groups into the **Post Hoc Tests for:** field, check the **LSD** option from the **Equal Variances Assumed** list, and then left-click **Continue** to finalize your selection and return to the **Univariate** dialogue box. As discussed in Chapter 8, the LSD *t*-test is offered as a simple introduction to comparing means in an ANOVA framework.

READING THE OUTPUT FOR A TWO-WAY ANOVA

Figure 9.6 on the following page presents the first part of the output for the analyses requested. The first table, titled **Between-Subjects Factors**, shows which independent variables were included in the analysis. For each independent variable, it shows the numerical values representing the two groups, the value labels for each group, and the number of participants in each group. For example, the stimulus type variable used the values 1 and 2 to represent the "Words" and "Pictures" groups, respectively, and the two groups each consisted of 12 participants.

DESCRIPTIVE DATA

The second table in Figure 9.6 titled **Descriptive Statistics** reports the means, standard deviations, and group sizes (**N**) for several different groupings of the participants by independent variable. The sections labeled Ⓐ show the descriptive statistics calculated separately for each of the four groups representing the combination of the two independent variables. For example, the first row shows that the six participants exposed to words who had positive attitudes toward wearing food put Spam on their heads and cucumbers in their noses an average of 10.5 times during the week after exposure. The second row shows that the six participants exposed to words who had negative attitudes toward wearing food wore Spam and cucumbers an average of 10.6667 times when exposed to words.

Alternatively, the sections labeled Ⓑ show data calculated separately for the Words and Pictures groups, irrespective of their attitudes toward wearing food. For example, the third row of the table shows that the 12 participants who were exposed to words wore Spam and cucumbers an average of 10.5833 times. Notice that this value is the average of the means for the six participants exposed to words who have positive attitudes (10.5000) and the six participants exposed to words who have negative attitudes (10.6667).

The section labeled Ⓒ shows the data calculated separately for the positive and negative food-as-fashion-accessory attitudes groups, regardless of what type of subliminal message they were exposed to. The row labeled **Positive** shows that the 12 participants who had positive attitudes toward wearing food put Spam on their heads and cucumbers in their noses an average of 10.5 times a week. Notice that this value is the average of the means for the six participants who were exposed to pictures and had positive attitudes (10.5) and the six participants who were exposed to words and had positive attitudes (10.5). Finally, the section labeled Ⓓ presents the descriptive data for the entire sample, regardless of any group membership (N = 24).

▶**Figure 9.6** Factorial ANOVA Output

Univariate Analysis of Variance

Between-Subjects Factors

		Value Label	N
Stimulus Types (Words vs. Pictures)	1	Words	12
	2	Pictures	12
Food as Fashion Accessory Attitude (Positive vs. Negative)	1	Positive	12
	2	Negative	12

Descriptive Statistics

Dependent Variable:Wearing Spam on Head and Cucumbers in Nose (times per week)

Stimu...	Food ...	Mean	Std. Deviation	N	
Words	Positive	10.5000	2.34521	6	A
	Negative	10.6667	2.50333	6	
	Total	10.5833	2.31432	12	
Pictures	Positive	10.5000	2.58844	6	B
	Negative	4.8333	1.60208	6	
	Total	7.6667	3.60135	12	
Total	Positive	10.5000	2.35488	12	C
	Negative	7.7500	3.64629	12	
	Total	9.1250	3.31417	24	D

Tests of Between-Subjects Effects

Dependent Variable:Wearing Spam on Head and Cucumbers in Nose (times per week)

Source	Type III Sum of Squares	df	Mean Square	F	Sig.	Partial Eta Squared
Corrected Model	147.458[a]	3	49.153	9.348	.000	.584
Intercept	1998.375	1	1998.375	380.040	.000	.950
stimtype	51.042	1	51.042	9.707	.005	.327
foofacat	45.375	1	45.375	8.629	.008	.301
stimtype * foofacat	51.042	1	51.042	9.707	.005	.327
Error	105.167	20	5.258			
Total	2251.000	24				
Corrected Total	252.625	23				

a. R Squared = .584 (Adjusted R Squared = .521)

ANOVA SUMMARY TABLE

The third table of output in Figure 9.6 is titled **Tests of Between-Subjects Effects**, and shows the factorial ANOVA summary table. For the current discussion, we will ignore the first two rows of this table, **Corrected Model** and **Intercept.** In more advanced statistics courses you may be compelled to consider them, but for the questions we are asking they are not necessary to interpret.

The **Tests of Between-Subjects Effects** table is similar to the ANOVA table obtained in Chapter 8 for the one-way ANOVA (See Figure 8.5). However, there are a number of elements which are new. For the one-way ANOVA, we only had to consider the effect for one independent variable. For this factorial ANOVA we have to consider the main effects of two independent variables, **stimtype** and **foofacat,** as well as the interaction between the two independent variables, denoted in this table as **stimtype*foofacat.** However, the data given in these rows are analogous to the Between Groups data presented in the ANOVA table. As you can see, the statistics given in the first five columns of this table are the same as those in the ANOVA table: Sum of Squares (SS), degrees of freedom (df), Mean Square (MS), F statistic, and Level of Significance (Sig.). Like one-way ANOVA, the F statistic for each row represents the ratio of variability attributable to group membership (MS for the row of interest) relative to the variability unaccounted for (MS_{Error}). For example, the F statistic for **stimtype** is 9.707, which is obtained by dividing the MS from the **stimtype** row by the MS_{Error}:

$$MS_{stimtype} / MS_{Error} = 51.042 / 5.258 = 9.707$$

Also like one-way ANOVA, the MS in each row is obtained by dividing the sums of squares for that row by its respective degrees of freedom. For example, the MS for **stimtype** is 51.042 and is obtained in the following manner:

$$MS_{stimtype} = SS_{stimtype} / df_{stimtype} = 51.042 / 1 = 51.042$$

To evaluate the statistical significance of F, we look at the level of significance (alpha) found in the **Sig.** column. For example, the F statistic for **stimtype** is 9.707 and the level of significance is .005. This level of significance indicates that we would only expect to find mean differences this large in 5 out of 1000 samples by chance alone. Again, most researchers set the critical value for significance at the .05 alpha level, so if the level of significance reported by SPSS is less than or equal to .05, then the effect is generally considered significant. Given that the alpha value for **stimtype** is less than .05, we can say that exposing participants to subliminal messages using different stimuli resulted in a significant change in the frequency with which participants put Spam on their heads and cucumbers in their noses. Looking at the word and picture groups means presented in the **Descriptive Statistics** table (10.5833 and 7.6667, respectively) we can see that participants who were exposed to the subliminal message using words wore Spam on their heads and put cucumbers up their noses significantly more often than did participants who were exposed to the message using pictures.

The F statistic for the main effect of the food-as-fashion-accessory variable, **foofacat,** is 8.629. The alpha level of .008 given in the **Sig.** column for **foofacat** is less than .05, which indicates that the main effect of this variable is also significant. Looking at the means for positive and negative attitudes given in the **Descriptive Statistics** table (10.5000 and 7.7500, respectively), it appears that participants who have positive attitudes toward wearing food as a fashion accessory wore Spam on their head and put cucumbers in their noses significantly more often than did participants with negative attitudes toward accessorizing with food.

The F statistic for the interaction of the two independent variables, **stimtype*foofacat,** is 9.707. The significance level of .005 given in the **Sig.** column is less than .05, which indicates that the interaction between the independent variables is significant. This significant interaction suggests that the effectiveness of the word and picture messages is contingent upon whether participants have positive or negative attitudes toward wearing food as a fashion accessory. Further tests must be undertaken to interpret this effect. These tests are described below in the *Simple Effects Tests* section.

If you are using SPSS to check your hand calculations, you should note that the last row of the table, **Corrected Total,** will match the total sums of squares and degrees of freedom typically obtained using hand calculations. The sums of squares and degrees of freedom given in the next to last row, **Total,** includes the sums of squares and the degrees of freedom from the **Intercept** row (row 2) in its calculation. The value in this row is typically not required to interpret Factorial ANOVA or to check hand calculations.

When checking hand calculations, it is important to remember that SPSS rounds values to the third decimal place. Your hand-calculated values may differ slightly due to rounding error.

EFFECT SIZE

The **Partial Eta** (pronounced ā-tuh) **Squared** is presented in the last column of the **Tests of Between-Subjects Effects** table. Partial Eta Squared (η^2) is a measure of effect size. Values for Partial Eta Squared reflect the proportion of variability in the dependent variable that is accounted for by the effect of either an independent variable or of an interaction between variables. It is important to consider the size of a statistical effect, measured using η^2, because it provides information about how much influence variables have on one another, independent of how they are measured and how large the sample is. This allows effects from different studies to be compared in meaningful ways. When multiplied by 100, η^2 can be thought of as a percentage. As shown in the **Test of Between-Subjects Effect** table, the main effect of the **stimtype** variable has a η^2 equal to .327. This indicates that 33% of the variance in the number of times participants wore Spam on their heads and cucumbers in their noses is predicted by the type of stimulus to which they were exposed. In 1992, statistician Jacob Cohen suggested standards for interpreting effect sizes in ANOVA. These standards are as follows: small effects account for around 1% of the variance in the dependent variable, medium effects account for about 6%, and large effects account for 13% or more. Given these standards, you can see that both main effects of the two independent variables in the Spam and cucumber subliminal message study and the interaction effect of the two would be considered quite large with respect to the effects typically found in social and behavioral science research.

POST HOC TESTS

In this example, each independent variable has only two groups, but if any of the independent variables had three or more groups, we would need to request Post Hoc tests in order to interpret significant main effects. When you request Post Hoc tests, the output will include a table headed *Post Hoc Tests*. These results are interpreted in the same way as the Post Hoc tests presented in the one-way ANOVA chapter.

PLOTS

The three line charts of means presented in Figure 9.7 plot the dependent variable means for the stimulus type variable, **stimtype**, the food-as-fashion-accessory variable, **foofacat**, and the interaction between the two variables, **stimtype*foofacat**, labeled Ⓐ, Ⓑ, and Ⓒ, respectively. The means in these charts are the same as the means presented in the **Descriptive Statistics** table in Figure 9.6. If these charts seem unfamiliar to you, then refer to Chapter 4, where they were introduced. The first chart, labeled Ⓐ,

▶**Figure 9.7** Factorial ANOVA Output Continued

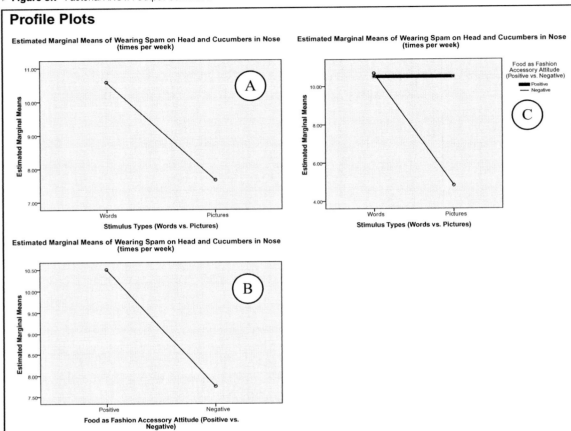

shows that the average number of times that participants wore Spam on their heads and cucumber in their noses after being exposed to subliminal messages is higher when the message took the form of words rather than pictures. The second chart, labeled Ⓑ, shows that the Spam- and cucumber-wearing averages is higher among participants who have positive attitudes toward wearing food as a fashion accessory than among participants with negative attitudes.

With respect to the plot of the interaction, labeled Ⓒ, the stimulus type groups are represented on the X-axis (words on the left and pictures on the right), and the food-as-fashion-accessory attitudes groups are represented by different lines (positive attitudes with a thick line and negative attitudes with a thin line). This graph shows that among participants with positive attitudes toward wearing food, exposure to subliminal messages through words or pictures results in relatively frequent Spam- and cucumber-wearing behavior. In contrast, among participants with negative food-wearing attitudes, exposure through words resulted in higher levels of Spam and cucumber wearing than did exposure through pictures, though further testing is required to know if this difference is significant. We can also see in this graph that for participants with negative attitudes, exposure through words resulted in levels of Spam and cucumber wearing equivalent to participants with positive attitudes.

When interpreting charts plotting interactions, remember that there are many different patterns that means can take when an interaction is significant. A rule of thumb to consider is that the presence of a significant interaction is reflected in a pattern where the lines of the chart are clearly not parallel to each other. In this case, the lines of chart Ⓒ are nowhere close to parallel, which is consistent with the significant test of the interaction.

SIMPLE EFFECTS TESTING

Finding that two independent variables have a significant interaction with each other is only the first step in learning about the effects of the interaction between the independent variables. In general, the presence of a significant interaction tells us that the effect of one independent variable on the dependent variable is not the same for the different groups of the second independent variable. For our example, the presence of a significant interaction means that the effect of changing the method (pictures or words) used to present the subliminal message on participants with positive attitudes toward food as a fashion accessory is not the same as it is for people with negative attitudes.

This is a very general piece of information. It does not tell us what the effect of changing the stimulus type is at either level of the food-as-fashion-accessory variable. It only tells us that whatever the effect of the stimulus type variable is, it will be different for people with positive attitudes toward food as a fashion accessory than for people with negative attitudes. Logically, this leads another set of tests. It suggests that we ought to first test the effects of the stimulus type variable using *only* the data from people with positive attitudes. After that, we ought to test the effect of the stimulus type variable using *only* the data for participants with negative attitudes. Each of these tests is an example of a *simple effect*. In factorial ANOVA with two independent variables, a simple effect is the effect of one independent variable on the dependent variable using only the data for members of a single group in the second independent variable.

A simple effect test is very similar, conceptually, to the one-way ANOVA covered in Chapter 8. The simple effect test itself is really just a one-way ANOVA that (a) only uses subjects from one level of a second independent variable and (b) uses the MS_{Error} from the Factorial ANOVA as part of the F statistic formula. Unlike the one-way ANOVA, the final F statistics will not be computed by SPSS. We have to compute the F statistic by hand, and the significance of F needs to be assessed by using a table of critical Fs found in most statistics textbooks or by having SPSS compute exact levels of significance.

RUNNING THE ANALYSES

We will approach the SPSS Simple Effects procedures in three parts. First, we will demonstrate the use of the **Split File...** command. This command instructs SPSS to run multiple one-way ANOVAs testing the effects of the first independent variable at each level of the second independent variable separately. After enabling the split file for the **foofacat** variable (positive vs. negative attitudes toward food as a fashion accessory), we can request one-way ANOVAs that will compare the **shcin_wear** scores for the words and pictures conditions. SPSS will automatically run two different analyses, one for each of the groups for the food-as-fashion-accessory variable. Finally, we will finish with a demonstration of the hand calculations for the simple effects and a description of how SPSS can compute significance values for your hand-calculated F statistics.

PROCEDURE FOR ENABLING SPLIT FILE

(1) Select **Data** from pull-down menu.

(2) Select **Split File....** This will open the **Split File** dialogue box.

(3) Select the **Organize output by groups** option.

(4) Select the independent variable for which you want the analyses to be run separately for each group. This example uses **foofacat**, which is entered into the **Groups Based on:** field by left-clicking on the boxed arrow.

(5) Finally, double-check the variables and all selected options and either select **OK** to run, or **Paste** to create syntax to run at a later time.

If you chose the paste option, you should have the following syntax:

```
SORT CASES BY foofacat .
SPLIT FILE
  SEPARATE BY foofacat .
```

▶**Figure 9.8** Running the Split File Command

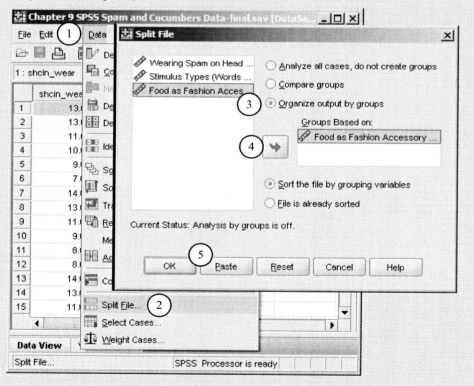

Before proceeding, we should note that the choice of which simple effects to test is largely based on what makes the most sense with respect to the research question at hand. For our example, a researcher could just as reasonably choose to test the effects of having positive vs. negative food-as-fashion attitudes separately for people exposed to words and people exposed to pictures. Some researchers may even choose to look at both sets of simple effects.

When you use the **Split File...** command and finish the analyses you are interested in, it is best to disable the command before proceeding. Otherwise it is easy to forget that it is enabled, and when running other analyses, you might get some rather confusing results. To disable the **Split File...** command, follow steps ① and ② in the above procedure box and check to make sure that the **Analyze all cases, do not create groups** option has been selected. Then either select **OK** to run or **Paste** to create syntax. If you chose the paste option, you should have generated the following syntax:

    SPLIT FILE

    OFF .

Once split file has been enabled, request the one-way ANOVA (See Figure 8.3 in Chapter 8 for a detailed review) and enter the appropriate independent variable into the **Factor:** field. In this case, because we used **foofacat,** for the **Split File...** command, we need to use **stimtype** as the factor. Next, enter the dependent variable, **shcin_wear,** into the **Dependent List:** field. No other options are necessary. Finish by either running the analysis (clicking **OK**) or pasting the syntax. If you chose the paste option, you should have generated the following syntax:

    ONEWAY
      shcin_wear BY stimtype
      /MISSING ANALYSIS .

READING THE OUTPUT

The first table, labeled Ⓐ in Figure 9.9, presents the results for participants with positive attitudes toward wearing food. This table shows the results of the simple effect one-way ANOVA, which compares the two stimulus type groups (words versus pictures) with respect to the frequency with which participants with positive attitudes put Spam on their heads and cucumbers in their noses. The Mean Square Between Groups ($MS_{between}$) presented in this table is the numerator for the simple effect F statistic that we must calculate by hand. For this analysis, the $MS_{between}$ is .000. The denominator of the simple effect F statistic is the MS_{Error} (5.258) reported in the **Test of Between-Subjects Effects** table shown in Figure 9.5. We have calculated the simple effect F statistic in Formula 9.1.

Formula 9.1 Participants with Positive Attitudes

$$F = \frac{MS_{between}}{MS_{Error}} = \frac{.000}{5.258} = .000$$

The **ANOVA** table, labeled Ⓑ, of Figure 9.9 presents the results of the simple effect one-way ANOVA conducted for participants with negative attitudes toward wearing

▶ **Figure 9.9** One-Way ANOVA: Simple Effects of Stimulus Type Separate for Negative and Positive Attitudes

Oneway

Food as Fashion Accessory Attitude(Positive vs. Negative) = Positive

ANOVA[a]

Wearing Spam on Head and Cucumbers in Nose (times per week)

	Sum of Squares	df	Mean Square	F	Sig.
Between Groups	.000	1	.000	.000	1.000
Within Groups	61.000	10	6.100		
Total	61.000	11			

Ⓐ

a. Food as Fashion Accessory Attitude (Positive vs. Negative) = Positive

Food as Fashion Accessory Attitude(Positive vs. Negative) = Negative

ANOVA[a]

Wearing Spam on Head and Cucumbers in Nose (times per week)

	Sum of Squares	df	Mean Square	F	Sig.
Between Groups	102.083	1	102.083	23.113	.001
Within Groups	44.167	10	4.417		
Total	146.250	11			

Ⓑ

a. Food as Fashion Accessory Attitude (Positive vs. Negative) = Negative

food as a fashion accessory. This table compares the subjects of the two stimulus type groups (words versus pictures) with respect to the frequency with which participants with negative food-wearing attitudes put Spam on their heads and cucumbers in their noses. To compute the F statistic for this analysis, we use the $MS_{between}$ presented here, 102.083, and again the MS_{Error} from Figure 9.5, which is 5.258. The completed computations are presented in Formula 9.2.

Formula 9.2 Participants with Negative Attitudes

$$F = \frac{MS_{between}}{MS_{Error}} = \frac{102.083}{5.258} = 19.415$$

SIGNIFICANCE LEVELS OF SIMPLE EFFECT *F* STATISTICS

Significance values for each simple effect F statistic can be determined using traditional tables of the critical values for F, found in most statistics textbooks and widely available online. SPSS can also compute exact significance values for you. These values can be obtained by making a new data file with three variables: **F**, **df_between**, and **df_error**. The **df_between** comes from the one-way ANOVA tables for the simple effects, and the

▶**Table 9.1** Significance (Alpha) Levels for Simple Effect *F* Statistics

Analysis	F	$df_{between}$	df_{Error}	Alpha level
Positive Attitudes: Words vs. Pictures	.000	1	20	1.000
Negative Attitudes: Words vs. Pictures	19.415	1	20	.001

df_error comes from the **Test of Between–Subjects Effects** table in Figure 9.5. We have presented these values for the Spam and cucumber example in Table 9.1. The data for each simple effect analysis is represented in its own row. Using the following compute procedure, SPSS can generate the significance level of each *F* statistic. These significance levels will be presented in a new column that is added to the Data Editor when the **Compute Variable...** procedure is completed. In our example, we have named this new column of values "**alpha_level**."

As you can see in Table 9.1, the simple effect of the **stimtype** variable is significant (has an alpha level less than or equal to .05) only among participants with negative attitudes toward wearing food. This information can be combined with what we know about the group means representing the interaction to fully interpret the interaction between the stimulus type variable and the food-as-fashion-accessory variable. Among participants with positive attitudes toward food as a fashion accessory, high levels of Spam and cucumber wearing were found regardless of whether participants were exposed to words ($M = 10.5000$) or pictures ($M = 10.5000$). Participants who had negative attitudes toward food as fashion and received the subliminal message through pictures had the lowest levels of Spam and cucumber wearing ($M = 4.8333$). The average number of times these subjects wore Spam on their heads and cucumbers in their noses is significantly lower than participants with negative attitudes who received the subliminal message through words ($M = 10.6667$).

PROCEDURE FOR COMPUTING THE SIGNIFICANCE OF *F* FOR SIMPLE EFFECTS

- Select **Data** from the pull-down menu.
- Select **Compute Variable....**
- To name the new variable representing the significance levels for each *F* statistic, type **alpha_level** in the **Target Variable:** field.
- To write the formula that instructs SPSS to generate significance levels for each *F* statistic, type the following in the **Numeric Expression:** field: **SIG.F(F, df_between, df_error)**
  - Note that **F, df_between,** and **df_error** represent variable names that we defined when we created the new data file. If you use different variable names in your files, you will need to adjust the formula accordingly.
- Left-click **OK** or **Paste** to finish.

SIMPLE EFFECT POST HOC TESTS

A significant simple effect F is like any F statistic. If you have more than two groups represented in the simple effect F, you will need to use follow-up tests to determine which means are significantly different. For example, if we had three types of stimuli (e.g., words, pictures, and animated video), a significant simple effect for positive or negative food-wearing attitudes would not show which group means are different. Like one-way ANOVA, the LSD t-tests utilizing the MS_{Error} from the Factorial ANOVA can be used here. These too will have to be computed by hand using Formula 9.3, and the significance levels will need to be determined using a table of critical values for t.

Formula 9.3 Simple Effect LSD t-Tests

$$t_{lsd} = \frac{Mean_{group1} - Mean_{group2}}{\sqrt{MS_{Error}\left(\frac{1}{n_{group1}} + \frac{1}{n_{group2}}\right)}}$$

SUMMARY

This chapter reviewed the basic procedures for conducting Factorial ANOVA with two categorical independent variables, each with two groups. The research example tested the effects of exposing participants to a subliminal message prompting them to wear Spam on their heads and cucumbers in their noses using two different methods of exposure: words and pictures. The study also considered whether having positive or negative attitudes toward wearing food as a fashion accessory would influence Spam and cucumber wearing after subliminal message exposure. The main effects portion of the factorial ANOVA tested whether the frequency with which participants wore Spam and cucumbers after exposure to the subliminal message differed between participants exposed to words and participants exposed to pictures. The main effects analyses also tested whether Spam and cumber wearing differed between participants with positive attitudes toward wearing food and participants with negative attitudes. It was found that words were more effective than pictures at increasing the number of times participants put Spam on their heads and cucumbers in their noses, and it was found that people with positive attitudes toward wearing food as an accessory wore Spam and cucumbers more often than people with negative attitudes. The factorial ANOVA also tested for the presence of an interaction effect, examining whether the effect of the type of stimulus used on Spam and cucumber wearing was dependent upon whether one had a positive or negative attitude toward wearing food as a fashion accessory. A significant interaction was found. Simple effects follow-up tests indicated that words and pictures were very effective at eliciting high levels of Spam and cucumber wearing among people with positive attitudes toward wearing food as a fashion accessory, but only words were effective at eliciting high levels of Spam and cucumber wearing among people with negative attitudes.

This chapter presented the simplest form of Factorial ANOVA, the 2×2 design, where two independent variables each have two groups. Factorial models can get far more complicated. For example, you can have 2×3, 3×3, or 4×4 models. These models will be tested in the same way as the 2×2 example we provide, but the simple effects tests will be more complex. You can also include more than two independent variables. Again, these models are tested in basically the same way, but there will be more main effects and interaction effects to consider. For example, a $2 \times 2 \times 2$ model will have three main effects, three two-way interactions (the first independent variable with the second, the first independent variable with the third, and the second independent variable with the third), and one three-way interaction that determines whether all three independent variables interact at the same time.

PRACTICE EXERCISES

Assume that a consortium of 10 year-olds fund a study to determine the feasibility of using subliminal messages to get parents to increase their allowance. Pilot testing indicated that "parental cheapness" (the tendency to be conservative about spending money) may impact the effectiveness of subliminal mes-

▶ **Table 9.2** Practice Exercise Data

No Subliminal Message		Subliminal Message	
Cheap	Generous	Cheap	Generous
3	18	18	3
4	19	19	4
5	20	20	5
5	20	20	5
6	21	21	6
7	22	22	7

sages encouraging increases in allowance. To investigate this research question, parents were randomly assigned to one of two groups. One group received a subliminal message and the other did not. Participants were also classified with respect to parental cheapness (cheap versus generous). Table 9.2 presents the result of the final study. Use a factorial ANOVA and simple effects tests to determine what effect, if any, subliminal priming and parental cheapness have on the amount of allowance 10 year-olds receive. For the overall analysis, report the means, the standard deviations, and the sample sizes. For the main and interaction effects report the F, the N, the degrees of freedom for the effect, the degrees of freedom for the error terms, the alpha level (level of significance), and indicate whether the analysis was significant. If the interaction is significant, report the simple effect ANOVA results (F, df between, df error, alpha, and interpretation). What can you conclude from these results?

REFERENCES

Cohen, J. (1992). A Power Primer. *Psychological Bulletin, 112,* 115–159.

Repeated-Measures
Analysis of Variance

This chapter introduces the analysis of data from studies that include a Repeated-Measures variable, which is called a *Within-Subjects Factor* in SPSS. Before starting this chapter, you may want to review the discussion of Repeated-Measures variables presented in Chapter 1. Again, a within-subjects independent variable is one where every participant has provided data in every condition. For example, if we gave pre- and post-tests to all the participants in a study, the scores on the two tests would represent a within-subjects factor. We will cover the use of SPSS to analyze data from two different designs: a One-Way Repeated Measures ANOVA and a Mixed-Model Repeated-Measures ANOVA. A One-Way Repeated-Measures ANOVA has only one independent variable, which is a within-subjects factor. A Mixed-Model Repeated-Measures ANOVA has two independent variables; one is a within-subjects (i.e., repeated) factor and the other is a between-subjects (i.e., non-repeated) factor.

Cartoon 10.1 illustrates a study that includes a repeated–measures (within–subjects) independent variable: a cat's behavior prior to exposure to music and after listening to 60 hours of music. Based on the results of this small study of animal behavior, our researchers are awarded a large grant from the National Institutes of Health to determine whether the effects found for cats can be generalized to humans. In a new study, the researchers administer a measure of anti-social attitudes to 20 college-age participants. Next, the researchers give each participant an iPod that is pre-loaded with one of two types of music: heavy metal (e.g., Ozzy Osbourne, Judas Priest, and Metallica) or easy listening (e.g., Barry Manilow, Kenny G, and Josh Groban). Participants are instructed to listen to their iPods continually throughout the day, even when going to class, driving, or operating heavy machinery. Participants are asked to complete the measure of anti-social attitudes three times: first, before listening to music; the second time after listening to the iPod for four hours; and the third time after listening for eight hours.

Figure 10.1 shows the Variable View of the SPSS Data Editor, where four variables have been created. The first variable corresponds to the anti-social attitude scores of participants recorded before they listened to any music. It is named **anti_soc1** and has the variable label "Pre-test – Anti-Social Attitudes." The second variable is named **anti_soc2** and has the variable label "After Four Hours – Anti-Social Attitudes." The third variable is named **anti_soc3** and has the variable label "After Eight Hours – Anti-Social Attitudes." The fourth variable listed corresponds to the type of music the participant listened to. It is named **music_type** and has the variable label "Type of Music." Subjects in the Heavy Metal condition are given a value of "1" and subjects in the Easy Listening

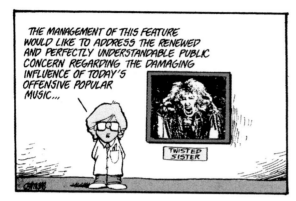

© Berkeley Breathed, dist. By The Washington Post. Reprinted with Permission.

▶**Figure 10.1** Variable View for Heavy Metal Data

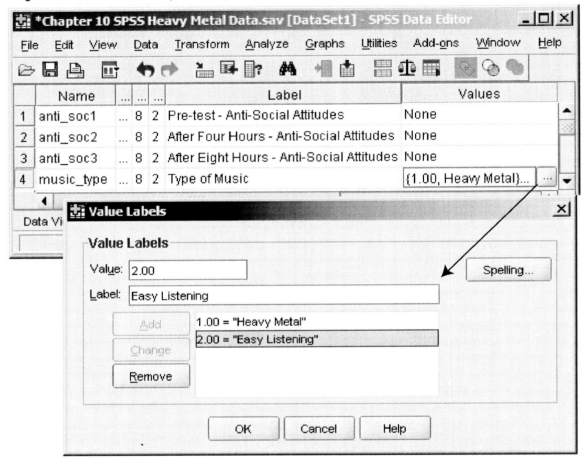

condition are given a value of "2." The Data View of the SPSS Data Editor for this data set is presented in Figure 10.2.

The researchers want to test two basic questions. First, are there significant changes in anti–social attitudes across the 8-hour period, regardless of the type of music the participants listen to? This will be addressed by a One-Way Repeated-Measures ANOVA. Second, is the pattern of change in anti-social attitude scores across the three times of measurement different for participants who listen to heavy metal music than for participants who listen to easy listening music? The second question will be addressed using a Mixed-Model Repeated-Measures ANOVA.

ONE-WAY REPEATED-MEASURES ANOVA

The researchers' first question regards whether the duration of listening to music has an effect on anti-social attitudes. Here, the investigators are not interested in the type of music the participants listened to, but only in whether there are any differences among the mean scores for anti–social attitudes obtained at each of the three times of testing.

▶ **Figure 10.2** Data View for Heavy Metal Data

	anti_soc1	anti_soc2	anti_soc3	music_type
1	10.00	9.00	10.00	Heavy Metal
2	12.00	14.00	13.00	Heavy Metal
3	15.00	13.00	14.00	Heavy Metal
4	9.00	10.00	11.00	Heavy Metal
5	13.00	12.00	11.00	Heavy Metal
6	18.00	16.00	18.00	Heavy Metal
7	14.00	16.00	18.00	Heavy Metal
8	12.00	12.00	14.00	Heavy Metal
9	14.00	17.00	15.00	Heavy Metal
10	16.00	15.00	16.00	Heavy Metal
11	13.00	17.00	21.00	Easy Listening
12	19.00	22.00	14.00	Easy Listening
13	20.00	25.00	16.00	Easy Listening
14	12.00	15.00	16.00	Easy Listening
15	14.00	13.00	16.00	Easy Listening
16	16.00	21.00	24.00	Easy Listening
17	11.00	16.00	18.00	Easy Listening
18	17.00	23.00	26.00	Easy Listening
19	14.00	18.00	18.00	Easy Listening
20	16.00	24.00	25.00	Easy Listening

Unlike the One-Way ANOVA presented in Chapter 8, where data for each condition were collected separately from each of three different groups, the design of the current study has only one group of 20 subjects. However, in this study, every subject provided data for all three conditions (i.e., at three different times of testing). Because the same group of subjects is repeating the process of providing data for the dependent variable, many textbooks label the independent variable as a *repeated-measures independent variable* or a *repeated-measures factor*. Other textbooks refer to the independent variable as a *within-subjects factor* because the comparison among the conditions takes place *within* one group of subjects. The terms "repeated-measures" and "within-subjects" are interchangeable and both appear in this chapter.

In this study, the only thing that is changing about the conditions under which the data are collected is the number of hours that subjects have been listening to music. Therefore, we are going to name this independent variable Hours of Music. Now we are going to use SPSS to conduct a One-Way Repeated-Measures ANOVA to see if there are any differences among the means for the scores collected at the three times of testing.

PROCEDURE FOR RUNNING A ONE-WAY REPEATED-MEASURES ANOVA:

① Select **Analyze** from the pull-down menu.

② Select **General Linear Model**.

③ Select **Repeated Measures…** from the side menu. This will open the **Repeated Measures Define Factor(s)** dialogue box.

④ Enter the name you want to use for the within-subjects variable in the **Within-Subject Factor Name:** field. We have named the repeated factor **Hours_of_Music**.

⑤ Enter the number of times each participant's score is measured in the **Number of Levels:** field. We have entered a value of "3" because we have taken three different measurements.

⑥ Left-click the **Add** button to include the term **Hours_of_Music(3)** in the field to the right. This indicates that SPSS is prepared to create a new repeated factor named "Hours_of_Music" and that this repeated factor has three levels.

⑦ Left-click **Define**. This will open the **Repeated Measures** dialogue box.

⑧ In the **Within-Subjects Variables (Hours_of_Music):** field, there are three rows of text consisting of _?_(1), _?_(2), and _?_(3). We have already told SPSS that we want to construct a repeated-measures independent variable named **Hours_of_Music** that has three levels. These entries represent place holders for the variables that make up this factor.

⑨ To define the repeated-measures independent variable, enter each variable that makes up the repeated factor in the order in which the variables were collected. Enter each variable by left-clicking on the variable name and then left-clicking the boxed arrow that points to the **Within-Subjects Variables (Hours_of_Music):** field. In this example, we have entered **anti_soc1** for _?_(1), **anti_soc2** for _?_(2), and **anti_soc3** for _?_(3) because this is the order in which each of the variables were collected.

⑩ To request descriptive statistics (Means and Standard Errors) for the scores at each time of testing, left-click the **Options…** button. This will open the **Repeated Measures: Options** dialogue box, which is shown in Figure 10.4.

⑪ Select the variable of interest (**Hours_of_Music**) from the **Factor(s) and Factor Interactions:** field. Left-click the boxed arrow to move this variable to the **Display Means for:** field.

⑫ Left-click **Continue** to return to the **Repeated Measures** dialogue box (in Figure 10.3).

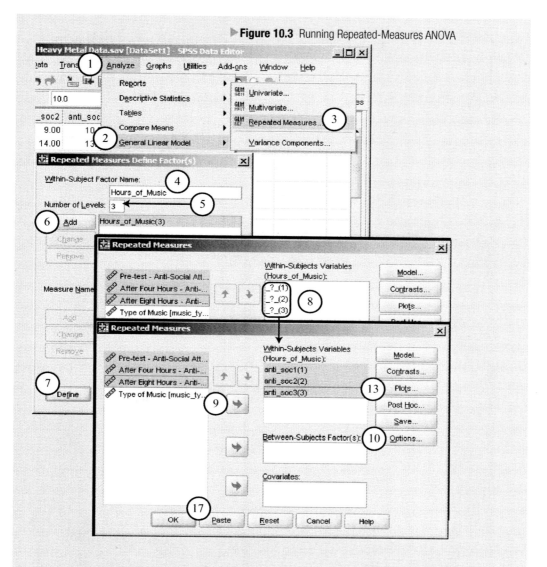

▷**Figure 10.3** Running Repeated-Measures ANOVA

⑬ To obtain a graph of the three means for the repeated-measures (within-subjects) independent variable, left click the **Plots…** button. This will open the **Repeated Measures: Profile Plots** dialogue box, which is shown in Figure 10.4.

⑭ Move the repeated factor (i.e., **Hours_of_Music**) to the **Horizontal Axis:** field by left-clicking the boxed arrow beside the field.

⑮ Left-click **Add** to move the request for a graph of the means into the **Plots:** field.

⑯ Left-click **Continue** to return to the **Repeated Measures** dialogue box (in Figure 10.3).

⑰ Finally, double-check your variables and all selected options and either select **OK** to run or **Paste** to create syntax to run at a later time.

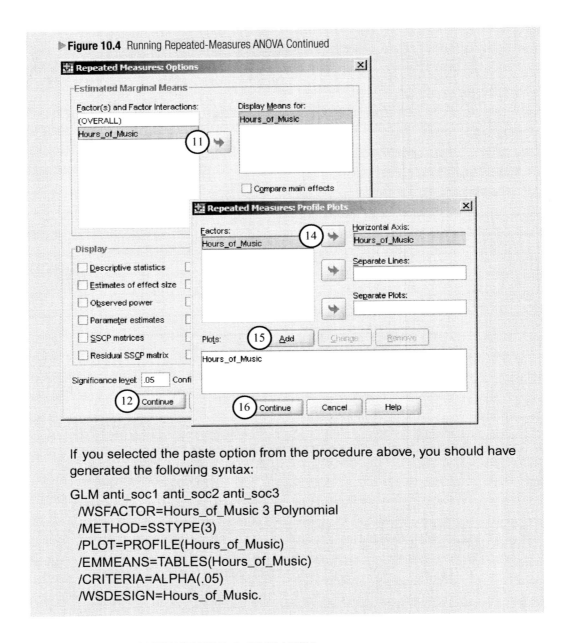

▶**Figure 10.4** Running Repeated-Measures ANOVA Continued

If you selected the paste option from the procedure above, you should have generated the following syntax:

```
GLM anti_soc1 anti_soc2 anti_soc3
  /WSFACTOR=Hours_of_Music 3 Polynomial
  /METHOD=SSTYPE(3)
  /PLOT=PROFILE(Hours_of_Music)
  /EMMEANS=TABLES(Hours_of_Music)
  /CRITERIA=ALPHA(.05)
  /WSDESIGN=Hours_of_Music.
```

READING THE OUTPUT FOR A ONE-WAY REPEATED-MEASURES ANOVA

The F-ratio used to test the effect of a repeated-measures independent variable is interpreted in the same way as an F-ratio used to test a non-repeated-measures independent variable (as presented in Chapter 8). The value for F still represents how much of the variance in the dependent variable is accounted for by the independent variable. The biggest difference in the output for a repeated-measures independent variable is that SPSS allows researchers to choose from among at least eight different versions of this F-test! Choice is good, but it does make the output more of a challenge to work with. We will just have to work our way through the choices one table at a time.

The output from our example is presented in Figures 10.5 and 10.6. One reason for the large number of tables in the output is the need to report results separately for both multivariate (MANOVA) and univariate (ANOVA) strategies. The distinction between the multivariate and univariate approaches is beyond the scope of this book. For now, you should know that both have proponents among professionals who analyze repeated-measures data. The multivariate approach has the advantage that it is not subject to a statistical assumption, referred to as *sphericity*, which will be discussed shortly. However, one disadvantage of multivariate tests is that they tend to have lower levels of statistical power than univariate tests (and thus are more likely to overlook effects that are really there). Full appreciation of the multivariate approach requires a substantial background in statistical analysis. Consequently, we will focus most of our attention on the more widely used univariate ANOVA results. As you can see in Figure 10.5, multivariate results appear in the output first, followed by univariate results.

The **Multivariate Tests** table [labeled Ⓐ in Figure 10.5] presents results of four multivariate *F*-tests: Pillai's Trace, Wilks' Lambda, Hotelling's Trace, and Roy's Largest Root. All four multivariate tests yield the same *F*-ratio of 5.458 and are statistically significant with a reported alpha level of .014, which falls well below the critical alpha level of .05. These tests indicate that there is a significant overall effect of listening to music on anti-social attitudes. This means that anti-social attitudes changed significantly across the three times they were measured.

Moving on to univariate results, the next table [labeled Ⓑ in Figure 10.5] is titled **Mauchly's Test of Sphericity**. Sphericity is one of the assumptions in testing the effect of a repeated-measures independent variable. Violating the assumption can produce significance levels that are lower than they should be and thus puts the researcher at increased risk of committing a Type I error (saying an effect is significant when it is not). We suggest you consult your textbook or instructor for a more complete explanation, but basically, a data set meets the assumption of sphericity when the consistency of change among subjects for one pair of conditions is roughly the same as the consistency of change among subjects for all pairs of conditions. Mauchly's Test of Sphericity is a direct test of this assumption. A significant value for **Mauchly's W** in the table indicates that the assumption has been violated. In our example, Mauchly's Test is not significant ($p = .184$).

The key table in the output for the current analysis is titled **Tests of Within-Subjects Effects** [labeled Ⓒ in Figure 10.5]. The first section of the **Source** columns contains the name of the within-subjects independent variable **Hours_of_Music** and presents the values used to calculate the numerators of the corresponding *F*-ratios. The four entries in this section (Sphericity Assumed, Greenhouse-Geisser, Huynh-Feldt, Lower-bound) present the results of four different ways of conducting the *F*-test. If Mauchly's Test of Sphericity is not significant, as with our example, one can use the results in the **Sphericity Assumed** row. If the result of Mauchly's Test is significant and the assumption of sphericity has been violated, then the researcher has a choice of the three remaining options. These options are based on different strategies for calculating unbiased significance levels. Although there are arguments to be made for all three, the **Greenhouse-Geisser** correction is probably the best known and most widely used. It is common practice for a researcher to report the results of the Greenhouse-Geisser-corrected version of the *F*-test, regardless of whether the result of the Mauchly's Test of Sphericity is significant.

Figure 10.5 Output for Repeated-Measures ANOVA: Part I

General Linear Model

Within-Subjects Factors

Measure:MEASURE_1

Hours_...	Dependent Variable
1	anti_soc1
2	anti_soc2
3	anti_soc3

Multivariate Tests[b]   A

Effect		Value	F	Hypothesis df	Error df	Sig.
Hours_of_Music	Pillai's Trace	.377	5.458[a]	2.000	18.000	.014
	Wilks' Lambda	.623	5.458[a]	2.000	18.000	.014
	Hotelling's Trace	.606	5.458[a]	2.000	18.000	.014
	Roy's Largest Root	.606	5.458[a]	2.000	18.000	.014

a. Exact statistic

b. Design: Intercept
Within Subjects Design: Hours_of_Music

Mauchly's Test of Sphericity[b]   B

Measure:MEASURE_1

Within Subjects Effect	Mauchly's W	Approx. Chi-Square	df	Sig.	Epsilon[a] Greenhouse-Geisser	Huynh-Feldt	Lower-bound
Hours_of_Music	.829	3.382	2	.184	.854	.930	.500

Tests the null hypothesis that the error covariance matrix of the orthonormalized transformed dependent variables is proportional to an identity matrix.

a. May be used to adjust the degrees of freedom for the averaged tests of significance. Corrected tests are displayed in the Tests of Within-Subjects Effects table.

b. Design: Intercept
Within Subjects Design: Hours_of_Music

Tests of Within-Subjects Effects   C

Measure:MEASURE_1

Source		Type III Sum of Squares	df	Mean Square	F	Sig.
Hours_of_Music	Sphericity Assumed	71.433	2	35.717	5.786	.006
	Greenhouse-Geisser	71.433	1.708	41.834	5.786	.010
	Huynh-Feldt	71.433	1.859	38.421	5.786	.008
	Lower-bound	71.433	1.000	71.433	5.786	.027
Error(Hours_of_Music)	Sphericity Assumed	234.567	38	6.173		
	Greenhouse-Geisser	234.567	32.443	7.230		
	Huynh-Feldt	234.567	35.325	6.640		
	Lower-bound	234.567	19.000	12.346		

Estimated Marginal Means

Hours_of_Music

Measure:MEASURE 1

Hours_ of_...	Mean	Std. Error	95% Confidence Interval	
			Lower Bound	Upper Bound
1	14.250	.652	12.884	15.616
2	16.400	1.024	14.256	18.544
3	16.700	1.006	14.595	18.805

Figure 10.6 Output for Repeated-Measures ANOVA: Part II

Profile Plots

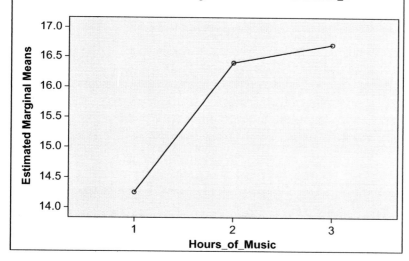

The second section of the **Source** columns is labeled **Error (Hours_of_Music)**. These rows contain the values used to calculate the denominators of the F-ratios that were used to test the effect of **Hours_of_Music**. Again, the row of results to look in depends on the version of the test the researcher has decided to use.

The **Tests of Within-Subjects Effects** table shows that when sphericity is assumed, as it is it is in our example, the F-ratio for the **Hours_of_Music** effect is 5.786 with 2 degrees of freedom in the numerator and 38 degrees of freedom in the denominator. The significance level of .006 indicates that the effect is significant. This tells us that mean anti-social attitude scores for participants changed significantly across the three times of testing. Looking in the row for the **Greenhouse-Geisser** version of the test, we see that the observed value for F is identical to that found in the **Sphericity Assumed** row, but that the significance level of .01 is slightly higher. Increased significance levels associated with the Greenhouse-Geisser, Huynh-Feldt, and Lower-bound versions of the F-test depend on the degree to which each test corrects for departures from sphericity.

In Figure 10.6, the table labeled **Estimated Marginal Means** provides the means and standard errors of the anti-social attitudes scores measured for participants at each of the three levels of the **Hours_of_Music** variable: before listening to any music (row 1), after four hours of listening (row 2), and after eight hours of listening (row 3). A graph of the means for the three levels of **Hours_of_Music** is provided in the final section of the output labeled **Profile Plots**. We can see from the graph that the means for anti-social attitudes are higher after listening to music than before the experiment began.

COMPARING PAIRS OF MEANS FOR A ONE-WAY REPEATED-MEASURES ANOVA

The results of the previous analysis showed that there are differences among the means for the three levels of **Hours_of_Music**, but it does not tell us *which* differences among these means are significant. To determine which means differ significantly, the researcher has several options. One strategy would be to conduct a Paired-Samples *t*-Test on each pair of scores that comprise levels of the repeated-measures independent variable, as covered in Chapter 7. A second option would be to conduct the comparison as a One-Way Repeated-Measures ANOVA that includes only the two levels of the repeated-measures independent variable that are being compared. In other words, the researcher creates a repeated-measures independent variable that has two levels instead of all three. The analysis can be repeated for as many pair-wise comparisons of means as desired.

Using the repeated-measures ANOVA method, assume the researchers decide to compare the means for participant scores on the anti-social attitude measure collected before listening to music and after listening to music for four hours. We will call these two levels of the repeated-measures variable Time 1 and Time 2. The researchers simply need to repeat the steps described in Figures 10.3 and 10.4, with a few minor modifications.

PROCEDURE FOR COMPARING PAIRS OF MEANS USING ONE-WAY REPEATED-MEASURES ANOVA:

- Select **Analyze** from the pull-down menu.
- Select **General Linear Model**.
- Select **Repeated Measures...** from the side menu. This will open the **Repeated Measures Define Factor(s)** dialogue box.

① Enter the name for the repeated factor in the **Within-Subject Factor Name:** field. We have named the repeated factor **Time 1 vs. Time 2**.

② Enter the value of **2** in the **Number of Levels:** field because we only want to include scores from two conditions: prior to any music listening and after four hours of music listening.

③ Click **Add**. The term **Time1_vs_Time2(2)** now appears in the box beside the **Add** button.

④ Click **Define**, which will open the **Repeated Measures** dialogue box.

⑤ In the **Within-Subjects Variables (Time1_vs_Time2):** field, you will see two rows of text consisting of _?_(1) and _?_(2).

⑥ Enter the variables representing the two levels of the within-subjects factor that you want to compare in the **Within-Subjects Variables (Time1_vs_ Time2):** field. For each variable, left-click the variable and then left-click on the boxed arrow that points into the box. In this example, we have entered **anti_soc1** for **_?_(1)** and **anti_soc2** for **_?_(2)**.

⑦ Finally, double-check your variables and all selected options and either select **OK** to run or **Paste** to create syntax to run at a later time.

If you selected the paste option from the procedure above, you should have generated the following syntax:

```
GLM anti_soc1 anti_soc2
  /WSFACTOR=Hours_of_Music 2 Polynomial
  /METHOD=SSTYPE(3)
  /EMMEANS=TABLES(Hours_of_Music)
  /CRITERIA=ALPHA(.05)
  /WSDESIGN=Hours_of_Music.
```

▶**Figure 10.7** Comparing Pairs of Means with Repeated-Measures ANOVA

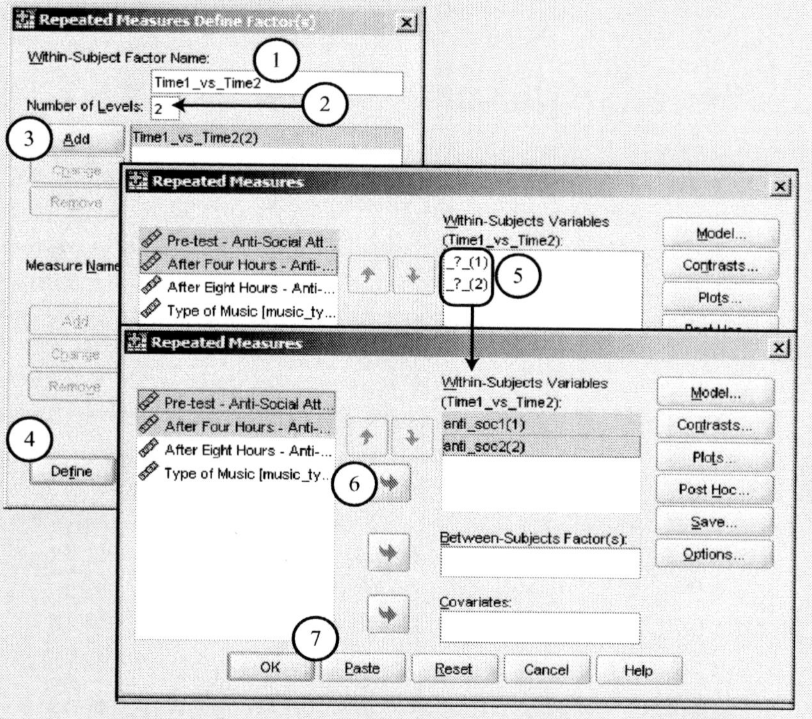

READING THE OUTPUT

The **Tests of Within-Subjects Effects** table from the output for the analysis is presented in Figure 10.8. We can see that the *F*-ratio of 10.806 is statistically significant at a significance level of .004. These values are the same for either the Sphericity Assumed or the Greenhouse-Geisser versions of the test. On the basis of this result, the researchers can

Figure 10.8 Output for Comparing Pairs of Means with Repeated-Measures ANOVA

Tests of Within-Subjects Effects

Measure:MEASURE 1

Source		Type III Sum of Squares	df	Mean Square	F	Sig.
Time1_vs_Time2	Sphericity Assumed	46.225	1	46.225	10.806	.004
	Greenhouse-Geisser	46.225	1.000	46.225	10.806	.004
	Huynh-Feldt	46.225	1.000	46.225	10.806	.004
	Lower-bound	46.225	1.000	46.225	10.806	.004
Error (Time1_vs_Time2)	Sphericity Assumed	81.275	19	4.278		
	Greenhouse-Geisser	81.275	19.000	4.278		
	Huynh-Feldt	81.275	19.000	4.278		
	Lower-bound	81.275	19.000	4.278		

conclude that anti–social attitudes increase significantly after listening to music for four hours. These same procedures can be used to compare other pairs of means. For example, we could compare Time 1 (pre-test) with Time 3 (eight hours of music listening), or we could compare Time 2 (four hours of music listening) with Time 3 (eight hours of music listening).

MIXED-MODEL REPEATED-MEASURES ANOVA

From the One-Way Repeated-Measures ANOVA reported above, we learned that listening to music, regardless of the type, resulted in significant increases in anti–social attitudes. The researchers' second question is whether the pattern of change in anti–social attitude scores across the three times of testing is different for participants who listen to heavy metal music than it is for participants in the easy listening condition. Specifically, this second question asks if there is an interaction between the two independent variables: Hours of Music (a repeated–measures variable) and Music Type (a non–repeated variable). Because the independent variables represent a mixture of repeated–measures and non–repeated–measures variables, the analysis of the study is commonly referred to as a *Mixed-Model Repeated-Measures ANOVA*.

PROCEDURE FOR RUNNING A MIXED-MODEL REPEATED-MEASURES ANOVA:

- First, repeat the procedures for defining the within-subjects independent variable (see steps 1 to 9 of Figure 10.3). To complete the Mixed-Model Repeated-Measures procedure, follow the steps below, which are shown in Figure 10.9.

① At the top of Figure 10.9, you can see the **Repeated Measures** dialogue box. In the **Within-Subjects Variable (Hours_of_Music):** field, the anti-social attitudes scores for the three times of testing (**anti_soc1**, **anti_soc2**, and **anti_soc3**) have been assigned to levels 1 through 3 of the repeated-measures independent variable.

② At this point, we need to tell SPSS to include a between-subjects (non-repeated-measures) independent variable. Left-click on the variable **music_type** and then left-click on the boxed arrow pointing to the **Between-Subjects Factor(s):** field.

③ To get the descriptive data (means and standard errors) for the two main effects and the interaction effect, click on the **Options…** button. This will open the **Repeated Measures: Options** dialogue box.

④ The names for the two main effects and the interaction effect are displayed in the **Factor(s) and Factor Interactions:** field (i.e., **music_type**, **Hours_of_Music**, and **music_type** * **Hours_of_Music**). Select each one in turn and left-click the boxed arrow to move each variable into the **Display Means for:** field.

⑤ Left-click **Continue** to return to the **Repeated Measures** dialogue box.

⑥ To get a graph of the means for the interaction between **Hours_of_Music** and Type of Music, click the **Plots…** button. This will open the **Repeated Measures: Profile Plots** dialogue box.

⑦ Select the variable **Hours_of_Music** in the **Factors:** field and left-click the boxed arrow beside the **Horizontal Axis:** field.

▶**Figure 10.9** Running a Mixed-Model ANOVA

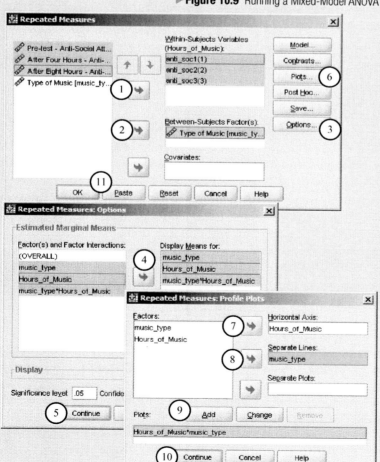

⑧ Select the variable **music_type** in the **Factors:** field and click the boxed arrow beside the **Separate Lines:** field.

⑨ Click the **Add** button. The term **Hours_of_Music** ∗ **music_type** will now appear in the **Plots:** field.

⑩ Click **Continue** to return to the **Repeated Measures** dialogue box.

⑪ Finally, double-check your variables and all selected options and either select **OK** to run or **Paste** to create syntax to run at a later time.

If you selected the paste option from the procedure above, you should have generated the following syntax:

```
GLM anti_soc1 anti_soc2 anti_soc3 BY music_type
 /WSFACTOR=Hours_of_Music 3 Polynomial
 /METHOD=SSTYPE(3)
 /PLOT=PROFILE(Hours_of_Music*music_type)
 /EMMEANS=TABLES(music_type)
 /EMMEANS=TABLES(Hours_of_Music)
 /EMMEANS=TABLES(music_type*Hours_of_Music)
 /CRITERIA=ALPHA(.05)
 /WSDESIGN=Hours_of_Music
 /DESIGN=music_type.
```

READING THE OUTPUT

Selected output from the mixed-models analysis is presented in Figures 10.10 and 10.11. You will notice that we have omitted several tables of output from the figures. In a couple of cases, this is because the information is the same as or similar to that presented in Figures 10.5 and 10.6. To keep things simple, we have skipped over the multivariate results.

A different error term is used as the denominator to calculate the F-ratios for every effect involving the repeated-measures independent variable, **Hours_of_Music**, than is used to calculate F-ratios for tests involving only the non-repeated-measures variable, **music_type**. Because of this, the output for the univariate analyses is split into two different tables. The **Tests of Within-Subjects Effects** table reports F-ratios of both the main effect of **Hours_of_Music** and the **Hours_of_Music** ∗ **music_type** interaction. The table for the **Tests of Between-Subjects Effects** reports the F-test of the main effect of **music_type**.

The top section of the **Tests of Within-Subjects Effects** table [labeled Ⓐ in Figure 10.10] contains four versions of the test of the main effect of the repeated measures variable: **Sphericity Assumed**, **Greenhouse-Geisser**, **Huynh-Feldt**, and **Lower-bound**. According to the **Sphericity Assumed** row, the main effect of **Hours_of_Music** is statistically significant at the .003 level, with an observed value for F of 6.93. If the **Greenhouse-Geisser** correction for departures from sphericity is used, the main effect for **Hours_of_Music** is still significant at the .007 level. The observed value for F remains the same at 6.93. This significant main effect of **Hours_of_Music** indicates that if we average the data from the two types of music, the mean scores for anti-social attitudes do not remain the same after listening to music.

> ▶**Figure 10.10** Output for Mixed-Model ANOVA: Part I

Tests of Within-Subjects Effects

Measure:MEASURE 1

Source		Type III Sum of Squares	df	Mean Square	F	Sig.
Hours_of_Music	Sphericity Assumed	71.433	2	35.717	6.930	.003
	Greenhouse-Geisser	71.433	1.470	48.586	6.930	.007
	Huynh-Feldt	71.433	1.658	43.086	6.930	.005
	Lower-bound	71.433	1.000	71.433	6.930	.017
Hours_of_Music * music_type	Sphericity Assumed	49.033	2	24.517	4.757	.015
	Greenhouse-Geisser	49.033	1.470	33.350	4.757	.026
	Huynh-Feldt	49.033	1.658	29.575	4.757	.021
	Lower-bound	49.033	1.000	49.033	4.757	.043
Error(Hours_of_Music)	Sphericity Assumed	185.533	36	5.154		
	Greenhouse-Geisser	185.533	26.464	7.011		
	Huynh-Feldt	185.533	29.842	6.217		
	Lower-bound	185.533	18.000	10.307		

A   B   C

Tests of Between-Subjects Effects

Measure:MEASURE_1
Transformed Variable:Average

D

Source	Type III Sum of Squares	df	Mean Square	F	Sig.
Intercept	14946.817	1	14946.817	647.723	.000
music_type	294.817	1	294.817	12.776	.002
Error	415.367	18	23.076		

The middle section of the **Tests of Within-Subjects Effects** table [labeled Ⓑ in Figure 10.10] presents results for tests of the interaction effect between the two independent variables: **Hours_of_Music** and **music_type**. If sphericity is assumed, the interaction between Hours of Music and Music Type is statistically significant at the .015 significance level, with an observed value for F of 4.757. If the Greenhouse-Geisser correction is used, the interaction effect is still significant at the .026 level. This can be interpreted to mean that the effect of Hours of Music is not the same for people who listen to heavy metal music as it is for people subjected to easy listening music.

The last section of the **Test of Within-Subjects Effects** table [labeled Ⓒ in Figure 10.10] contains the information needed to generate the denominators (error terms) for the F-ratios used to test the main effect and interaction term involving the repeated-measures independent variable (i.e., Hours of Music). You should consult your textbook for a full description of the nature of this error term.

The **Tests of Between-Subjects Effects** table [labeled Ⓓ in Figure 10.10] provides the results of the F-test of the main effect of the non–repeated independent variable **music_type**. Two F-tests are reported. The F-test of the **Intercept** in the top row is something that can be ignored because it does not provide information about the major research question (does the type of music listened to have an effect on anti-social attitudes?). The results of the F-test for the main effect of the type of music a participant

▶ **Figure 10.11** Output for Mixed-Model ANOVA: Part II

Estimated Marginal Means

1. Hours_of_Music

Measure:MEASURE 1   Ⓔ

Hours_ of_...	Mean	Std. Error	95% Confidence Interval	
			Lower Bound	Upper Bound
1	14.250	.632	12.923	15.577
2	16.400	.780	14.762	18.038
3	16.700	.814	14.990	18.410

2. Type of Music

Measure:MEASURE 1   Ⓕ

Type of Music	Mean	Std. Error	95% Confidence Interval	
			Lower Bound	Upper Bound
Heavy Metal	13.567	.877	11.724	15.409
Easy Listening	18.000	.877	16.157	19.843

3. Type of Music * Hours_of_Music

Measure:MEASURE 1   Ⓖ

Type of Music	Hours_ of_...	Mean	Std. Error	95% Confidence Interval	
				Lower Bound	Upper Bound
Heavy Metal	1	13.300	.893	11.423	15.177
	2	13.400	1.103	11.084	15.716
	3	14.000	1.151	11.582	16.418
Easy Listening	1	15.200	.893	13.323	17.077
	2	19.400	1.103	17.084	21.716
	3	19.400	1.151	16.982	21.818

Profile Plots

Estimated Marginal Means of MEASURE_1

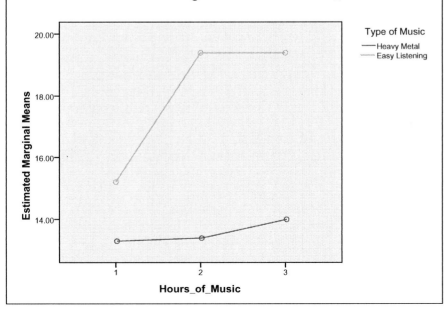

listened to is presented in the row labeled with the variable name, **music_type**. We can see that the main effect of **music_type** is significant at the .002 level. The *F*-ratio for the effect is 12.776, with 1 degree of freedom in the numerator and 18 degrees of freedom in the denominator. The **Error** row in the table provides the information used to calculate the denominator of this *F*-ratio.

The **Estimated Marginal Means** section of the output is presented in Figure 10.11 and contains three numbered tables. The table titled **1. Hours_of_Music** [labeled Ⓔ in the figure] contains the means and standard errors for the main effect of this independent variable. The **2. Type of Music** [labeled Ⓕ in the figure] table contains the means and standard errors for this main effect. The **3. Type of Music ∗ Hours_of_Music** table [labeled Ⓖ in the figure] contains the means and standard errors for the six conditions involved in the "Hours of Music by Type of Music" interaction.

The **Profile Plots** section of the output in Figure 10.11 presents a graph of means for the Hours of Music by Music Type interaction. The three levels of Hours of Music are located on the *X*-axis, and separate lines are displayed for each of the two types of music. We can see from the graph that there is very little change over time in anti-social attitudes for listeners to heavy metal music. In contrast, it appears that exposure to easy listening music led to a sharp increase in anti-social attitudes after four hours and that higher levels of anti-social attitudes were maintained at the end of a second 4-hour period.

TESTING SIMPLE EFFECTS OF THE REPEATED FACTOR AT SINGLE LEVELS OF THE NON-REPEATED FACTOR

The presence of a significant interaction between two independent variables indicates that the effect of one independent variable (on the dependent variable) is not the same at every level of the second independent variable. The significant interaction between Hours of Music and Music Type noted in the example above can be interpreted to show that the effect of listening to music on anti-social attitudes for people who listen to heavy metal music is not the same as it is for people exposed to easy listening music. This piece of information is important, but it does not tell us everything we need to know about the effects of music on anti-social attitudes. For example, it does not tell us *how* the effect of heavy metal is different from the effect of easy listening. To explore the issue further, we will need to first examine the effect of Hours of Music on Anti-Social Attitudes using only the data for the 10 subjects who listened to heavy metal and then examine the effects using only the data for the 10 subjects who were exposed to easy listening music. As discussed in Chapter 9, these effects are referred to as *simple effects* because each test is examining the effect of one independent variable at a single level of the second independent variable.

Testing the simple effect of a repeated-measures independent variable at one level of a non-repeated-measures independent variable is easy. Because the independent variable being tested is a repeated factor, every effect being tested needs its own separate error term, rather than some type of pooled or overall error term. This means that a simple effect needs to be evaluated using an error term that is based on only the data that contribute to this simple effect.

Using the select cases option As an example, we will test the simple effect of Hours of Music for subjects assigned to the Heavy Metal condition. First, we need to tell SPSS that we only want to use the data for subjects in the Heavy Metal condition. An easy way to do this is through the **Select Cases** option.

PROCEDURE FOR USING THE SELECT CASES OPTION:

(1) Select **Data** from the pull-down menu.

(2) Left-click the **Select Cases** option. This will open the **Select Cases** dialogue box.

- We have a number of options in the **Select** section of the dialogue box.

  The default **All cases** setting obviously tells SPSS to use the data from every subject. We want to use a subset of this overall number of subjects, so we need to click the option labeled **If condition is satisfied**.

(3) We still need to tell SPSS which subjects we want to include in our analysis, so click the **If...** button. This brings up the **Select Cases: If** dialogue box. So far, we've told SPSS to "select cases if some condition is satisfied." Now we need to specify what that condition is. In this example,

▶**Figure 10.12** Using the Select Cases Option

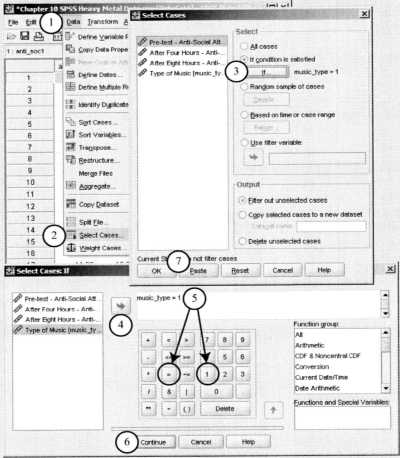

we want to use the type of music participants listened to as the variable on which we base the inclusion or exclusion of participants.

④ Left-click the variable **music_type** in the list of variables on the left-hand side of the dialogue box, and then left-click the boxed arrow to move that variable name into the field to the right of the arrow.

⑤ Now we need to complete the statement that specifies the condition that needs to be met to include a participant's data in the analysis. The participants in the Heavy Metal condition were given a value of 1 for the variable **music_type** in the Variable View of the SPSS Data Editor. Thus, we need to add the text "= 1" after the variable name **music_type**. You can do this by simply typing this text into the box or you can click on the buttons for these symbols that are provided in the dialogue box. Left-click the "=" button and then the "**1**" button. You should now see the phrase "**music_type** = 1" in the box to the right of the arrow. We have now completed an if-then statement that reads "*If music_type = 1, then select that case for inclusion in subsequent analyses.*"

⑥ Left-click **Continue** to return to the **Select Cases** dialogue box.

⑦ Finally, double-check your variables and all selected options and either select **OK** to run or **Paste** to create syntax to run at a later time.

If you selected the paste option from the procedure above, you should have generated the following syntax:

```
USE ALL .
COMPUTE filter_$=(music_type = 1) .
VARIABLE LABEL filter_$ 'music_type = 1 (FILTER)' .
VALUE LABELS filter_$ 0 'Not Selected' 1 'Selected' .
FORMAT filter_$ (f1.0) .
FILTER BY filter_$ .
EXECUTE .
```

If you look at the Data View of the SPSS Data Editor, you will see that a slash now appears in the case number for subjects with a value of "2" for **music_type**. A slash through a case number means that this case will not be included in any analysis that follows. To turn the selection condition off, return to the **Select Cases** dialogue box and select the **All Cases** option. It is generally good practice to turn off the selection condition after running the analysis of interest. Otherwise it's easy to forget that it's on, and when you run other analyses, it only uses part of your sample.

After running the **Select Cases** option, the only subjects available for us to use are the 10 subjects who listened to Heavy Metal music. Now we can run a One-Way Repeated-Measures ANOVA with **Hours_of_Music** as the repeated-measures independent variable. And you already know how to do this! Just go back and follow the same steps we went through for the one-way Repeated-Measures ANOVA procedure presented at the start of the chapter and shown in Figures 10.3 and 10.4.

The output for the simple effect test is shown in Figure 10.13. In the first **Tests of Within-Subjects Effects** table [labeled (A) in the figure], we can see that the observed value for *F* for the effect is 1.054 and that it does not reach significance when evaluated using significance levels from either the **Sphericity Assumed** (*p* = .369) or **Greenhouse-Geisser** (*p* = .366) versions of the test. This tells us that listening to heavy metal music has no effect on anti-social attitudes.

At this point, the researchers would test the other simple effect in the set to see if exposure to easy listening music has an effect on anti-social attitudes. The one difference in the procedure to test this simple effect is that we need to go back and change the **Select Cases** option so that the selection condition reads "**music_type = 2**." Now the only subjects available for analysis are the 10 participants in the Easy Listening condition. Again, run the one-way Repeated-Measures ANOVA with **Hours_of_Music** as the repeated-measures variable. The resulting **Tests of Within-Subjects Effects** table for this analysis is displayed in the bottom half of Figure 10.13 [labeled (B)]. The table shows that the observed value for *F* for this second simple effect is 6.571 and that the effect is statistically significant using either the **Sphericity Assumed** (*p* = .007) or **Greenhouse-Geisser**

▶ **Figure 10.13** Output for Mixed-Model ANOVA: Simple Effect of Hours of Music for the Heavy Metal and Easy Listening Groups

Tests of Within-Subjects Effects (A)

Measure:MEASURE 1

Source		Type III Sum of Squares	df	Mean Square	F	Sig.
Hours_of_Music	Sphericity Assumed	2.867	2	1.433	1.054	.369
	Greenhouse-Geisser	2.867	1.876	1.528	1.054	.366
	Huynh-Feldt	2.867	2.000	1.433	1.054	.369
	Lower-bound	2.867	1.000	2.867	1.054	.331
Error(Hours_of_Music)	Sphericity Assumed	24.467	18	1.359		
	Greenhouse-Geisser	24.467	16.888	1.449		
	Huynh-Feldt	24.467	18.000	1.359		
	Lower-bound	24.467	9.000	2.719		

Tests of Within-Subjects Effects (B)

Measure:MEASURE 1

Source		Type III Sum of Squares	df	Mean Square	F	Sig.
Hours_of_Music	Sphericity Assumed	117.600	2	58.800	6.571	.007
	Greenhouse-Geisser	117.600	1.328	88.533	6.571	.019
	Huynh-Feldt	117.600	1.471	79.958	6.571	.015
	Lower-bound	117.600	1.000	117.600	6.571	.031
Error(Hours_of_Music)	Sphericity Assumed	161.067	18	8.948		
	Greenhouse-Geisser	161.067	11.955	13.473		
	Huynh-Feldt	161.067	13.237	12.168		
	Lower-bound	161.067	9.000	17.896		

($p = .019$) versions of the test. This result shows that the means for anti-social attitudes at the three times of testing are not the same when subjects are exposed to easy listening music. In other words, easy listening music has a significant effect on anti-social attitudes. This is shocking!

The purpose of our set of simple effects tests was to show us why there was a significant interaction between the number of hours spent listening to music and the type of music that people listen to. Together, the results of the two simple effects tests show us that the effects of one independent variable, Hours of Music, are not the same at the two levels of Music Type. In other words, there is no significant change in anti-social attitudes when people listen to heavy metal music, but anti-social attitudes do change significantly when people are exposed to easy listening music. This pattern is consistent with the definition of an interaction effect.

TESTING SIMPLE COMPARISONS OF MEANS INVOLVING THE REPEATED FACTOR

This significant simple effect found for those exposed to easy listening music tells us that there are differences among the means of anti-social attitude scores for the three times of testing, but it does not tell us which means are significantly different from one another. A *simple comparison* tests the difference between two of the means that comprise a particular simple effect. The goal of this section is to describe how to use SPSS to test a simple comparison involving the repeated-measures independent variable.

Assume that our researchers want to test the difference between the means for subjects in the Easy Listening group collected before any music was administered (Time 1) and after they had listened to music for four hours (Time 2). The procedure is identical to that already described in testing a comparison between means in the context of a One-Way Repeated-Measures ANOVA with only one difference: we need to make sure we have set the **Select Cases...** option to include only the subjects for the particular level of the non-repeated factor we want to work with, which for our current example is those subjects who were exposed to easy listening music.

PROCEDURE FOR TESTING A SIMPLE COMPARISON OF THE REPEATED-MEASURES VARIABLE AT A SINGLE LEVEL OF A NON-REPEATED-MEASURES INDEPENDENT VARIABLE:

- Using the **Select Cases...** option, make sure the selection condition is set to include the data from the correct level of Type of Music. In this example, we only want to use the data from the subjects in the Easy Listening condition, so the selection condition should be "**music_type = 2**". Refer back to Figure 10.12 for a demonstration.

- To conduct the One-Way Repeated-Measures ANOVA for the simple contrast, repeat the procedures outlined in Figure 10.7.

▶**Figure 10.14** Output for Mixed-Model ANOVA: Simple Comparison Between
Time 1 and Time 2 for the Easy Listening Group

Measure:MEASURE 1

Source		Type III Sum of Squares	df	Mean Square	F	Sig.
Hours_of_Music	Sphericity Assumed	88.200	1	88.200	32.008	.000
	Greenhouse-Geisser	88.200	1.000	88.200	32.008	.000
	Huynh-Feldt	88.200	1.000	88.200	32.008	.000
	Lower-bound	88.200	1.000	88.200	32.008	.000
Error (Hours_of_Music)	Sphericity Assumed	24.800	9	2.756		
	Greenhouse-Geisser	24.800	9.000	2.756		
	Huynh-Feldt	24.800	9.000	2.756		
	Lower-bound	24.800	9.000	2.756		

The **Tests of Within-Subjects Effects** table from the output for the simple comparison analysis is presented in Figure 10.14. As shown, the F-ratio of 32.008 is statistically significant at the .001 significance level with 1 degree of freedom in the numerator and 9 degrees of freedom in the denominator. These values are the same for both the **Sphericity Assumed** and the **Greenhouse-Geisser** versions of the test. The researchers can therefore conclude that exposure to easy listening music for four hours results in a significant increase in anti-social attitudes compared to the pre-exposure levels. To get a complete picture of our data, we may want to follow this up with other simple comparisons among participants exposed to easy listening music. For example, we could compare the anti-social attitudes scores at four hours (time 2) with the scores taken at eight hours (time 3).

TESTING SIMPLE EFFECTS OF THE NON-REPEATED FACTOR AT SINGLE LEVELS OF THE REPEATED FACTOR

One can interpret an interaction from the point of view of either set of simple effects. This section will describe how you can use SPSS to test a simple effect of the between-subjects or non-repeated independent variable at a single level of the repeated-measures independent variable. In our design, we have a non-repeated variable with two levels and a repeated-measures variable with three levels. This means that there are three possible simple effects: the effect of Music Type at each of three levels of Hours of Music.

In terms of the analysis, we have chosen to treat each simple effect in the set as a separate Between-Subjects One-Way ANOVA, as covered in Chapter 8. In fact, the procedures in SPSS are exactly the same as those presented in Chapter 8. The independent variable is the non-repeated variable, Music Type, and the dependent variable consists of scores from a single level of Hours of Music (i.e., a single time of testing). For example, assume the researchers want to test the simple effect of Music Type for scores obtained after subjects had been listening to music for eight hours (Time 3). We would simply do the following:

PROCEDURE FOR TESTING THE SIMPLE EFFECT OF A NON-REPEATED INDEPENDENT VARIABLE AT A SINGLE LEVEL OF A REPEATED-MEASURES INDEPENDENT VARIABLE:

- Select **Analyze** from the pull-down menu.
- Select **Compare Means**.
- Select **One-Way ANOVA...** from the side menu.
- Select **anti_soc3** as the variable to go in the **Dependent List:** field.
- Select **Type of Music** as the **Factor:**.
- Click **OK** to run the analysis:

▶ **Figure 10.15** Output for Mixed-Model ANOVA: Simple Effects for Type of Music at Time 3

ANOVA

After Eight Hours — Anti-Social Attitudes

	Sum of Squares	df	Mean Square	F	Sig.
Between Groups	145.800	1	145.800	11.008	.004
Within Groups	238.400	18	13.244		
Total	384.200	19			

The ANOVA table in the generated output is displayed in Figure 10.15. The F-ratio of 11.008, with 1 degree of freedom in the numerator and 18 degrees of freedom in the denominator, is statistically significant, with a significance level of .004. This indicates that anti-social attitudes after eight hours of exposure to easy listening music are significantly higher than anti-social attitudes after listening to eight hours of heavy metal music. To test the other simple effects in the set, we only need to repeat the analysis, substituting the variable name for a different level of Hours of Music each time.

If the between-subjects (non-repeated) variable has more than two levels or groups, then it would be necessary to follow up significant simple effects with simple comparisons. To obtain the desired simple comparisons, simply apply the same methods covered in Chapter 8 for testing comparisons between pairs of group means and use the appropriate level of the repeated factor.

The approach presented above assumes the researcher wants to use a different error term for each simple effect. A common alternative approach is to use a pooled error term to test each effect involving the non–repeated factor. To apply this approach, the researcher would (a) use the procedures outlined above to obtain the numerators for the F-ratios testing each simple effect, and then (b) divide each numerator by the desired pooled error term. You should consult your statistics textbook for advice on the appropriate pooled error term to use.

SUMMARY

This chapter focused on testing the effects of repeated-measures independent variables. We used SPSS to test the overall effect of one repeated factor and learned how to compare the means for two levels of this repeated factor. We then covered the analysis of data from a more complicated design that included one repeated factor and one non-repeated factor. We tested the interaction between the two independent variables and the main effects for each. We then described procedures for testing simple effects and simple comparisons from two points of view: (a) the effect of the repeated-measures variable at unique levels of the non-repeated-measures variable and (b) the effect of the non-repeated-measures variable at unique levels of the repeated-measures variable. Finally, we learned that easy listening music is a dark and dangerous source of anti-social attitudes in today's society.

PRACTICE EXERCISES

1. The data set displayed in Table 10.1 contains scores for a measure of empathy that have been obtained from the same 20 subjects used in the anti-social attitude music study and collected at the same three testing times (prior to listening to music, after four hours of music, and after eight hours of music). Enter these data into an SPSS spreadsheet using variable names of your choice.

   a. Test for the presence of a significant interaction between the repeated factor (Hours of Music) and the non-repeated factor (Type of Music).

   b. Test the main effect of Hours of Music and the main effect of Type of Music.

   c. Test the simple effects of Hours of Music at each of the two levels of Type of Music.

   d. Test the simple comparison of Pre-Test vs. Four Hours for subjects in the Easy Listening group.

   e. Test the simple comparison of Four Hours vs. Eight Hours for subjects in the Easy Listening group.

   f. Test the simple effects of Type of Music for scores collected at each of the three levels of Type of Music.

2. Make up a data set that has three levels of a repeated factor and three levels of a non-repeated factor. Make sure your study has as little to do with music, penguins, cats, and anti-social behavior as possible. Construct the data so that the interaction between the two variables is significant. Conduct the appropriate analyses to fully explain the pattern of results displayed in a graph of all nine means. After you've done that, try at least one example of everything we covered in this chapter.

▶ **Table 10.1** Practice Exercise Data

Participants	Empathy Pre-Test	Empathy After Four Hours	Empathy After Eight Hours	Type of Music
1	43	41	40	Heavy Metal
2	38	39	38	Heavy Metal
3	35	33	34	Heavy Metal
4	27	25	24	Heavy Metal
5	26	27	27	Heavy Metal
6	35	35	36	Heavy Metal
7	40	41	40	Heavy Metal
8	42	39	40	Heavy Metal
9	38	35	36	Heavy Metal
10	34	30	31	Heavy Metal
11	26	27	34	Easy Listening
12	30	26	22	Easy Listening
13	36	30	31	Easy Listening
14	37	37	37	Easy Listening
15	28	20	22	Easy Listening
16	46	33	34	Easy Listening
17	35	35	32	Easy Listening
18	32	25	22	Easy Listening
19	46	28	28	Easy Listening
20	38	29	27	Easy Listening

Regression and Correlation

This chapter covers procedures for testing the association between two score variables using the SPSS **Regression** and **Correlate** procedures. Specifically, we demonstrate procedures for running Bivariate Correlations (reporting the Pearson's r statistic), running a Simple Linear Regression, and producing Scatterplots. Both regression and correlation analyses will allow us to identify the strength and direction of the relationship between two score variables. Regression will also allow us to make predictions: once we know how two variables are related, we can use the values of one variable (called the predictor) to predict the values of the second variable (called the criterion or outcome variable).

SETTING UP THE DATA

For the following examples, we turn to Cartoon 11.1, where Santa uncharacteristically threatens his reindeer. Assume that Santa allows us to measure 1) the number of times in a month that the reindeer file formal complaints, and 2) the number of reindeer that are "fired" each month across a full year. With this data, we can determine whether there is an association between complaining and being "fired." The data are presented in Table 11.1.

▶**Table 11.1** Complaints and Reindeer "Fired"

Month	Number of Complaints Received Per Month (X)	Number of Reindeer "Fired" Per Month (Y)
January	2	1
February	1	2
March	3	2
April	4	3
May	3	4
June	5	6
July	4	6
August	7	8
September	8	9
October	10	12
November	11	14
December	14	17

"And I've only one thing to say about all these complaints I've been hearing about ... *Venison!*"

Figure 11.1 on page 154 presents the Variable View of the SPSS Data Editor, where two score variables have been created. The first variable, **complain**, represents the frequency with which the reindeer complain per month during the 12 months sampled. The variable label for **complain** is "Number of Complaints Received per Month." The second variable, **fired**, represents the number of reindeer "fired" each month. The variable label for **fired** is "Number of Reindeer 'Fired' Each Month."

Figure 11.2 on page 154 presents the Data View of the SPSS Data Editor, where the complaint and firing data have been entered. Remember that the columns represent each variable and the rows represent each observation, which in this case is each month sampled. For example, during the first month, two reindeer complained and one was fired. Similarly, during the 12th month, 14 reindeer complained and 17 were fired.

CORRELATION

Pearson's *r* correlation coefficient can be obtained using the **Bivariate Correlation** option. This statistic indicates the strength, direction, and significance of the association

▶**Figure 11.1** Variable View for Reindeer Data

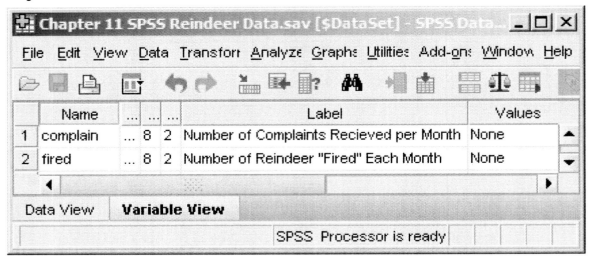

▶**Figure 11.2** Data View for Reindeer Data

	complain	fired
1	2.00	1.00
2	1.00	2.00
3	3.00	2.00
4	4.00	3.00
5	3.00	4.00
6	5.00	6.00
7	4.00	6.00
8	7.00	8.00
9	8.00	9.00
10	10.00	12.00
11	11.00	14.00
12	14.00	17.00

between two score variables. The values of Pearson's *r* correlation can range between 1 and –1. The closer the value of *r* is to 0, the weaker the association between the variables of interest. Correlations also tell us whether variables are directly related (with a positive linear relationship) or inversely related (with a negative linear relationship). If the value of *r* is positive, we know that an increase in one variable results in an increase in the second variable. If the value of *r* is negative, we know that an increase in one variable results in a decrease in the second variable, and vice versa. For positive and negative correlations, the size of the increase in the second variable depends upon the strength of the association, or how far *r* is from 0. Like the statistics covered in earlier chapters, the test of significance for correlation will tell us whether the value of *r* should be considered meaningful or whether it is likely to have occurred by chance. Also like previous statistics we have covered, the .05 alpha level is generally considered the cutoff for establishing significance.

RUNNING THE ANALYSES

In our example, Pearson's *r* will tell us whether a significant association exists between the number of Santa's reindeer that complain each month and the number of reindeer that meet an unfortunate end. Further, if the association is significant, the Pearson's *r* will indicate whether more reindeer are "fired" when more complaints are lodged—a positive correlation—or whether fewer reindeer are "fired" when more complaints are lodged—a negative correlation.

PROCEDURE FOR RUNNING A BIVARIATE CORRELATION:

① Select **Analyze** from the pull-down menu.
② Select **Correlate**.

▶ **Figure 11.3** Running Correlation Analyses

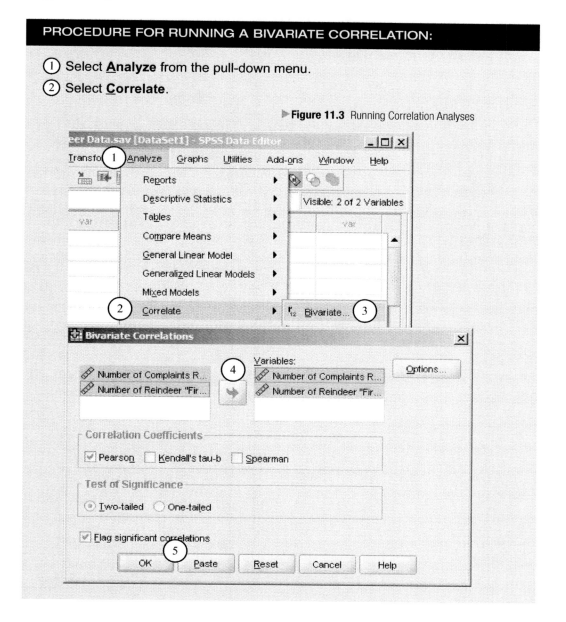

③ Select **Bivariate…** from the side menu. This will open the **Bivariate Correlations** dialogue box.

④ Enter the variables **fired** and **complain** in the **Variables:** field by either double-clicking on each variable or by left-clicking on each variable and left-clicking on the boxed arrow pointing to the **Variables:** field.

⑤ Finally, double check your variables and either select **OK** to run or **Paste** to create syntax to run at a later time.

If you selected the paste option from the procedure above, you should have generated the following syntax:

CORRELATIONS
 /VARIABLES=complain fired
 /PRINT=TWOTAIL NOSIG
 /MISSING=PAIRWISE .

READING THE OUTPUT

The Correlation output is presented in Figure 11.4. In our current example, the results are organized in a 2 × 2 matrix, where the variables **complain** and **fired** are represented in both the rows and the columns. Each cell of this matrix reports (a) the Pearson's r correlation between the variables, (b) the significance levels for each correlation, and (c) the number of subjects contributing data to each correlation, from which the degrees of freedom can be obtained (for Pearson's r, $df = n–2$). The cells forming the diagonal of this matrix; row 1, column 1 and row 2, column 2; represent each variable's correlation with itself. Both are equal to 1.0 because a variable is always perfectly correlated with itself. In Figure 11.4, the cells forming the diagonal are labeled Ⓐ. These correlations are rather meaningless and therefore no significance levels are provided. It is also important to notice that the analyses above and below the diagonal are redundant. The correlation in the cell below the diagonal, labeled Ⓑ, is identical to the correlation reported in the cell above the diagonal. Thus, even though there are four cells reported in this matrix, there is only one correlation statistic to interpret. The correlation between the number of complaints reindeer make and the number of reindeer fired is .983 with 10 degrees of freedom. The significance level is reported as .000, but we should interpret this as .001 because we can never be 100% sure the results are meaningful. We can conclude that

▶**Figure 11.4** Output for Correlation Analyses

Correlations

Correlations

		Number of Complaints Recieved per Month	Number of Reindeer "Fired" Each Month
Number of Complaints Recieved per Month	Pearson Correlation	Ⓐ 1.000	.983**
	Sig. (2-tailed)		.000
	N	12.000	12
Number of Reindeer "Fired" Each Month	Pearson Correlation	Ⓑ .983**	Ⓐ 1.000
	Sig. (2-tailed)	.000	
	N	12	12.000

**Correlation is significant at the 0.01 level (2-tailed).

these two variables are significantly and strongly positively correlated. That is, when there is an increase in the number of complaints that Santa receives, there is a strong tendency for Santa to "fire" more reindeer that month. Though correlations cannot determine whether complaints cause firings or firings cause complaints, the prudent reindeer may wish to err on the side of caution and keep complaints to a minimum.

SIMPLE LINEAR REGRESSION

Like correlation, Simple Linear Regression allows us to determine the direction and significance of the association between two variables. However, regression also identifies the least squares regression line that best fits the data. The least squares regression line can be written with the formula: $Y = a + bX$, where a is the point where the regression line meets the Y-axis, also called the Y-intercept, and b represents the slope of the regression line, also called the regression coefficient. Identifying the least squares regression line allows us to make predictions about the value of Y for known values of X, where Y is used to represent the criterion variable and X is used to represent the predictor variable. The Y-intercept tells us what the expected value of Y is when the value of X is 0. The regression coefficient b indicates how much Y is expected to change each time X increases by 1 unit. When b has a positive value, an increase in X results in an increase in Y, a positive association. When b has a negative value, an increase in X results in a decrease in Y, a negative association.

RUNNING THE ANALYSES

Like the correlation procedure conducted earlier, the following simple linear regression procedure will allow us to determine whether reindeer complaints are significantly associated with reindeer "firings" within Santa's herd. It will also allow us to determine whether complaints and firings are positively or negatively associated. Further, this analysis will give us the Y-intercept and b values that make up the regression equation. The Y-intercept will tell us how many reindeer we should expect to get fired during a month when no complaints have been lodged. Combined with the Y-intercept, b will allow us to predict how many reindeer will get fired as the number of complaints increases.

PROCEDURE FOR RUNNING A SIMPLE LINEAR REGRESSION:

1. Select **Analyze** from the pull-down menu.
2. Select **Regression**.
3. Select **Linear...** from the side menu. This will open the **Linear Regression** dialogue box.
4. Enter the variable **fired** in the **Dependent:** field by left-clicking on the variable and left-clicking on the boxed arrow pointing to the **Dependent:** field.
5. Next, enter the variable **complain** in the **Independent(s):** field by left-clicking on the variable and left-clicking on the boxed arrow pointing to the **Independent(s):** field.
6. Finally, double-check your variables and either select **OK** to run or **Paste** to create syntax to run at a later time.

▶**Figure 11.5** Running Simple Linear Regression

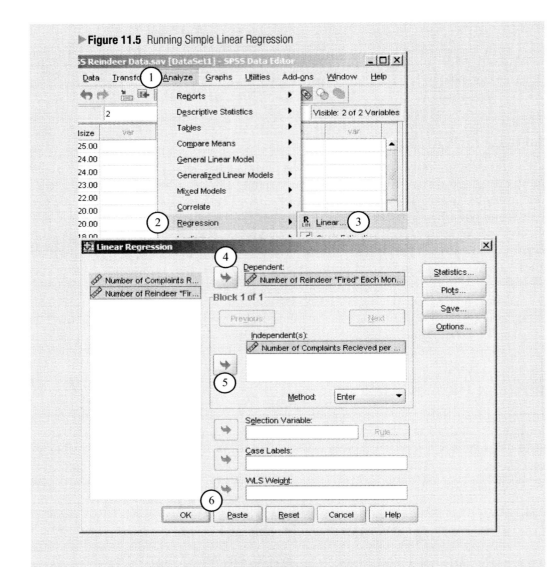

If you selected the paste option from the procedure above, you should have generated the following syntax:

```
REGRESSION
 /MISSING LISTWISE
 /STATISTICS COEFF OUTS R ANOVA
 /CRITERIA=PIN(.05) POUT(.10)
 /NOORIGIN
 /DEPENDENT fired
 /METHOD=ENTER complain .
```

READING THE SIMPLE LINEAR REGRESSION OUTPUT

The Linear Regression Output consists of four parts: **Variables Entered/Removed**, **Model Summary**, **ANOVA**, and **Coefficients**. We will only be looking at the output table labeled **Coefficients**. For this reason, we have omitted all but the **Coefficients** table in Figure 11.6. Interpretation of the tables of the output not shown in Figure 11.6 is provided in Chapter 12, *Multiple Regression*.

The first row of the **Coefficients** table, labeled **(Constant)**, reports the Y-intercept (a) in the first column, labeled **B**. The second column of this row reports the Standard Error (SE) of the Y-intercept. Like the standard errors reported in previous chapters, the SE of the Y-intercept is an estimate of the average amount that sample Y-intercepts differ from the Y-intercept found in the population. The last two columns of this row report a t value and the associated significance level, which tests whether the Y-intercept is significantly different from zero. The t value is obtained by dividing the Y-intercept by the Standard Error of the Y-intercept. In this case, the Y-intercept for our data is -.551, the SE of the Y-intercept is .537, and the resulting t value is -1.025, which is not significant since the alpha level (.330) is greater than .05. The non-significant t indicates that the Y-intercept is not significantly different from 0. Again, the value of the Y-intercept indicates how many reindeer you would expect to be "fired" when there are no complaints lodged by Santa's herd. Literally, less than zero (-.551) reindeer are fired, but it is more practical to say that zero reindeer are expected to be fired when zero complaints are lodged.

The second row of this output, labeled with the predictor variable, number of complaints received per month, presents the slope of the regression line (b) in the first column, labeled **B**. In our example, b is 1.258. That is, for every complaint that the reindeer lodge, the number of reindeer fired increases by 1.258. The second column of this row presents the Standard Error (SE) of b. The SE of b is an estimate of the average amount that values for b obtained from samples differ from the value of b in the population. Skipping now to the last two columns of the second row, SPSS reports a t statistic that allows us to determine whether the relationship between X and Y is significant. Specifically, this t test tells us whether the slope of the regression equation is significantly different from zero. It is obtained by dividing b by the SE of b. In this example, b is 1.258, SE of b is .075, and t is 16.696, which is significant at least at the .001 level. Thus, we can conclude that the number of complaints made by reindeer is a meaningful predictor of the number of reindeer that are "fired."

Combining the information obtained for the Y-intercept and b we can estimate the number reindeer that would be "fired" when different numbers of complaints have

▶ **Figure 11.6** Output for Regression Analyses

Coefficients[a]

Model		Unstandardized Coefficients		Standardized Coefficients	t	Sig.
		B	Std. Error	Beta		
1	(Constant)	-.551	.537		-1.025	.330
	Number of Complaints Recieved per Month	1.258	.075	.983	16.696	.000

a. Dependent Variable: Number of Reindeer "Fired" Each Month

been lodged. We know that –.551 reindeer get fired when no complaints are lodged, and we know that each complaint lodged tends to increase the number of firings by 1.288 reindeer. Based on this information, we can expect that if 1 reindeer complains, then .707 reindeer would get fired (–.555 + 1.258). If 2 reindeer complained, then 1.965 reindeer would be expected to get fired [–.551 + (1.258 * 2) = –.551 + 2.516]. If 10 reindeer complained, then 12.029 reindeer would be expected to get fired [–.551 + (1.258 * 10) = –.551 + 12.58].

The third column of the output reports the Standardized Regression Coefficient, commonly referred to as Beta. This coefficient represents the slope of the regression line predicting Y from X after scores for both variables have been converted to Z-scores. With one predictor variable, Beta is the same as the Pearson's r coefficient and similarly tells us the strength and direction of the relationship between X and Y. The Beta for our reindeer data is .983, indicating that there is a strong positive linear relationship between complaints and firings. You may note that no value is displayed in the **(Constant)** row for the Standardized Coefficients column. When scores for X and Y are expressed in standard score units, the Y-intercept for the equation is always 0.

OBTAINING THE SCATTERPLOT

The **Graphs** options of SPSS can generate a scatterplot for X and Y. Also, the **Graphs** options can be used to plot the least squares regression line within the scatterplot. In the following example, we present the steps for obtaining the scatterplot for our reindeer data. The X-axis (abscissa) will represent the number of complaints, and the Y-axis (ordinate) will represent the number of reindeer "fired."

PROCEDURE FOR OBTAINING A SCATTERPLOT:

① Select **Graphs** from the pull-down menu.

② Select **Legacy Dialogs**.

③ Select **Scatter/Dot...** from the side menu. This opens the **Scatter/Dot** dialogue box

④ Select the **Simple Scatter** option.

⑤ Left-click **Define**. This will open the **Simple Scatterplot** dialogue box.

⑥ Enter the **fired** variable in the **Y Axis:** field by left-clicking the **fired** variable and left-clicking the boxed arrow pointing to the **Y Axis:** field.

⑦ Enter the **complain** variable in the **X Axis:** field by left-clicking the **complain** variable and left-clicking the boxed arrow pointing to the **X Axis:** field.

⑧ To add a descriptive title to the scatterplot, left-click the **Titles...** button. This will open the **Titles** dialogue box.

⑨ Enter the major heading desired in the **Line 1:** field. In this case, we have entered the title "Reindeer Data Scattergram."

⑩ Left-click **Continue** to return to the **Simple Scatterplot** dialogue box.

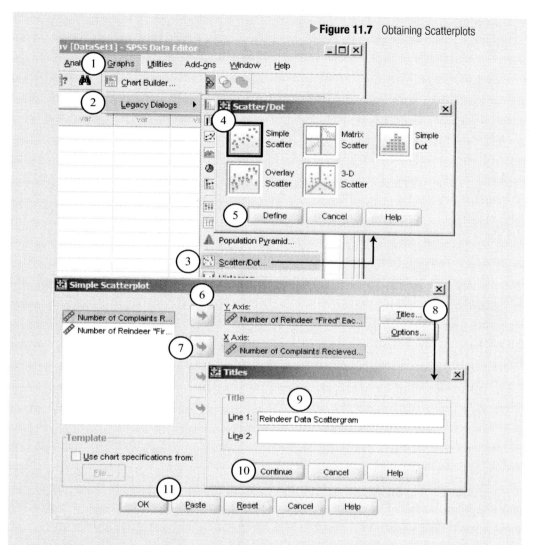

▶**Figure 11.7** Obtaining Scatterplots

⑪ Finally, double-check your variables and either select **OK** to run or **Paste** to create syntax to run at a later time.

If you selected the paste option from the procedure above, you should have generated the following syntax:

```
GRAPH
  /SCATTERPLOT(BIVAR)=complain WITH fired
  /MISSING=LISTWISE
  /TITLE= 'Reindeer Data Scattergram' .
```

▶**Figure 11.8** Output for Scatterplot

Graph

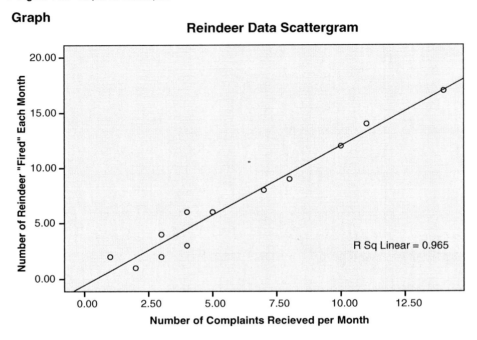

Figure 11.8 presents the scatterplot we requested and includes the least squares regression line that best fits our data. However, the procedure above did not include the steps required to insert a regression line. We must add the regression line while in the Output Navigator. The steps are described in the procedure below.

PROCEDURE FOR ADDING THE REGRESSION LINE TO A SCATTERPLOT:

- In the **Output Navigator**, double-click on the scatterplot to open the SPSS **Chart Editor**.

① In the **Chart Editor**, select the **Elements** pull-down menu.

② Select **Fit Line at Total**. This will open the **Properties** dialogue box. Ensure that the **Linear** option is selected in the **Fit Method** section.

③ Left-click **Close** to return to the **Chart Editor**.

④ To return to the **Output Navigator**, close the **Chart Editor** by left-clicking the boxed X in the upper right-hand corner of the **Chart Editor**.

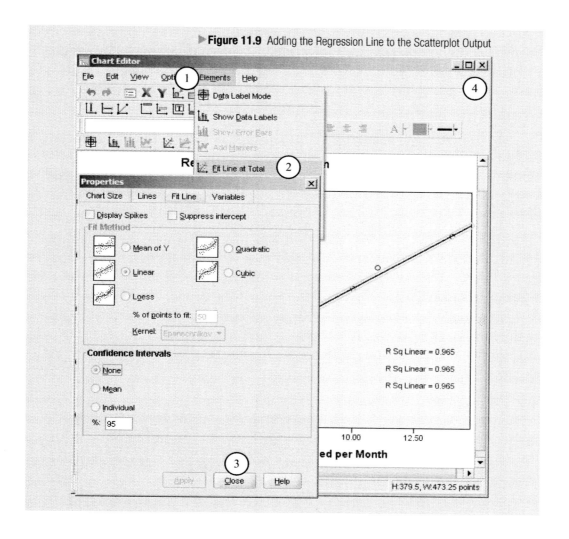

▶**Figure 11.9** Adding the Regression Line to the Scatterplot Output

Each circle shown in the scatterplot in Figure 11.8 represents the data for each month relative to the number of complaints—on the X-axis—and the number of reindeer "fired"—on the Y-axis. Eyeballing the chart, we can see a clear trend where months with fewer complaints also had fewer firings, and months with more complaints had more firings. This reflects a positive linear relationship.

The figure also displays the least squares regression line, which represents the expected values of Y—reindeer firings—for a range of possible values of X—complaints. This line represents the straight line that comes closest to all the data points in the scatterplot. The point where this line is parallel to 0 on the X-axis is the Y-intercept, and the slope of this line is b. In our example, the line rises as it moves from left to right. Had a negative linear relationship existed, the line would have dropped from left to right, indicating that as complaints increased firings tended to decrease.

Adding the least square regression line also added a new statistic that will be covered more fully in the next chapter. R^2, which is labeled **R Sq. Linear** in the chart, represents the proportion of variability in Y that is accounted for or predicted by X. In this case, the number of complaints lodged by Santa's reindeer accounts for 96.5% of the variability in the number reindeer that are "fired" each month. Thus we can conclude that complaints very strongly predict firings in our sample of reindeer.

SUMMARY

This chapter presented procedures for generating Pearson's *r* correlation and simple linear regressions using the **Correlate** and **Regression** procedures. In the example, correlation and regression analyses were used to determine the nature of the relationship between the number of time Santa's reindeer complained each month and the number of reindeer that Santa had "fired." Together, the Pearson's *r* correlation, Simple Linear Regression, and the Scatterplot indicated that the number of complaints Santa receives each month is strongly positively associated with the number of reindeer that get fired. That is, more reindeer complaints tend to coincide with more reindeer firings.

PRACTICE EXERCISES

Assume a researcher is interested evaluating the relationship between the number of complaints lodged by each of 20 different reindeer over the past 25 years and the number of times each reindeer has been part of the team on Chrisman Eve in the past 25 years. These data are presented in Table 11.2. Enter the data into SPSS, complete the

▶**Table 11.2** Practice Exercise Data

Participant	Number of Complaints Made in Past 25 Years (*X*)	Number of Times Part of Sled Team on Big Night (*Y*)
1	1	25
2	3	25
3	4	17
4	5	15
5	6	23
6	10	12
7	12	22
8	13	12
9	14	23
10	15	20
11	15	19
12	17	20
13	18	18
14	18	23
15	20	21
16	23	14
17	24	13
18	27	18
19	28	15
20	30	10

following analyses, and for each analysis indicate what the results tell us about the relationship between the number of complaints lodged and being a part of the team on the "big night."

1. Conduct a Bivariate Correlation analysis and report the Pearson's r, N, df, and alpha level, and interpret the results.

2. Conduct a Simple Linear Regression and report the Y-intercept, b, t, and alpha level, and interpret the results.

3. Generate a scatterplot of the data and include the regression line in the chart.

4. What do these results tell us about the relationship between the two variables?

Multiple Regression

n Chapter 11, we talked about using SPSS to generate *Simple Linear Regression* equations, where the scores for one variable (i.e., the *predictor*) are used to predict the scores of a second variable (i.e., the *criterion*). In this chapter, we will take the process a little further by showing you how to include more than one predictor variable in a regression equation. Fortunately, because multiple regression is a natural extension of simple regression, the steps needed to include multiple predictor variables are very similar to those for including just one.

The ability to use multiple predictor variables makes multiple regression one of the most flexible and useful tools in data analysis. In this chapter, we will show you how to run three of the most common types of multiple regression procedures in SPSS. First, we will cover how to create a regression equation that includes two or more predictor variables. Second, we will show you how to determine the unique contribution of a predictor variable by seeing how much additional variability that predictor can account for when added to an equation that already contains one or more other predictor variables. Third, we will cover a number of methods for selecting the most effective set of predictor variables.

It's time to get started; but first, a word from our sponsor – Prozac (see Cartoon 12.1).

SETTING UP THE DATA

In Cartoon 12.1, we see that Bongo (the one-eared bunny) does not seem to display a great deal of respect for authority. Inspired by the cartoon, a researcher decides to examine the degree to which children's attitudes toward authority can be predicted from various combinations of three variables: (a) the dosage of Prozac the children take, (b) each child's score on a measure of Locus of Control (measuring whether one feels life is controlled by others, an external locus of control, or whether one feels in control of the events of his or her life, an internal locus of control), and (c) the extent to which children are introverts or extroverts. To assess this relationship, the researcher creates measures for all four variables and collects data from 30 fifth-graders for each measure.

Figure 12.1 shows the Variable View of the SPSS Data Editor where we have assigned variable names and variable labels to four variables. The criterion variable Attitude Toward Authority is given the variable name **authority**. Higher scores for this variable reflect more negative attitudes towards authority. The predictor variable Prozac Dosage is assigned the variable name **prozac**. Values for this variable represent the dosage of Prozac each child takes per day. The predictor variable Locus of Control is given the

variable name **locus**. Higher scores on this variable reflect an external locus of control and lower scores reflect an internal locus of control. The final predictor variable Introversion/ Extroversion is assigned the variable name **int_ext**. Extroverts produce higher scores on this measure and introverts produce lower scores.

Figure 12.2 displays the Data View of the SPSS Data Editor. Panel Ⓐ of the figure presents the data for the first half of the sample, participants 1–15. Panel Ⓑ shows the data for the remaining participants, numbered 16–30.

▶ **Figure 12.1** Variable View for Authority Attitudes and Prozac Data

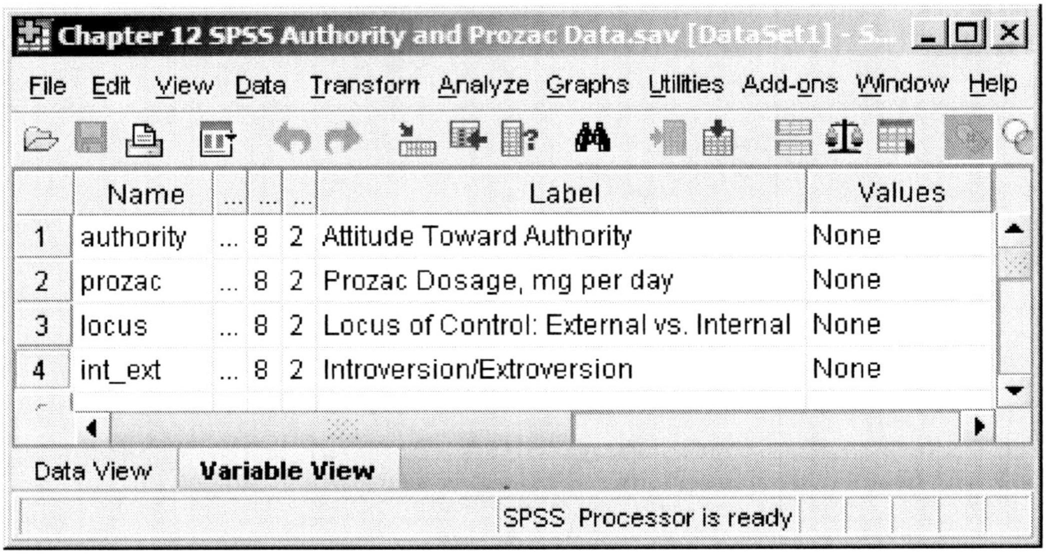

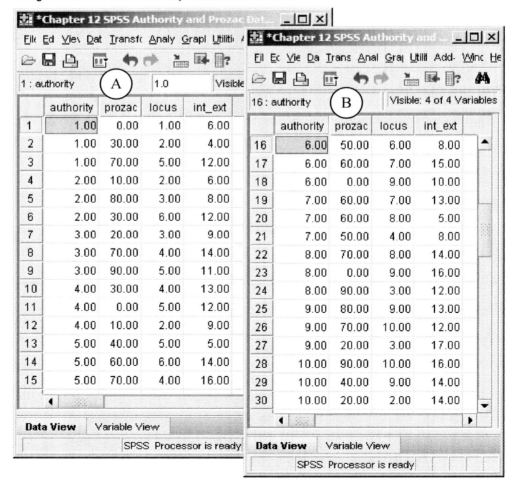

▶ **Figure 12.2** Data View for Authority Attitudes and Prozac Data

SIMULTANEOUS ENTRY OF TWO PREDICTOR VARIABLES

SPSS offers several methods for selecting predictor variables. The **Enter** method tells SPSS to use a particular set of predictors. In other words, if we tell SPSS to use variable X and variable Z as predictors, it will do so whether or not these variables do a good job of predicting scores for the criterion variable. Fortunately, SPSS will provide the same diagnostic information about the utility of a multiple regression equation that it provided in the output for simple regression described in Chapter 11. The output will supply such valuable information as the percentage of variability accounted for by the regression equation, the standard error of estimate, the *F*-ratio used to test the significance of the regression equation, as well as information about which of the individual predictor variables, if any, contribute significantly to the regression equation. Finally, the output for the **Enter** method will provide the regression coefficients needed to write the regression equation. Using this regression equation, we will be able to predict scores for the criterion variable when all we know about a person or case are the scores obtained on the predictor variables we instructed SPSS to use.

PROCEDURE FOR RUNNING MULTIPLE REGRESSION USING A PRE-SELECTED SET OF PREDICTOR VARIABLES:

1. Select **Analyze** from the pull-down menu.
2. Select the **Regression** option.
3. Select **Linear...** from the side menu. This will open the **Linear Regression** dialogue box.
4. Enter the criterion variable, **authority** for our example, into the **Dependent:** field by left-clicking on the variable and left-clicking on the boxed arrow next to the **Dependent:** field.
5. Enter the desired predictor variables (**prozac** and **locus**) in the **Independent(s):** field by left-clicking each variable while pressing the **Crtl** key and then left-clicking the boxed arrow next to the **Independent(s):** field.
6. Make sure the **Enter** option is selected on the **Method:** drop-down menu.
7. To obtain the means and standard deviations for each variable and the simple correlation between each pair of variables, left-click on **Statistics ... .** This will open the **Linear Regression: Statistics** dialogue box.
8. Select the **Descriptives** option.
   - The options for **Model fit** and **Estimates** will be checked by default. Leave them selected.
   - Note that the **Residuals** options are not displayed in Figure 12.3 due to space considerations.
9. Click **Continue** to return to the main **Multiple Regression** dialogue box.

▶ **Figure 12.3** Running Multiple Regression: Enter Method

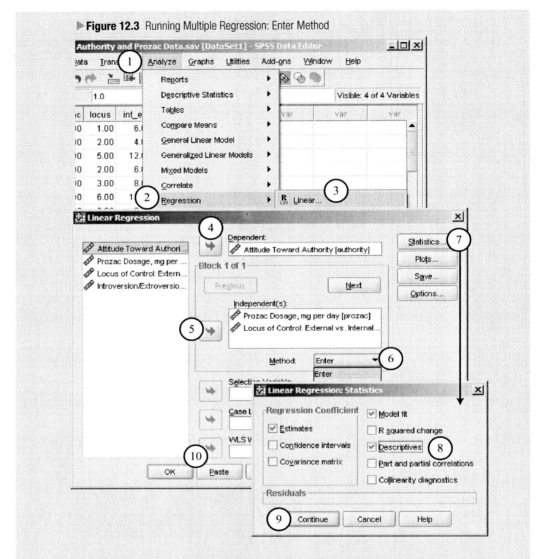

⑩ Finally, double-check your variables and options and either select **OK** to run or **Paste** to create syntax to run at a later time.

If you selected the paste option from the procedure above, you should have generated the following syntax:

```
REGRESSION
    /DESCRIPTIVES MEAN STDDEV CORR SIG N
    /MISSING LISTWISE
    /STATISTICS COEFF OUTS R ANOVA
    /CRITERIA=PIN(.05) POUT(.10)
    /NOORIGIN
    /DEPENDENT authority
    /METHOD=ENTER prozac locus .
```

READING THE OUTPUT FOR SELECTING TWO PREDICTOR VARIABLES

The output for the multiple regression procedures we ran are presented in Figures 12.4 and 12.5. Figure 12.4 presents the first two output tables for the analyses we requested (note that your output may differ if you selected different options). The first table in the output, titled **Descriptive Statistics**, provides the means, standard deviations, and sample size for each variable. The second table, titled **Correlations**, presents the Pearson correlations among all three variables, the significance level for each correlation, and the number of subjects providing data for each correlation. We have circled the relevant correlations below the diagonal. The correlation of .204 between Prozac Dosage and Attitude Toward Authority is not significantly different from zero. The significance level of .14 for this correlation is above the required .05 significance level. The correlation of .580 between Locus of Control and Attitude Toward Authority is significantly different from zero with a significance level less than .001. The correlation of .299 between the two predictor variables, Prozac Dosage and Locus of Control, does not reach significance with a significance level of .054, though it comes very close.

▶ **Figure 12.4** Multiple Regression Output: Descriptive Data

Regression

Descriptive Statistics

	Mean	Std. Deviation	N
Attitude Toward Authority	5.5000	2.92138	30
Prozac Dosage, mg per day	45.6667	29.79046	30
Locus of Control: External vs. Internal	5.3667	2.69717	30

Correlations

		Attitude Toward Authority	Prozac Dosage, mg per day	Locus of Control: External vs. Internal
Pearson Correlation	Attitude Toward Authority	1.000	.204	.580
	Prozac Dosage, mg per day	.204	1.000	.299
	Locus of Control: External vs. Internal	.580	.299	1.000
Sig. (1-tailed)	Attitude Toward Authority		.140	.000
	Prozac Dosage, mg per day	.140		.054
	Locus of Control: External vs. Internal	.000	.054	
N	Attitude Toward Authority	30	30	30
	Prozac Dosage, mg per day	30	30	30
	Locus of Control: External vs. Internal	30	30	30

Figure 12.5 presents the last four tables of the regression output. The **Variables Entered/Removed** table provides information about the predictor variables entered into the regression equation, the order in which they were entered, and the method used to enter the variables. There is not much to look at here for the current example because we asked for two predictor variables to be entered at the same time. On the other hand, this table provides a handy reminder of what we asked SPSS to do.

The **Model Summary** table provides a lot of useful information. The value in the column is referred to as the *Multiple Correlation,* and it represents the correlation between

▶**Figure 12.5** Multiple Regression Output: Regression Data

Variables Entered/Removed[b]

Model	Variables Entered	Variables Removed	Method
1	Locus of Control: External vs. Internal, Prozac Dosage, mg per day[a]		Enter

a. All requested variables entered.

b. Dependent Variable: Attitude Toward Authority

Model Summary

Model	R	R Square	Adjusted R Square	Std. Error of the Estimate
1	.581[a]	.337	.288	2.46479

a. Predictors: (Constant), Locus of Control: External vs. Internal, Prozac Dosage, mg per day

ANOVA[b]

Model		Sum of Squares	df	Mean Square	F	Sig.
1	Regression	83.470	2	41.735	6.870	.004[a]
	Residual	164.030	27	6.075		
	Total	247.500	29			

a. Predictors: (Constant), Locus of Control: External vs. Internal, Prozac Dosage, mg per day

b. Dependent Variable: Attitude Toward Authority

Coefficients[a]

Model		Unstandardized Coefficients		Standardized Coefficients	t	Sig.
		B	Std. Error	Beta		
1	(Constant)	2.038	1.111		1.834	.078
	Prozac Dosage, mg per day	.003	.016	.033	.204	.840
	Locus of Control: External vs. Internal	.617	.178	.570	3.470	.002

a. Dependent Variable: Attitude Toward Authority

actual scores for Attitude Toward Authority and predicted scores for this variable, as generated by the regression equation. It should be noted that R is always a positive value, regardless of the direction of the bivariate correlations between the criterion and the predictor variables. Logically enough, the value in the **R Square** column represents the *Multiple Squared Correlation,* or R^2, between the actual and predicted values of the criterion value. As we saw in Chapter 11, when multiplied by 100, this number can be interpreted as a percentage. Thus, the value of .337 for R^2 indicates that the two predictor variables combine to account for 33.7% of the variability in students' scores on the Attitude Toward Authority measure. The value for the **Adjusted R Square** (.288) provides an unbiased estimate of R^2 in the population. The **Standard Error of Estimate** of 2.46 tells us that predicted Attitude Toward Authority scores derived from our regression equation will differ on average from students' actual Attitude Toward Authority scores by 2.46 points.

The table titled **ANOVA** reports the results of a significance test of whether the regression model using the two predictor variables accounts for a significant amount of variability in the criterion variable. For our current example, the obtained value for **F** is 6.780 and is significant at the .004 level. This indicates that a linear combination of the amount of Prozac a student takes and his or her score on the locus of control measure accounts for a significant amount of variability in the scores on the Attitudes Toward Authority measure.

The **ANOVA** table also provides the **Sums of Squares** and degrees of freedom, **df**, for the **Regression** row (which refers to the variability in the criterion variable accounted for by the regression equation), the **Residual** row (which refers to the variability in the criterion variable not accounted for by the regression equation), and the **Total** of all sources of variability. In particular, you should note that there are 2 degrees of freedom associated with the Regression term because there are two predictor variables in this example.

The last table in Figure 12.5 is labeled **Coefficients**. There are two major sections of this table. The section labeled **Unstandardized Coefficients** provides the information needed to write the regression equation in raw score units, and the **Standardized Coefficients** section provides the information needed to express the regression equation in standard score units, or *Z*-score units. Starting with the **Unstandardized Coefficients** section, look at column **B**. This column contains the three regression coefficients needed to create the regression equation using the two selected predictor variables. The top value of 2.038 is the *Y*-intercept for the equation and is in the row labeled **(Constant)** in the **Model** column. Likewise, .003 is the regression coefficient that SPSS recommends applying to the predictor variable Prozac Dosage. The value of .617 is the regression coefficient applied to the predictor variable Locus of Control.

We can now use the three values provided in the column **B** to write our regression equation:

Predicted Attitude Toward Authority Score = 2.038 + .003 * (Prozac Dosage)
+ .617 * (Locus of Control score)

This equation can be used to calculate predicted values for the criterion variable when the values of the predictor variables are known. For example, if a child's Prozac dosage is

10 and the child has a locus of control score of 5, that child's predicted score for Attitude Toward Authority Score will be 5.153, calculated as follows:

$$5.153 = 2.038 + (.003 * 10) + (.617 * 5) = 2.038 + .03 + 3.085$$

The **Std. Error** column provides the standard errors associated with each regression coefficient. Each standard error represents the average amount that sample values for a regression coefficient differ from the actual value in the population. These standard errors can be used to determine whether each coefficient is significantly different from zero. The results for each test are provided in the **t** and **Sig.** columns of the table. The value for **t** is obtained by dividing each value for **B**, also known as a regression coefficient, by its respective standard error. Using our knowledge of *t* values, we can see from these columns that the *Y*-intercept of 2.028 is 1.834 standard deviations above a comparison value of zero, and it has a significance value of .078, which is not significant.

The regression coefficient of .003 for Prozac Dosage is .204 standard deviations from zero and has a significance value of .840, which is also not significant. This indicates that knowing the amount of Prozac that children take does not contribute significantly to our ability to predict how they feel about authority figures. In fact, Prozac Dosage could be removed from the regression equation without significantly reducing our ability to predict the children's attitudes toward authority.

The regression coefficient of .617 for Locus of Control is 3.47 standard deviations above zero and is significantly different from zero with a significance value of .002. This indicates that a child's locus of control contributes significantly to the prediction of children's attitudes toward authority. In addition, because the regression coefficient is positive, it appears that having a more external locus of control, feeling that events of your life are controlled more by others than yourself, is associated with having more positive attitudes toward authority.

Now let's go back to the Standardized Coefficients column of the Coefficients table. Notice that the term **Beta** also shows up at the top of this column. This is because standardized regression coefficients are often referred to as values for "beta," while unstandardized coefficients are referred to as values for "b." Also notice that there is just a blank spot in the row for the Constant, where the values corresponding to the *Y*-intercept are provided. The reason for this is that when all of the variables are in standard score units, the *Y*-intercept for the regression equation is always zero. The values for beta applied to Prozac Dosage and Locus of Control are .033 and .570, respectively. This allows us to write the following regression equation for obtaining predicted standard scores for Attitude Toward Authority:

$$Z_{\text{Attitude Toward Authority}} = (.033) * Z_{\text{Prozac Dosage}} + (.570) * Z_{\text{Locus of Control}}$$

Again, we can use known *Z*-score values of the predictor variables to predict the *Z*-score value for the criterion variable. A child whose Prozac Dosage was 1 standard deviation above the mean, $Z_{\text{Prozac Dosage}} = 1$, and whose Locus of Control score was 1 standard deviation above the mean, $Z_{\text{Locus of Control}} = 1$, would be expected to have an Attitude Toward Authority score of .603 standard deviations above the mean, $Z_{\text{Attitude Toward Authority}} = .603$.

To review, the values in the **t** column just to the right of the values for Beta provide significance tests for each predictor variable. The *t* value of .204 for Prozac Dosage, which has a beta of .033, is not statistically significant (p = .840). However, the *t* value of 3.27 for Locus of Control, which has a beta of .570, is significantly different from zero (p = .002). These results show that children's scores on the Attitude Toward Authority measure are quite strongly predicted by a combination of two predictor variables, the amount of Prozac children are taking and whether children feel that their lives are controlled externally or internally. With respect to the influence each specific predictor has on the criterion, the amount of Prozac children take does not appear to meaningfully contribute to the prediction of children's attitudes toward authority. However, Locus of Control is a significant predictor of children's attitudes toward authority. Specifically, children who report having a more external locus of control tend to report having more positive attitudes toward authority.

VARYING THE ORDER OF ENTRY: HIERARCHICAL MULTIPLE REGRESSION

In the last section, we covered using SPSS to enter two or more predictor variables at the same time in a single regression equation. There are situations, however, where you might want to create a multiple regression equation by adding predictors one variable, or one block of variables, at a time. For example, we can use multiple regression to address theoretical questions about the variables involved in the analyses, rather than use it purely for the sake of obtaining accurate predicted scores for a particular criterion variable. This technique is often referred to as *Hierarchical Regression* because the researcher is specifying a specific order, or hierarchy, in which predictor variables are entered into the regression model.

For example, let's say that the researcher wants to test the theoretical question of whether Locus of Control can account for a significant amount of the variability in children's scores on the Attitude Toward Authority measure *that the predictor variable Prozac Dosage does not already account for.* In other words, does Locus of Control make a significant *unique contribution* to the regression equation beyond the variability already accounted for by Prozac Dosage? SPSS makes it easy to answer this question by allowing us to enter predictor variables in separate steps. All we have to do is to enter Prozac Dosage in the first step and see what proportion of variability it accounts for by itself. Then we can add Locus of Control to the regression model in a second step and see how much the proportion of variability accounted-for goes up. This additional variability accounted-for represents the unique contribution of the Locus of Control variable, meaning the amount of variability in a child's attitude towards authority that Locus of Control is able to account for but that Prozac Dosage cannot.

PROCEDURE FOR RUNNING A HIERARCHICAL MULTIPLE REGRESSION ANALYSIS:

- Select **Analyze** from the pull-down menu.
- Select **Regression**.
- Select **Linear...** from the side menu. This will open the **Linear Regression** dialogue box.

① Enter the criterion variable, **authority**, into the **Dependent:** field by left-clicking on the variable and left-clicking on the boxed arrow next to the **Dependent:** field.

② Enter the predictor variable(s) that will be added in the first step—in this example, **prozac**—by left-clicking the variable and then left-clicking the boxed arrow next to the **Independent(s):** field.

③ Make sure the **Enter** option is selected on the **Method:** drop-down menu.

▶**Figure 12.6** Running Hierarchical Multiple Regression

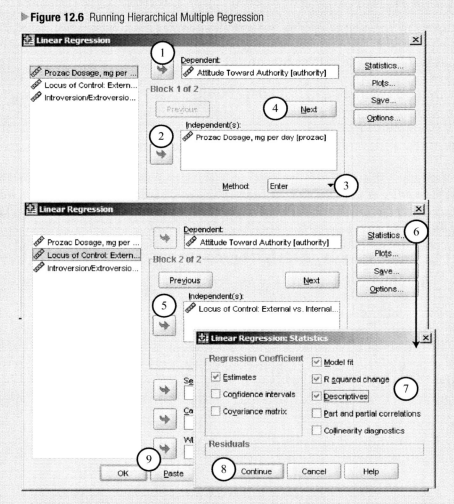

④ At the top of the part of the dialogue box for specifying predictor variables there is the statement **Block 1 of 1** (Note: In the figure it says "Block 1 of 2" because we eventually used two sets of predictors). A "block" of predictors is a set of predictor variables that is being added to the regression equation at a particular step. What we have said so far is that we want to enter Prozac Dosage all by itself in a first step. But we now want to add a second predictor variable in a second step, or block. Click the button labeled **Next**. The statement at the top of this section of the dialogue box should now say **Block 2 of 2**.

⑤ Enter the predictor variable(s) that will be added in the second step—in the current example, **locus**—by left-clicking the variable name and then left-clicking the boxed arrow next to the **Independent(s):** field.

⑥ Click the **Statistics…** button. This will open the **Linear Regression: Statistics** dialogue box.

⑦ Select the **R squared change** option. Selecting this option instructs SPSS to tell us in the output how much the proportion of variability accounted-for increases when this second predictor variable is added. In essence, the R-Squared change *is* the unique contribution of Locus of Control, beyond the variability accounted for by Prozac Dosage.

• Select the **Descriptives option**.

• Make sure the default options **Estimates** and **Model fit** are selected.

⑧ Click **Continue** to return to the main Linear Regression dialogue box.

⑨ Finally, double-check your variables and options and either select **OK** to run or **Paste** to create syntax to run at a later time.

If you selected the paste option from the procedure above, you should have generated the following syntax:

```
REGRESSION
    /DESCRIPTIVES MEAN STDDEV CORR SIG N
    /MISSING LISTWISE
    /STATISTICS COEFF OUTS R ANOVA CHANGE
    /CRITERIA=PIN(.05) POUT(.10)
    /NOORIGIN
    /DEPENDENT authority
    /METHOD=ENTER prozac /METHOD=ENTER locus .
```

READING THE OUTPUT FOR A HIERARCHICAL REGRESSION ANALYSIS

The output for the hierarchical regression analysis, presented in Figures 12.7 and 12.8, contains the same information we saw before when two predictors were entered at the same time, with several notable exceptions. We have chosen not to display the output from the **Descriptives** option, the **Descriptives Statistics** and **Correlations** tables, because it is the same as that contained in Figure 12.4.

▶**Figure 12.7** Hierarchical Regression Output: Part I

Regression

Variables Entered/Removed[b]

Model	Variables Entered	Variables Removed	Method
1	Prozac Dosage, mg per day[a]	.	Enter
2	Locus of Control: External vs. Internal[a]	.	Enter

a. All requested variables entered.
b. Dependent Variable: Attitude Toward Authority

Model Summary C

Model	R	R Square	Adjusted R Square	Std. Error of the Estimate	R Square Change	F Change	df1	df2	Sig. F Change
					Change Statistics				
1	.204[a]	.042	.007	2.91054	.042	1.217	1	28	.279
2	.581[b]	.337	.288	2.46479	.296	12.043	1	27	.002

a. Predictors: (Constant), Prozac Dosage, mg per day
b. Predictors: (Constant), Prozac Dosage, mg per day, Locus of Control: External vs. Internal

A, B, D

At the top of Figure 12.7, you will notice that the **Variables Entered/Removed** table, labeled Ⓐ in Figure 12.7, now contains rows for two different models. The table reminds us that we asked SPSS to enter Prozac Dosage in step 1 to produce a regression equation with one predictor variable and then Locus of Control in step 2 to produce a regression equation containing both predictor variables.

The **Model Summary** table presents information about the two regression models generated in this analysis. Note that the bottom of the table, labeled Ⓑ in Figure 12.7, lists the predictor variables contained in each model. We can see that the squared multiple correlation, **R Square**, is .042 when Prozac Dosage is the only predictor and that **R Square** rises substantially to .337 when Locus of Control is added to the model.

The part of the **Model Summary** table that is new to this analysis is the section labeled **Change Statistics**. The **R Square Change** column is useful because it tells us how much the proportion of variability accounted for increases when Locus of Control is added as a second predictor. As you can see, **R Square Change** values are provided for each model. The value of .042 for Model 1 indicates that going from zero predictors to one predictor results in an increase of 4.2% in the proportion of variability accounted for. The more useful number is the **R Square Change** associated with Model 2 in the bottom row, labeled Ⓒ in Figure 12.7. The value of .296 indicates that although Prozac Dosage accounts for 4.2% of the variability by itself, Locus of Control accounts for an additional 29.6% of the variability beyond what Prozac Dosage can account for. In other words, we can say that *the unique contribution of the Locus of Control variable is 29.6% of the variability*. The remaining columns in the **Change Statistics** section provide information about whether the change in the proportion of variability accounted-for is significant. The **F Change**, **df1**, **df2**, and **Sig. F Change** columns display the statistical results of an *F*-test of the significance of the change in the proportion of variability accounted-for. For the Model 2 row, labeled Ⓓ in Figure 12.7, we see that there is an observed value for

▶**Figure 12.8** Hierarchical Regression Output: Part II

ANOVA[c]

Model		Sum of Squares	df	Mean Square	F	Sig.
1	Regression	10.305	1	10.305	1.217	.279[a]
	Residual	237.195	28	8.471		
	Total	247.500	29			
2	Regression	83.470	2	41.735	6.870	.004[b]
	Residual	164.030	27	6.075		
	Total	247.500	29			

a. Predictors: (Constant), Prozac Dosage, mg per day

b. Predictors: (Constant), Prozac Dosage, mg per day, Locus of Control: External vs. Internal

c. Dependent Variable: Attitude Toward Authority

Coefficients[a]

Model		Unstandardized Coefficients		Standardized Coefficients	t	Sig.
		B	Std. Error	Beta		
1	(Constant)	4.586	.984		4.659	.000
	Prozac Dosage, mg per day	.020	.018	.204	1.103	.279
2	(Constant)	2.038	1.111		1.834	.078
	Prozac Dosage, mg per day	.003	.016	.033	.204	.840
	Locus of Control: External vs. Internal	.617	.178	.570	3.470	.002

a. Dependent Variable: Attitude Toward Authority

Excluded Variables[b]

Model		Beta In	t	Sig.	Partial Correlation	Collinearity Statistics
						Tolerance
1	Locus of Control: External vs. Internal	.570[a]	3.470	.002	.555	.910

a. Predictors in the Model: (Constant), Prozac Dosage, mg per day

b. Dependent Variable: Attitude Toward Authority

F of 12.043, with 1 degree of freedom in the numerator and 27 degrees of freedom in the denominator. The significance level of .002, well below the .05 alpha level, indicates that the unique contribution of Locus of Control in predicting scores for Attitude Toward Authority is statistically significant.

The structure of the remaining tables of output, shown in Figure 12.8, is essentially the same as the output we obtained when we entered both predictors in a single step (see Figure 12.5 for review). The only exception is that separate information is presented for both models. Thus, you will quickly notice that the information for Model 2 is identical to that presented in Figure 12.5, when both predictors were entered into the regression equation at the same time. The only new element is the **Excluded Variables** table, which reports that Locus of Control was not included as part of Model 1 and shows some of the statistical information that would have been obtained had Locus of Control been included as part of Model 1. For the most part, this information is redundant with information provided for Model 2, where Locus of Control is included in the model.

USING AUTOMATED STRATEGIES FOR SELECTING PREDICTOR VARIABLES

We used the **Enter** method in each of our two previous examples because it allowed us to specify the variables we wanted to use as predictors and the order in which those variables were entered. The **Enter** method is like flying an airplane manually; you decide what happens and when. This makes sense when the selection of variables is based on a particular theory or predetermined strategy. In other situations, however, it makes sense to select predictor variables on the basis of a set of rules, or algorithm, for identifying an efficient set of predictors. If the goal is *to account for the greatest amount of variability using the fewest number of predictors,* then the researcher should consider using one of several automated strategies for identifying predictor variables, such as the **Stepwise**, **Forward**, or **Backward** options. Tell SPSS which method to use and which potential predictors to pick from, and it will then make a recommendation about the predictors you should use. Employing these methods is like putting an airplane on autopilot; you tell SPSS which variables to pick from and it will pick the best set of predictors. We present the Stepwise procedure as an example. Examples for the Forward and Backward methods are not provided because the procedures for running them and the formats of the resulting output are essentially the same as those for the Stepwise method.

PROCEDURE FOR RUNNING A MULTIPLE REGRESSION ANALYSIS USING THE STEPWISE METHOD:

- Select **Analyze** from the pull-down menu.
- Select **Regression**.
- Select **Linear...** from the side menu. This will open the **Linear Regression** dialogue box.
- ① Enter the criterion variable, **authority**, into the **Dependent:** field by left-clicking on the variable and left-clicking on the boxed arrow next to the **Dependent:** field.
- ② Enter the predictor variables that you want SPSS to pick from by left-clicking each variable while pressing the **Crtl** key and then left-click the boxed arrow next to the **Independent(s):** field. In this case we have entered **prozac**, **locus**, and **int_ext**.
- ③ Select the **Stepwise** option from the **Method:** drop down menu.
- ④ Left-click the **Statistics...** button. This will open the **Linear Regression: Statistics** dialogue box.

⑤ Select the **R squared change** and **Descriptives** options.

• Make sure the default options **Estimates** and **Model fit** are selected.

⑥ Left-click **Continue**.

⑦ Finally, double-check your variables and options and either select **OK** to run or **Paste** to create syntax to run at a later time.

• If you selected the paste option from the procedure above, you should have generated the following syntax:

```
REGRESSION
    /DESCRIPTIVES MEAN STDDEV CORR SIG N
    /MISSING LISTWISE
    /STATISTICS COEFF OUTS R ANOVA CHANGE
    /CRITERIA=PIN(.05) POUT(.10)
    /NOORIGIN
    /DEPENDENT authority
    /METHOD=STEPWISE prozac locus int_ext .
```

▶**Figure 12.9** Running Stepwise Multiple Regression

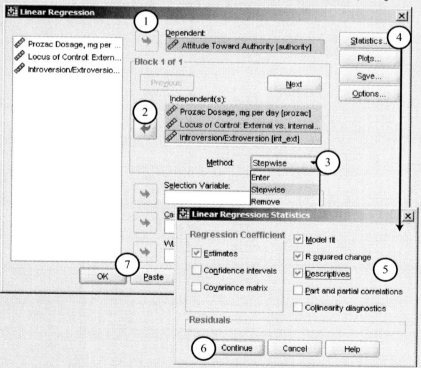

READING THE OUTPUT OF THE STEPWISE PROCEDURE

The output from the Stepwise procedure looks very similar to the output obtained when we added predictor variables in two different steps using the hierarchical regression procedures. In this section, we will devote most of our time to noting places where the output for the Stepwise procedure is different from what we have seen before. The output for the Stepwise procedure is displayed in Figures 12.10 and 12.11.

At the top of Figure 12.10, we see the **Variables Entered/Removed** table. Implementing the algorithm for the stepwise entry of predictor variables, SPSS has entered predictor variables in two steps. In step 1 it entered the Locus of Control variable.

▶**Figure 12.10** Stepwise Regression Output: Part I

Regression

Variables Entered/Removed[a]

Model	Variables Entered	Variables Removed	Method
1	Locus of Control: External vs. Internal	.	Stepwise (Criteria: Probability-of-F-to-enter <= .050, Probability-of-F-to-remove >= .100).
2	Introversion/Extroversion	.	Stepwise (Criteria: Probability-of-F-to-enter <= .050, Probability-of-F-to-remove >= .100).

a. Dependent Variable: Attitude Toward Authority

Model Summary

Model	R	R Square	Adjusted R Square	Std. Error of the Estimate	Change Statistics				
					R Square Change	F Change	df1	df2	Sig. F Change
1	.580[a]	.336	.313	2.42223	.336	14.184	1	28	.001
2	.664[b]	.441	.399	2.26387	.105	5.054	1	27	.033

a. Predictors: (Constant), Locus of Control: External vs. Internal

b. Predictors: (Constant), Locus of Control: External vs. Internal, Introversion/Extroversion

ANOVA[c]

Model		Sum of Squares	df	Mean Square	F	Sig.
1	Regression	83.218	1	83.218	14.184	.001[a]
	Residual	164.282	28	5.867		
	Total	247.500	29			
2	Regression	109.122	2	54.561	10.646	.000[b]
	Residual	138.378	27	5.125		
	Total	247.500	29			

a. Predictors: (Constant), Locus of Control: External vs. Internal

b. Predictors: (Constant), Locus of Control: External vs. Internal, Introversion/Extroversion

c. Dependent Variable: Attitude Toward Authority

Notice that in the far right-hand column, the Method listed is Stepwise, [labeled Ⓐ in Figure 12.10]. In a second step, SPSS entered the Introversion/Extroversion variable. At that point SPSS stopped adding predictor variables because the third potential predictor variable, Prozac Dosage, must not have made a significant unique contribution to the model.

In the **Model Summary** table, we have circled the most noteworthy values. Specifically, we can see that when Locus of Control was entered first in the regression, it accounted for 33.6% of the variability (**R Square** = .336). In the row for Model 2, we see that when Introversion/Extroversion was added to the regression equation, the proportion of variability accounted for increased to 44.1% (**R Square** = .441). Looking at the **Change Statistics** for Model 2, we also find that Introversion/Extroversion accounted for an additional 10.5% of the variability (**R Square Change** = .105), beyond that accounted for by Locus of Control (**R Square Change** = .336). The table also shows us that this unique contribution of 10.5% for Introversion/Extroversion is statistically significant with a value of 5.54 in the **F Change** column and a value of .033 in the **Sig. F Change** column.

The **ANOVA** section of the output shows the ANOVA tables for *F*-tests of both models, the first with Locus of Control as the only predictor and the second with both Locus of Control and Introversion/Extroversion as predictors. From these ANOVA

▶**Figure 12.11** Stepwise Regression Output: Part II

Coefficients[a]

Model		Unstandardized Coefficients B	Std. Error	Standardized Coefficients Beta	t	Sig.
1	(Constant)	2.129	.998		2.133	.042
	Locus of Control: External vs. Internal	.628	.167	.580	3.766	.001
2	(Constant)	-.223	1.402		-.159	.875
	Locus of Control: External vs. Internal	.485	.168	.448	2.879	.008
	Introversion/Extroversion	.277	.123	.349	2.248	.033

a. Dependent Variable: Attitude Toward Authority

Excluded Variables[c]

Model		Beta In	t	Sig.	Partial Correlation	Collinearity Statistics Tolerance
1	Prozac Dosage, mg per day	.033[a]	.204	.840	.039	.910
	int_ext	.349[a]	2.248	.033	.397	.857
2	Prozac Dosage, mg per day	-.009[b]	-.061	.952	-.012	.896

a. Predictors in the Model: (Constant), Locus of Control

b. Predictors in the Model: (Constant), Locus of Control, int_ext

c. Dependent Variable: attitude toward authority

tables, we see that both models account for significant amounts of variability in scores on the Attitude Toward Authority measure.

In Figure 12.11, the **Coefficients** table gives the regression coefficients for both models. Because the ultimate goal of the Stepwise procedure is to generate the most efficient regression equation possible (at least according to the rules for that particular algorithm), the last model listed in the output is always the one that SPSS recommends. In this example, the unstandardized regression coefficients for Model 2, labeled Ⓑ in Figure 12.11, consist of a Y-intercept of -.223, given in the (Constant) row, a value for "b" applied to Locus of Control of .485, and a regression coefficient applied to Introversion/Extroversion of .277. Expressing this information in the form of a regression equation, we have:

Predicted Attitude Toward Authority Score = −.223 + .485 * (Locus of Control)
+ .277 * (Introversion/Extroversion)

The final table in the output is labeled **Excluded Variables**. This table provides information about why SPSS selected the variables it did at each step and why it eventually stopped adding predictors. In this example, Locus of Control was entered first, which left two predictor variables remaining to compete for the privilege of entering the equation. In the rows for Model 1 we see values for **Beta In** for both variables, followed by t-tests of these beta values. Of the remaining predictor variables, SPSS identifies the predictor that would have the largest standardized regression coefficient if it were added to the equation. In this case, it is Introversion/Extroversion, with a value of .349. For SPSS to go ahead and add this predictor, this value for beta has to be significantly different from zero. The significant t-test for Introversion/Extroversion (**t** = 2.248, **Sig.** = .033) indicates that this is the case. After both Locus of Control and Introversion/Extroversion have been included in the regression equation, SPSS then considered whether to add Prozac Dosage to the equation. In the section of the table for Model 2, we see that the value for **Beta In** of −.009 is not significantly different from zero (**t** = −.061, **Sig.** =.952), so SPSS didn't add Prozac Dosage as a third predictor.

SUMMARY

This chapter demonstrated three multiple regression procedures: entering a group of predictor variables in a single step, entering predictor variables in separate, hierarchical steps, and using a Stepwise procedure to select the most efficient set of predictors. With respect to the researcher's study of children's attitudes toward authority, these three procedures gave different types of information. First, the Single-Step Enter Method analysis indicated that as a group, the variables Prozac Dosage and Locus of Control predicted children's attitudes toward authority, but that Locus of Control contributed the most to the prediction of those attitudes. The hierarchical regression analysis indicated that the unique contribution of Locus of Control to the prediction of authority attitudes was quite substantial, even after the influence of Prozac had been taken into account. Finally, using the Stepwise strategy for selecting predictors, when SPSS had all three potential predictor variables to pick from, the combination of Locus of Control and Introversion/Extroversion as predictors was found to provide the most efficient regression equation.

PRACTICE EXERCISES

As a follow-up study, our researcher has shifted attention to the use of Prozac among teachers. Specifically, the researcher is interested in factors that predict how much Prozac (in milligrams) is taken daily in a sample of 20 elementary school teachers. We have named this variable **teacher_proz**. The potential predictor variables are the following: Average Prozac Dosage of the students in each teacher's class, named **class_proz** here, the size of each teacher's class, named **class_size**, and each teacher's score on a measure of authoritarian teaching style, **auth_teach**. The data are presented in Table 12.1.

1. Conduct a Single Step Multiple Regression using the Enter Method, where **teacher_proz** is the criterion variable and the predictors are **class_proz** and **class_size**.

   a. What is the total amount of variability accounted for by the predictor variables? Is it significant?

   b. Which predictors (if any) significantly contribute to the prediction of the teacher's daily Prozac dosage?

   c. If a teacher has 15 students and on average the teacher's students take 60 milligrams of Prozac per day, then what is the Prozac dosage we could expect the teacher to have?

▶**Table 12.1** Practice Exercise Data

Participant	teach_proz	class_proz	class_size	teach_auth
1	0	80	12	1
2	0	80	11	1
3	10	80	13	2
4	10	90	16	2
5	20	80	15	3
6	20	70	17	1
7	30	20	14	3
8	30	60	12	2
9	40	10	15	3
10	40	50	15	4
11	50	80	16	5
12	50	40	12	5
13	60	20	17	4
14	60	30	18	5
15	70	10	18	7
16	70	20	16	6
17	80	10	19	6
18	80	10	15	5
19	90	20	20	7
20	90	0	12	7

2. Conduct a hierarchical multiple regression analysis using the **Enter** method, where **teacher_proz** is the criterion variable, **class_proz** is entered in the first step as a predictor, **block 1** within SPSS, and **class_size** is entered in the second step as a predictor, what SPSS will call **block 2**.

   a. What is the amount of variability accounted for by **class_proz** alone? Is it significant?

   b. What is the unique contribution of **class_size**? Is it significant?

3. Conduct a Stepwise Multiple Regression, where **teacher_proz** is the criterion variable and the potential predictors are **class_proz**, **class_size**, and **auth_teach**.

   a. What set of predictors does SPSS recommend as the most efficient set of predictors?

   b. Which variables, if any, are excluded from the analysis?

   c. How much of the variability in **teach_proz** is accounted for by this recommended set of predictors?

thirteen

Chi-Square

Τhis chapter covers the steps for running Chi-Square analyses using the SPSS **Crosstabs** and **Nonparametric Tests** procedures. Specifically, we demonstrate steps for running two separate types of nonparametric Chi-Square tests: The Goodness-of-Fit Chi-Square and Pearson's Chi-Square, also called the Test of Independence. As discussed in earlier chapters, every statistical test is designed for a specific type of data, group data or score data. Both Chi-Square procedures shown here are meant to be used with group data. The Goodness-of-Fit Chi-Square is used when you have one group variable and you want to know whether the frequency of occurrence (e.g., the number of people in each group) differs from the frequencies expected by chance alone. Pearson's Chi-Square is used to ask questions about two group variables, and it can be used to determine whether two group variables are associated in some way.

▶ **Cartoon 13.1**

RUBES ® By Leigh Rubin

7-27

"That's it! If you kids don't start behaving, I'm taking you both to McDonald's!"

SETTING UP THE DATA

The examples in this chapter are based on Cartoon 13.1, where a frustrated parent seems to be making the ultimate threat. To investigate bovine parent-adolescent interactions, researchers observe a sample herd and record whether each adolescent misbehaves— recorded yes or no—and whether they are "taken to McDonald's" by their parents—also recorded yes or no. The results of this study are presented in Table 13.1.

Figure 13.1 presents the Variable View of the SPSS Data Editor where we have defined two group variables. The first variable represents two groups of bovine adolescents: those

▶ **Table 13.1** Comparison of Behavior and McDonald's Visits for Adolescent Bovines

		Misbehaves?	
		Yes	*No*
Visited McDonald's?	*Yes*	38	15
	No	7	70

▶ **Figure 13.1** Variable View for Visiting McDonald's Data

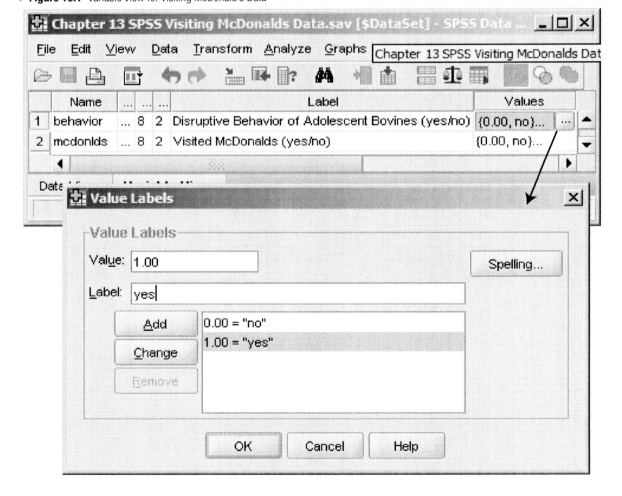

that demonstrate disruptive behavior and those that do not. We have given it the variable name **behavior** and given it the variable label "Disruptive Behavior of Adolescent Bovines (yes/no)." The second variable also represents two groups of bovine adolescents; those that are taken to McDonald's and those that are not. We have given it the variable name **mcdonlds** and the variable label "Visited McDonald's (yes/no)."

For each variable, we have assigned values to each of the two groups represented and created corresponding value labels. For the **behavior** variable, we have paired 1 with the label "yes," representing the bovine adolescents who have been disruptive, and 0 with the label "no," representing the bovine adolescents who did not demonstrate disruptive behavior. For the **mcdonlds** variable, 1 is paired with the label "yes," representing the bovine adolescents whose parents took them to McDonald's, and 0 is paired with the label "no," representing the bovine adolescents whose parents did not take them to McDonald's.

Figure 13.2 presents the Data View of the SPSS Data Editor, where we have entered the data for the 100 adolescents in our sample. Remember that the columns represent

Figure 13.2 Data View for Visiting McDonald's Data

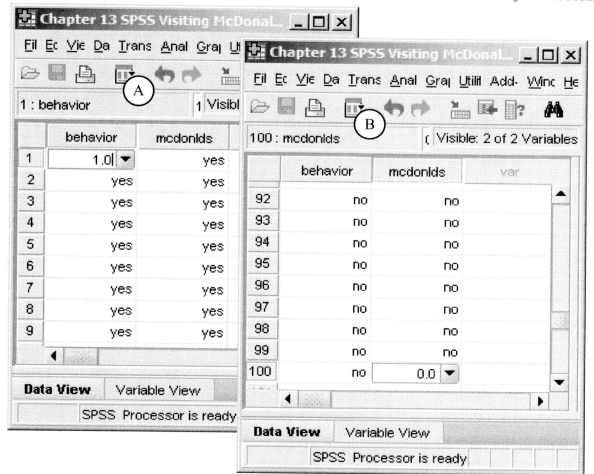

each of the different variables and the rows represent each observation, which in this case is each bovine adolescent. For example, the first adolescent, found in part Ⓐ of the figure, behaved disruptively and was taken to McDonald's by his parent. The 100th adolescent bovine, found in part Ⓑ of the figure, did not behave disruptively and was not taken to McDonald's by his parent.

GOODNESS-OF-FIT CHI-SQUARE

The Goodness-of-Fit Chi-Square allows us to determine whether the observed group frequencies for a single variable differ from what is expected by chance alone. That is, it tells us whether or not the observed pattern of group frequencies is significantly different from a random pattern. In many ways, the Goodness-of-Fit Chi-Square is identical to the Pearson's Chi-Square. In fact, they both use the same Chi-Square formula, and the significance of the statistic is tested in the same manner. However, the Goodness-of-Fit Chi-Square only evaluates one variable at a time, while the Pearson's Chi-Square evaluates the pattern of frequencies across two variables. In addition, because the Goodness-of-Fit Chi-Square only evaluates one variable at a time, it does not tell us anything about relationships between variables.

An important characteristic of the Goodness-of-Fit Chi-Square is the flexibility in the type of questions it can answer. Often we are interested in knowing whether the group frequencies we obtain differ from expected values associated with groups or outcomes that are equally proportional. For example, if we were flipping a coin, we would expect 50% of our flips to be heads and 50% to be tails. Alternatively, if we had a herd of cows made up of equal numbers of Holstein, Jersey, and Guernsey cows and we drew a random sample from this herd, each type of cow would be expected to represent 33.33% of our sample. In some cases, however, the expected values for each group may not be equal. For example, if the variable of interest represented the ethnicity of groups of people (e.g., European American or African American), then we would not find equal numbers for each group in the population. Therefore, we would not expect equal numbers of people in each group if the sample were randomly drawn from the population. Fortunately, the Goodness-of-Fit Chi-Square allows us to determine whether the group frequencies obtained in our sample significantly differ from expected values that are not equal.

RUNNING THE ANALYSIS

For our present example, we will conduct two separate Goodness-of-Fit Chi-Square analyses, one for each variable in the data set. For the **behavior** variable, the results of the Chi-Square will show whether the bovine adolescents who do or do not misbehave are significantly over- or under-represented compared to a population where the distribution is 50/50. Similarly, for the **mcdonlds** variable, the results of the Chi-Square will show whether the bovine adolescents who are or are not taken to McDonald's by a parent are significantly over- or under-represented compared to a population where the distribution is 50/50.

PROCEDURE FOR RUNNING A GOODNESS-OF-FIT CHI-SQUARE:

① Select **Analyze** from the pull-down menu.

② Select **Nonparametric Tests**.

③ Select **Chi-Square...** from the side menu. This will open the **Chi-Square Test** dialogue box.

▶**Figure 13.3** Running Goodness-of-Fit Chi-Square

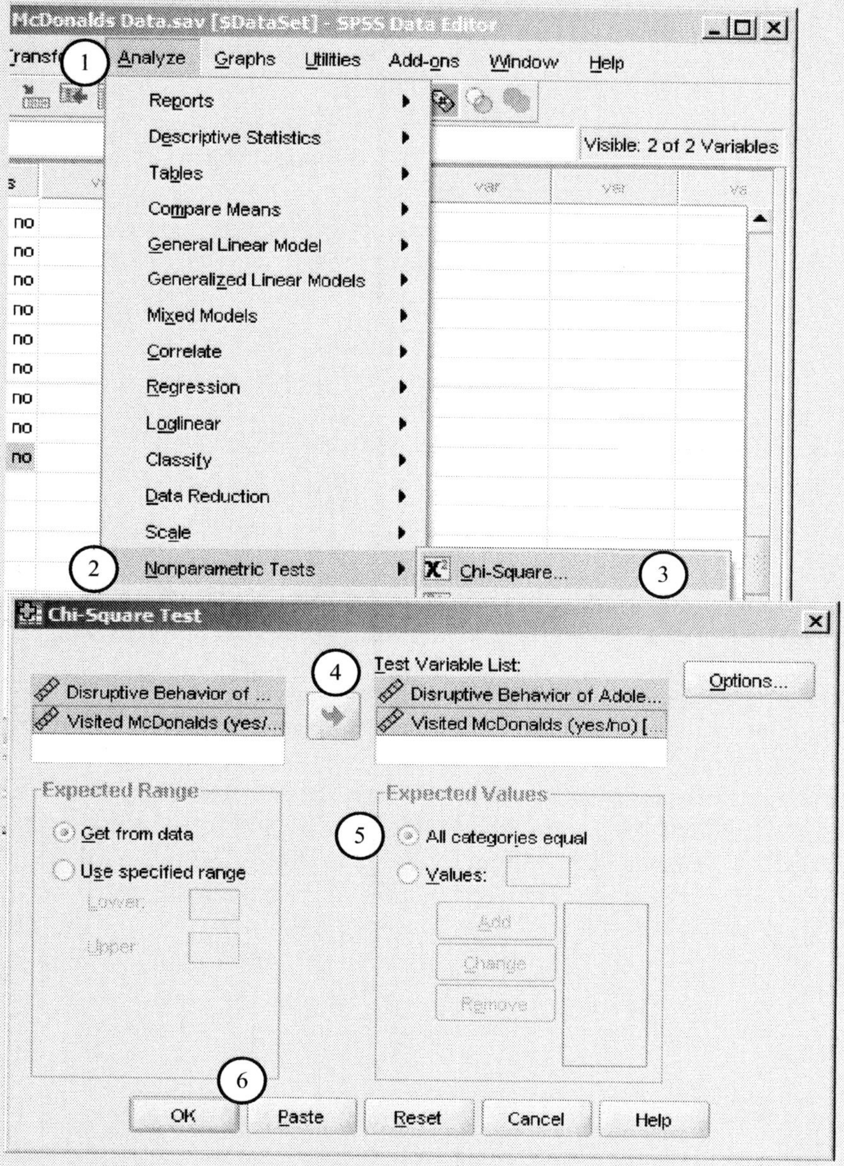

④ Enter the variables you wish to test; for the current example, **behavior** and **mcdonlds**; in the **Test Variables List:** field by either double-clicking on each variable or selecting each variable and left-clicking on the boxed arrow pointing to the right.

⑤ Decide whether the expected values for each group are equal or unequal. For unequal expected values, enter the number of cases expected to be found in each group in the **Values:** field and click **Add**. In this case, we are using equal expected frequencies for each group and have selected the **All categories equal** option under the **Expected Values** options.

⑥ Finally, double-check your variables and options and either select **OK** to run or **Paste** to create syntax to run at a later time.

If you selected the paste option from the procedure above, you should have generated the following syntax:

```
NPAR TEST
 /CHISQUARE=behavior mcdonlds
 /EXPECTED=EQUAL
 /MISSING ANALYSIS .
```

READING THE GOODNESS-OF-FIT CHI-SQUARE OUTPUT

The Goodness–of–Fit Chi–Square output is presented in Figure 13.4. This output consists of two parts: **Frequencies** and **Test Statistics**. The **Frequencies** output reports the observed, expected and residual frequencies for each group. The **Residual** frequency represents the difference between the expected and observed frequencies and is obtained by subtracting the value in the **Expected N** column from the values in **Observed N** column. In our example, because we requested two separate analyses, one for each variable, we are presented with two tables of frequency output.

The first table of the frequencies output represents the data for the **behavior** variable and is titled with its variable label, **Disruptive Behavior of Adolescent Bovines**. In our sample, 55 of the adolescent bovine did not misbehave, 50 were expected to not misbehave, and the difference between the observed and the expected values is 5.00. Also in our sample, 45 of the adolescent bovines did misbehave, 50 were expected to misbehave, and the difference between the observed and the expected values is -5.00.

The second table in the frequencies output represents the data for the **mcdonlds** variable and is titled with its variable label **Visited McDonald's (yes/no)**. In our sample, 47 of the adolescent bovine were not taken to McDonald's, 50 were expected to be taken, and the difference between the observed and expected values is -3.00. Also in our sample, 53 of the adolescents did visit McDonald's, 50 were expected to visit, and the difference between the observed and the expected values was 3.00.

The **Test Statistics** output reports the value for Chi–Square obtained, the degrees of freedom, and the exact level of significance in separate columns for each of the variables included in the analysis. For the **behavior** variable, the Chi–Square obtained is 1.00. With 1 degree of freedom (calculated by subtracting 1 from the number groups: 2 - 1 = 1) and

Figure 13.4 Goodness-of-Fit Chi-Square Output

NPar Tests

Chi-Square Test

Frequencies

Disruptive Behavior of Adolescent Bovines (yes/no)

	Observed N	Expected N	Residual
no	55	50.0	5.0
yes	45	50.0	-5.0
Total	100		

Visited McDonald's (yes/no)

	Observed N	Expected N	Residual
no	47	50.0	-3.0
yes	53	50.0	3.0
Total	100		

Test Statistics

	Disruptive Behavior of Adolescent Bovines (yes/no)	Visited McDonald's (yes/no)
Chi-Square	1.000[a]	.360[a]
df	1	1
Asymp. Sig.	.317	.549

a. 0 cells (.0%) have expected frequencies less than 5. The minimum expected cell frequency is 50.0.

a significance level of .317, which falls well above the .05 alpha level, we can conclude that the difference between the observed and expected values is not significant. Thus we can conclude that well-behaved or misbehaving bovine adolescents are not significantly over- or under-represented within our sample compared to a population where the distribution is 50/50.

With respect to the **mcdonlds** variable, the obtained value for Chi-Square is .360. With 1 degree of freedom and a significance level of .549, which falls well above the .05 alpha level, the difference between the observed and expected values is not significant.

Again we can conclude that the bovine adolescents who have visited McDonald's and those who have not are neither significantly over- nor under-represented within our sample compared to a population where the distribution is 50/50. Based on these results, we can say that each adolescent in our sample has a 50% chance of becoming a McDonald's hamburger.

A SECOND GOODNESS-OF-FIT CHI-SQUARE EXAMPLE: UNEQUAL EXPECTED VALUES

In the last example of the Goodness-of-Fit Chi-Square, the expected values for each group were the same because of the question we were asking. We wanted to know whether the group frequencies differed from each other and therefore differed from a 50/50 pattern. However, if we change the question of interest, then the expected values will need to change accordingly. Assume that we want to know whether the frequency of disruptive behavior in our sample differs from the frequencies found in a special population of adolescent bovines, happy California cows, where only 10% of the adolescent bovines demonstrate disruptive behavior. If our sample is representative of the population, then we should expect 10 bovines in our sample to show disruptive behavior and 90 bovines in our sample not to show disruptive behavior. Thus, the expected values are 10 for the "yes" group and 90 for the "no" group.

Figure 13.5 presents the **Chi-Square Test** dialogue box and the resulting output for a Goodness-of-Fit Chi-Square using unequal expected values for the **behavior** variable. In the **Expected Values** options of the **Chi-Square Test** dialogue box, we have selected the unequal expected values option by left-clicking on the **Values:** option [step ①]. In the **Values:** field, we first entered the expected percentage, 90, for the group which did not engage in disruptive behavior, and then left-clicked the **Add** button. Next, we entered the expected percentage, 10, for the group which did behave disruptively, and then left-clicked the **Add** button. Finally, we ran the analysis by clicking **OK** [step ②]. You should note that the order in which the expected values were entered was based on the numerical values with which the groups are labeled. The first expected value should correspond to the group with lowest numerical label, in this case 0 for the "no" group, and the order of the remaining expected values follow the increasing numerical order of the values labeling the groups.

Selecting the paste option from the procedure above generates the following syntax:

```
NPAR TEST
 /CHISQUARE=behavior
 /EXPECTED=90 10
 /MISSING ANALYSIS .
```

You should note that the expected values can be entered into SPSS as either group percentages or actual expected frequencies. In this example, the expected group percentages and actual expected frequencies are the same because there are 100 cows in the sample. However, if there were only 50 cows, we could have used the percentages of 90 and 10 or the expected values of 45 and 5. SPSS recognizes both sets of values as equivalent because they represent identical ratios.

The Chi-Square Test output for this analysis is provided in the bottom of Figure 13.5, and it is split into two parts: **Frequencies** and **Test Statistics**. The **Frequencies** table

Figure 13.5 Goodness-of-Fit Chi-Square with Unequal Expected Values

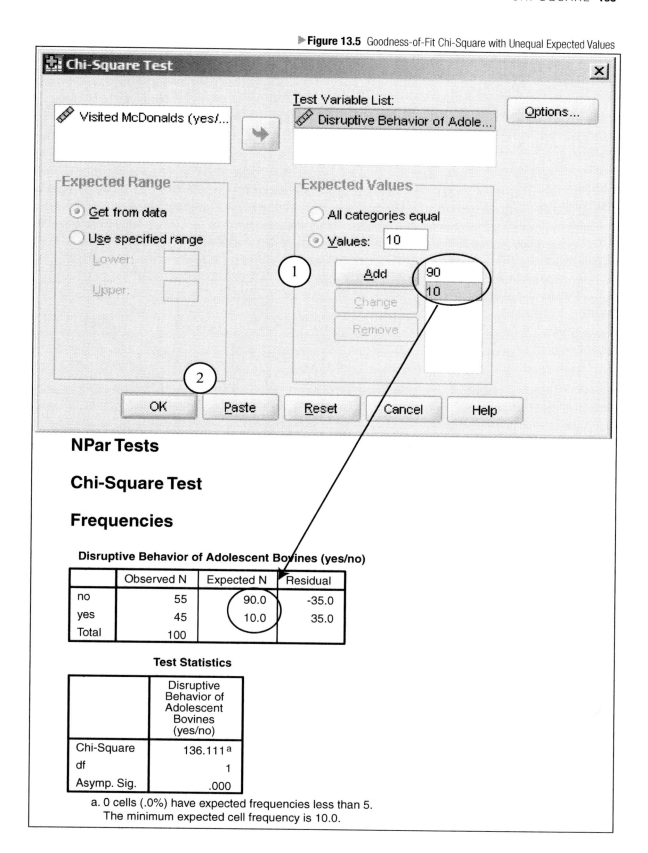

NPar Tests

Chi-Square Test

Frequencies

Disruptive Behavior of Adolescent Bovines (yes/no)

	Observed N	Expected N	Residual
no	55	90.0	-35.0
yes	45	10.0	35.0
Total	100		

Test Statistics

	Disruptive Behavior of Adolescent Bovines (yes/no)
Chi-Square	136.111[a]
df	1
Asymp. Sig.	.000

a. 0 cells (.0%) have expected frequencies less than 5.
The minimum expected cell frequency is 10.0.

reports the obtained, expected, and residual values for each group. As we requested in the **Chi-Square Test** dialogue box, the expected values for the "no" and "yes" groups are 90 and 10, respectively. These expected values are substantially different from the observed values and result in quite large residuals for the "no" and "yes" groups, −35 and 35, respectively.

The **Test Statistics** table reports the obtained Chi-Square values, the degrees of freedom, and the exact level of significance for the **behavior** variable. Compared to the analysis where the expected values were equal, the substantially larger residual values resulted in a substantially larger obtained value for Chi-Square, 136.111. Thus, the differences between the observed frequencies found within our sample and the frequencies expected in the special population are significant at least at the .001 level with 1 degree of freedom. This tells us that the odds are at least 1 in 1000 that the frequency of disruptive behavior observed in our sample of adolescent bovines differs from the frequency expected in the special population of cows. We can reasonably conclude that our sample is not representative of the special population of cows because disruptive adolescents are significantly over-represented and non-disruptive adolescents are significantly under-represented. As you can see, changing the research question substantially changes the results obtained using the same data and same statistical procedures.

PEARSON'S CHI-SQUARE

Like the Goodness-of-Fit Chi-Square, Pearson's Chi-Square tells us whether a particular pattern of group frequencies is likely due to chance alone. Pearson's Chi-Square differs from the Goodness-of-Fit in that it evaluates the pattern obtained from a combination of two different variables. Because Pearson's Chi-Square evaluates two variables, a significant Chi-Square value not only tells us that the pattern of frequencies is significantly different from a random pattern, but it also tells us that if the two variables are significantly associated with one another, that is, if changes in one variable tend to be matched with changes in the other. This association can also be expressed with a statistic called Cramer's V, which is interpreted in much the same way as the correlation coefficient introduced in Chapter 11.

RUNNING PEARSON'S CHI-SQUARE

With respect to our current example, the following procedure will determine whether the frequencies for bovine adolescents that behave or misbehave, relative to whether or not they visit McDonald's, are significantly different from frequencies resulting from chance alone. If the pattern of frequencies do differ from chance, then it means that a relationship exists between the adolescents' behavior and whether they are taken to McDonald's. It may be that misbehavior is associated with a greater likelihood of visiting McDonald's or it may be associated with a reduced likelihood. Careful inspection of the pattern of frequencies will be required to determine the nature a significant Pearson's Chi-Square.

PROCEDURE FOR RUNNING A PEARSON'S CHI-SQUARE:

1. Select **Analyze** from the pull-down menu.

2. Select **Descriptive Statistics**.

3. Select **Crosstabs...** from the side menu. This will open the **Crosstabs** dialogue box.

4. Enter the variable **behavior** in the **Column(s):** field by left-clicking the **behavior** variable and then clicking on the boxed arrow pointing to the **Column(s):** field.

5. Next, enter the variable **mcdonlds** in the **Row(s):** field by left-clicking on the variable and left-clicking on the boxed arrow pointing to the **Row(s):** field.

   • You should note that the decision regarding which variable goes in the rows and which goes in the columns is rather arbitrary. However, in cases where one variable has more groups than the other (e.g., a 2 × 3 design), it is preferable to put the variable with the fewest groups in the columns field as it makes the printout of the output easier to read (unless you use the landscape print option, in which case the opposite is true).

6. To select the Pearson's Chi-Square statistic left-click the **Statistics...** button, which will open the **Crosstabs: Statistics** dialogue box.

   7. Check the **Chi-square** option.

   8. In this example, we have also requested **Phi and Cramer's V** option which are effect size estimates similar to Pearson's *r*.

   9. Click **Continue** to return to the **Crosstabs** dialogue box.

10. To select the type of information that will be displayed for each cell of the Chi-Square table in the output, left-click the **Cells...** button, which will open the **Crosstabs: Cell Display** dialogue box.

    11. Select the **Observed** (already selected for you) and **Expected** options under the **Counts** options.

    12. Select the **Adjusted standardized** option under the **Residuals** options.

    13. Left-click **Continue** to return to the **Crosstabs** dialogue box.

14. Finally, double-check your variables and options and either select **OK** to run or **Paste** to create syntax to run at a later time.

    If you selected the paste option from the procedure above, you should have generated the following syntax:

    ```
    CROSSTABS
      /TABLES=mcdonlds BY behavior
      /FORMAT=AVALUE TABLES
      /STATISTICS=CHISQ PHI
      /CELLS=COUNT EXPECTED ASRESID
      /COUNT ROUND CELL .
    ```

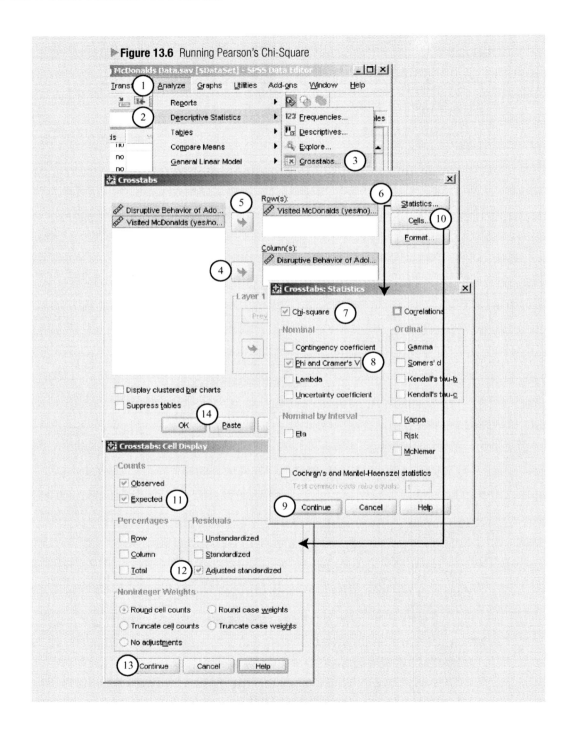

▶ **Figure 13.6** Running Pearson's Chi-Square

READING THE PEARSON'S CHI-SQUARE CROSSTABS OUTPUT

The Pearson's Chi-Square Crosstabs output is presented in Figure 13.7. This output consists of four parts: the **Case Processing Summary** table, labeled Ⓐ; the Cross-tabulation matrix titled **Visited McDonalds (yes/no)*Disruptive Behavior of adolescent Bovines (yes/no) Crosstabulation**, labeled Ⓑ; the **Chi-Square Tests** table, labeled

▶**Figure 13.7** Pearson's Chi-Square Output

Crosstabs

Case Processing Summary

(A)	Cases					
	Valid		Missing		Total	
	N	Percent	N	Percent	N	Percent
Visited McDonald's (yes/no) * Disruptive Behavior of Adolescent Bovines (yes/no)	100	100.0%	0	.0%	100	100.0%

Visited McDonald's (yes/no) * Disruptive Behavior of Adolescent Bovines (yes/no) Crosstabulation

(B)			Disruptive Behavior of Adolescent Bovines (yes/no)		
			no	yes	Total
Visited McDonald's (yes/no)	no	Count	40	7	47
		Expected Count	25.8	21.2	47.0
		Adjusted Residual	5.7	−5.7	
	yes	Count	15	38	53
		Expected Count	29.2	23.8	53.0
		Adjusted Residual	−5.7	5.7	
	Total	Count	55	45	100
		Expected Count	55.0	45.0	100.0

Chi-Square Tests

(C)	Value	df	Asymp. Sig. (2-sided)	Exact Sig. (2-sided)	Exact Sig. (1-sided)
Pearson Chi-Square	32.476[a]	1	.000		
Continuity Correction[b]	30.222	1	.000		
Likelihood Ratio	34.914	1	.000		
Fisher's Exact Test				.000	.000
Linear-by-Linear Association	32.151	1	.000		
N of Valid Cases	100				

a. 0 cells (.0%) have expected count less than 5. The minimum expected count is 21.15.

b. Computed only for a 2 × 2 table

Symmetric Measures

(D)		Value	Approx. Sig.
Nominal by Nominal	Phi	.570	.000
	Cramer's V	.570	.000
	N of Valid Cases	100	

Ⓒ; and the **Symmetric Measures** table, labeled Ⓓ. The **Case Processing Summary** table reports the number (**N**) and percentage of valid cases (cases for which there is no missing data), missing cases (cases where data for at least one variable is missing), and total cases in the sample regardless of their status as valid or missing. In this example, there is no missing data for either of the variables, so the valid and total numbers are the same.

The cross-tabulation matrix, labeled Ⓑ, presents tabulations or counts for each group of one variable separated *across* the groups of the second variable, thus the term crosstabulation. Here, the Disruptive Behavior groups are presented in the columns and the Visit to McDonald's groups are presented in the rows. Within each cell the observed values are listed first, labeled **Count** in the row heading. The expected values are listed below the observed values, labeled **Expected Count** in the row heading. Also for each cell, the **Adjusted Residual** is presented. As with Goodness-of-Fit Chi-Square, the residual represents the difference between the observed and expected frequencies. However, the adjusted residual has been standardized and can be interpreted like a Z-score. These adjusted residuals can be used to determine whether the difference between the observed and expected frequencies for any given group is significant. We will return to this after we interpret the values provided in the Chi-Square table. Note that in the cross-tabulation matrix, the row and column totals are also presented.

In the **Chi–Square Test** table, labeled Ⓒ, we are given an overwhelming number of statistics to interpret. For simplicity's sake, we will only concern ourselves with the first row of statistics, labeled Pearson Chi–Square, which we have circled in the output. This row reports the Chi–Square obtained, the degrees of freedom, and the alpha level (found in the column labeled **Asymp. Sig. (2–sided)**). The degrees of freedom for Pearson's Chi–Square are calculated with the following formula: $df = (R-1)(C-1)$, where R = number of rows and C = number of columns. In this case, we have a Chi–Square of 32.476, with 1 degree of freedom [$df = (2-1)(2-1) = 1$]. The Chi–Square value is significant at least at the .001 alpha level, meaning we would expect a pattern like this to occur by chance alone fewer than 1 in 1000 times. Thus we can conclude that there is a significant relationship between bovine adolescents misbehaving and being taken to McDonald's. However, similar to the interpretation of One-Way ANOVA with three or more groups, a significant Pearson's Chi–Square does not tell us which cross-tabulated groups are under- or over-represented with respect to the expected pattern of frequencies. It only tells us that the overall pattern of frequencies significantly differs from a random pattern.

To determine which cross-tabulated groups are significantly under- or over-represented, we can look at the adjusted residuals in each cell. If the adjusted residual is greater than or equal to 1.96 (the Z-Score associate with the two-tailed .05 alpha level) then we can conclude that the observed frequency is significantly different from the expected frequency for that cell. If the residual is positive, then that cross-tabulated group is over-represented, and if it is negative, the group is under-represented. In the cross-tabulation matrix for this example, the residuals for each cell were either 5.7 or −5.7, so the observed-expected difference is significant in each group. Given the pattern of positive and negative residuals, it appears that bovine adolescents who misbehave are over-represented among adolescents who get turned into McDonald's hamburgers and are under-represented among adolescents who do not get turned into hamburgers. Not surprisingly, those bovine adolescents who do not misbehave are over-represented among the adolescents who do not get turned into McDonald's hamburgers and are under-represented among adolescents who do. Thus we can conclude that the wise and well-behaved adolescent will have the greatest longevity.

Finally, the **Symmetric Measures** table, labeled (D), reports **Cramer's V** (also called Cramer's Phi or Φ_{Cramer}). This statistic can be used to indicate the size of the effect one group variable has on another. Unlike Chi-Square, the value of Cramer's V is independent of sample size, so we can compare the results of different studies that have utilized different sample sizes. It is quite similar to a correlation coefficient (e.g., Pearson's r), though it cannot have a negative value. Cohen & Cohen (1988) have suggested standards for interpreting this statistic, where the values of .10, .30, and .50 correspond to small, medium, and large effects, respectively. In our example, V = .57, which indicates that among adolescent bovine there is a very strong relationship between complaining and being turned into hamburgers.

SUMMARY

This chapter demonstrated some basic techniques for conducting Goodness-of-Fit and Pearson's Chi-Square. These analyses assess whether the number of cases (e.g., people, coin-flips, or cows) in different groups significantly differs from the number we might expect based on population frequencies, outcome probabilities, or theory. Further, this chapter showed how Pearson's Chi-Square can tell us whether or not two group variables are significantly associated. Cramer's V can also express the relationship between two group variables as a value which is interpreted in much the same way as the Pearson's r correlation coefficient.

PRACTICE EXERCISES

Assume a bovine researcher wants to know whether the breed (Jersey vs. Holstein) of adolescent bovines is related to "visiting" McDonald's. The data set the researcher collected is presented in Table 13.2. Enter the data separately for the two variables, Breed and Visited McDonald's. Using the data, run the following analyses within SPSS. For each analysis, report the Chi-Square statistic, degrees of freedom, sample size, and alpha level, and describe the results.

1. Compare the number of Jersey and Holstein cows to a 50/50 distribution.

2. Compare the number visits to McDonald's to a 50/50 distribution.

3. Compare the number of Jersey and Holstein cows to a distribution where 30% are Jersey and 70% are Holstein.

4. Conduct an analysis that would determine whether Breed is associated with Visiting McDonald's. For this analysis, report the Chi-Square statistic, degrees of freedom, sample size, alpha level, and Cramer's V. What do these results tell us?

▶ **Table 13.2** Practice Exercise Data

		Bovine Breed	
		Holstein	Jersey
Visited McDonald's?	Yes	4	6
	No	14	2

REFERENCES

Cohen, J. (1992). A Power Primer. *Psychological Bulletin, 112,* 115–159.

Reliability

I n the classical view of measurement, everything we measure is made up of two basic parts: *True Score* (what we intend to measure) and *Error* (factors that influence measures that are not of interest). For example, your score on a statistics test will partly reflect what you know about statistics, but it will also reflect things that have little to do with what you know about statistics: how tired you are, your ability to read and write English, and any random mistakes you may make (e.g., circling the wrong answer). On an accurate measure—a test, measurement, or assessment—your score will be based as much as possible on your true score (what you know) and as little as possible on sources of error. One way to evaluate how much true score is represented in a measure is by taking multiple measurements and looking at the consistency of the measurements. This approach to estimating true scores is called *reliability* and the reliability of a measure is typically represented by the strength of the correlation between the different measurements.

This chapter investigates the reliability of a specific measure to introduce procedures for conducting some common reliability analyses. Specifically, we will present methods for assessing reliability across time—*Test-Retest* and *Parallel Forms Reliability*—and assessing reliability across test items—*Split-Half Reliability* and *Cronbach's Alpha*.

SETTING UP THE DATA

Cartoon 14.1 will serve as the backdrop for the examples in this chapter. In this cartoon we are warned of the dangers of failing to develop children's computer literacy; they will grow up to be eccentric (if not insanely wealthy) members of rock bands. To test this theory, we first need to develop a method for assessing the degree to which individuals share characteristics with Gene Simmons, the bass player for the rock band KISS, shown in Cartoon 14.1. To this end, we have developed a scale of Gene Simmons Resemblance (GSR). This six-item measure asks participants to rate the frequency with which they engage in the behaviors listed below using the following scale: 1 = never, 2 = rarely, 3 = sometimes, 4 = often, and 5 = very often.

1. How often do you play bass guitar?

2. How often do you play in a rock band?

3. How often do you stick your tongue down to your kneecaps?

4. How often do you spit fire?

5. How often do you wear fishnet stockings?

6. How often do you use your computer? (This item is reverse scored.)

GENE SIMMONS NEVER HAD A PERSONAL COMPUTER WHEN HE WAS A KID

How do we know? We know because our own well-documented research has shown conclusively that a child who lacks his own personal computer during those earliest school years will very probably grow up to be a bass player in a heavy-metal rock band who wears women's fishnet pantyhose and sticks his tongue down to his kneecaps. Just like Gene Simmons.

Your child's future doesn't have to look like this. The Banana Junior 6000 Self-portable Personal Computer System, complete with its optional soft-ware— Bananawrite, Bananadraw, Bananafile and Bananamanager—is just what your four-year-old needs to compete in today's cut-throat world of high tech and high expectations.

The Banana Junior 6000... **Buy one before it's too late.** **Gene's mother wishes she had.**

Figure 14.1 on the following page shows the Variable View of the SPSS Data Editor, where eight variables have been defined. The first six variables represent the six items of the GSR scale, given at a single point in time. The last two variables—**GSR_Time1** and **GSR_Time2**—represent the average of participants' responses for the GSR taken at two different times with a three month interval between the two assessments. Note that we have not entered the individual responses to the GSR taken at time 2 into the Data Editor as they are not required for the following analyses.

Figure 14.2 on the following page shows the Data View of the Data Editor, where the responses of 10 college students are presented for each of the eight GSR items. In Chapter 6, we introduced some procedures for working with multi–item measures that make use of items that are reverse scored. Because more frequent computer use is expected to be associated with less Gene Simmons resemblance, item 6 of the GSR scale should be reversed so that high scores indicate high levels of Gene Simmons resemblance and low scores represent low levels. In the interest of simplicity, the data for item 6 in Figure 14.2 has already been reverse scored.

TEST-RETEST AND PARALLEL FORMS RELIABILITY

One method for assessing the degree to which measures reflect true scores is to look at their stability over time. The reliability of measures taken at different times can be estimated either by a) using the same measure both times, called *Test-Retest Reliability*, or b) using two different but equivalent versions of the measure each time, called *Parallel Forms Reliability*. Both test-retest and parallel forms reliability are estimated by correlating

Figure 14.1 Variable View for Gene Simmons Resemblance Data

Chapter 14 SPSS Gene Simmons Resemblance Data.sav [DataSet1] - SP...
File Edit View Data Transform Analyze Graphs Utilities Add-ons Window Help
Name
Label
1 GSR_1 ... 8 2 GSR 1 (Bass Playing Frequency)
2 GSR_2 ... 8 2 GSR 2 (Rock Band Playing Frequency)
3 GSR_3 ... 8 2 GSR 3 (Sticking Tongue Down to Kneecaps Frequency)
4 GSR_4 ... 8 2 GSR 4 (Spitting Fire Frequency)
5 GSR_5 ... 8 2 GSR 5 (Wearing Fishnet Stockings Frequency)
6 GSR_6r ... 8 2 GSR 6 (Computer Use Frequency - scores reversed)
7 GSR_Time1 ... 8 2 GSR Time 1
8 GSR_Time2 ... 8 2 GSR Time 2
Data View
Variable View
SPSS Processor is ready

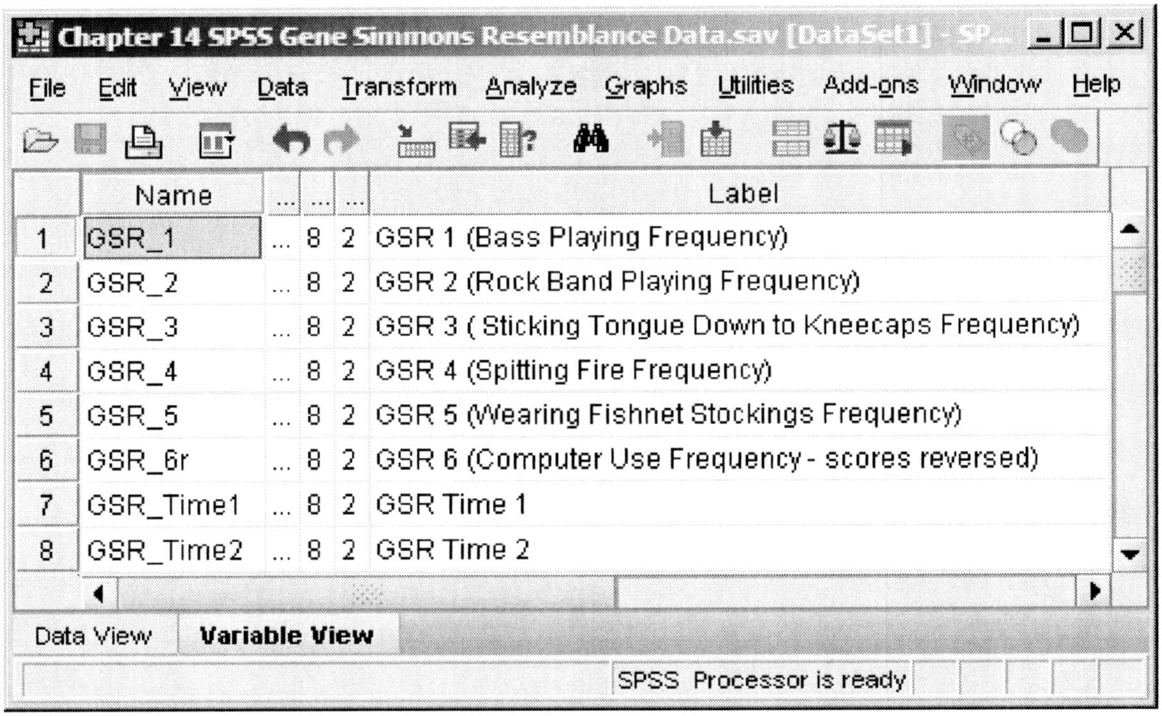

Figure 14.2 Data View for Gene Simmons Resemblance Data

	GSR_1	GSR_2	GSR_3	GSR_4	GSR_5	GSR_6r	GSR_Time1	GSR_Time2
1	1.00	1.00	1.00	1.00	4.00	4.00	2.00	2.00
2	1.00	2.00	1.00	1.00	4.00	3.00	2.00	3.00
3	2.00	2.00	2.00	2.00	4.00	4.00	2.67	2.67
4	2.00	3.00	2.00	2.00	1.00	1.00	1.83	2.83
5	3.00	3.00	3.00	4.00	4.00	4.00	3.50	3.50
6	3.00	3.00	3.00	3.00	2.00	2.00	2.67	2.67
7	4.00	4.00	4.00	4.00	1.00	2.00	3.17	3.17
8	4.00	5.00	3.00	4.00	2.00	3.00	3.50	4.50
9	5.00	5.00	5.00	4.00	4.00	4.00	4.50	4.50
10	5.00	5.00	5.00	5.00	3.00	3.00	4.33	4.33

the scores gathered at the first point in time with scores gathered at the second point in time. The stronger the correlation between the scores from each time, the higher the reliability of the measure.

These different approaches have their strengths and weaknesses. The test-retest approach is often easier to implement than parallel forms. However, the usefulness of test-retest methods can be limited by practice effects. That is, the second time respondents take a test, they may remember what was on the test and adjust their responses accordingly. The parallel forms approach fixes this by administering two forms of the measure that use different items but measure the same general concept/construct. However, this approach is limited by the difficulty of creating two forms of a measure that actually measure the exact same thing. Both approaches are limited by the degree to which the characteristic you are measuring remains stable over time. Some characteristics are less stable than others (i.e., a person's mood), and very little reliability over time should be expected. Similarly, some characteristics might be stable for short time periods but not long periods.

In SPSS, the **<u>Reliability</u> Analysis...** can be used to test reliability using either the test-retest or parallel forms reliability approaches. Whether the analysis results in a value for test-retest reliability or parallel forms reliability depends on the variables of interest. If the responses were obtained using the same measure given twice, then this procedure provides test-retest reliability. If they were obtained using two different forms of the same measure, then this procedure provides parallel forms reliability. For this reason, we will only present one example here.

Based on the Gene Simmons Resemblance example introduced earlier, we will demonstrate test–retest reliability. In this example, college students' GSR scores collected at time 1 will be correlated with their respective scores from time 2. The degree to which students' scores remain consistent across the two times will be represented as a correlation coefficient. The stronger the correlation is the greater the consistency between scores and therefore the higher the reliability.

PROCEDURE FOR OBTAINING TEST-RETEST OR PARALLEL FORMS RELIABILITY:

① Select **<u>A</u>nalyze** from the pull-down menu.

② Select **Sc<u>a</u>le**.

③ Select **Reliability Analysis...** from the side menu. This will open the **Reliability Analysis** dialogue box.

④ Enter the variables of interest (**GSR_Time1** and **GSR_Time2**) in the **<u>I</u>tems:** field either by double-clicking each variable or left-clicking each variable and left-clicking the boxed arrow pointing toward the **Items:** field.

⑤ Select the **Parallel** option from the **<u>M</u>odel:** drop-down menu.

- In this model, it is assumed that the variances (including error variance) for both forms are equal. Alternatively, you could select the **Strict Parallel** option, which assumes that both the means and the variances for each form are equal.

⑥ You can add a scale label to the output in the **Scale label:** field. Here, we have typed "GSR Test-Retest Reliability."

⑦ Finally, double-check your variables and options and either select **OK** to run or **<u>P</u>aste** to create syntax to run at a later time.

If you selected the paste option from the procedure above, you should have generated the following syntax:

```
RELIABILITY
 /VARIABLES=GSR_Time1 GSR_Time2
 /SCALE('GSR Parallel Forms') ALL
 /MODEL=PARALLEL .
```

▶ **Figure 14.3** Obtaining Test-Retest or Parallel Forms Reliability

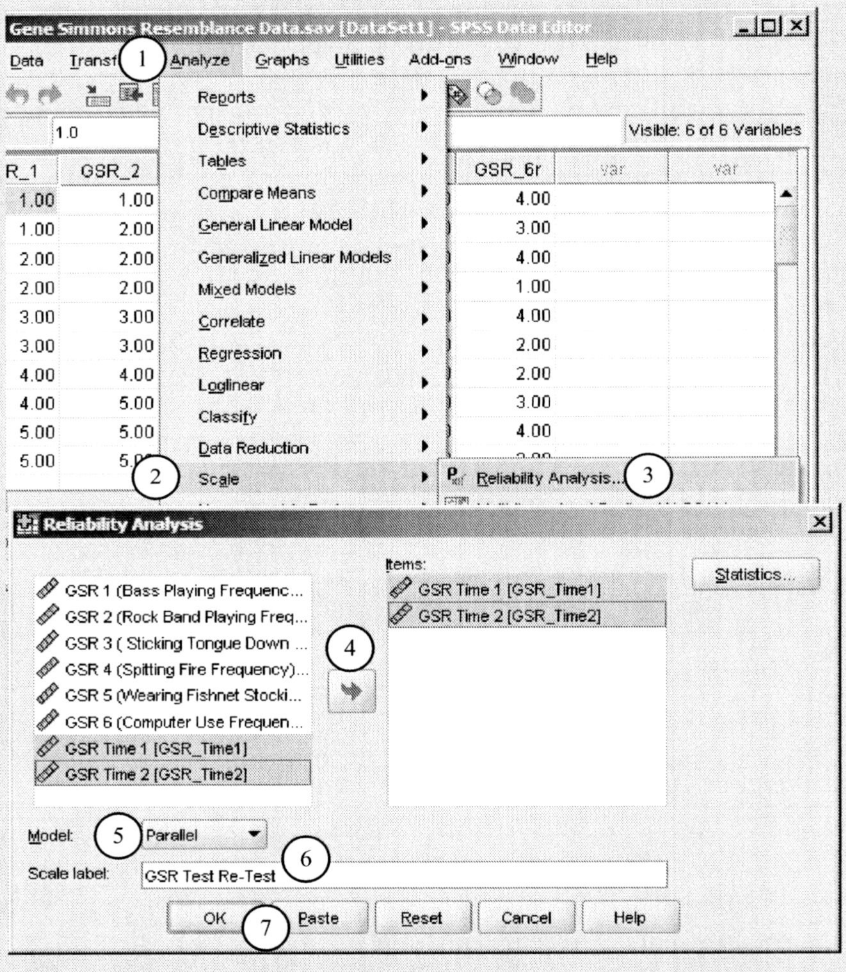

READING THE PARALLEL FORMS/TEST-RETEST OUTPUT

The output generated using the **Parallel** option for the **Reliability Analysis…** consists of four parts: **Case Processing Summary, Test for Model Goodness of Fit, Reliability Statistics**, and **Inter-item Correlation Matrix**. We have only shown the **Reliability Statistics** table in Figure 14.4 because the **Case Processing Summary** is similar to output covered in previous chapters, the **Test for Model Goodness of Fit** is not necessary for our current discussion, and the **Inter-Item Correlation Matrix** will

▶**Figure 14.4** Output for Test-Retest or Parallel Forms Reliability

Reliability

Scale: GSR Test-Retest Reliability

Reliability Statistics

Common Variance	.829
True Variance	.713
Error Variance	.116
Common Inter-Item Correlation	.860
Reliability of Scale	.925
Reliability of Scale (Unbiased)	.941

be covered later in this chapter. The correlation representing the test–retest reliability (or parallel forms if you used different forms of the measure at each time) is presented in the row labeled **Common Inter-Item Correlation**. For this example, the reliability is .860. Because this correlation is being used to represent reliability, we can interpret this to mean that 86% of the variability in scores at the two times is attributable to true score. This percentage reflects the ratio obtained by dividing the variability attributable to the true score by the total amount of variability across all the scores of the respondents. These values are also reported in the **Reliability Statistics** table: the value for **True Variance**, .713, is the amount of variability attributable to true scores, and the value for **Common Variance**, .829, is the total amount of variability across all scores. Dividing the true variance by the common variance will reproduce the value of the common inter–item correlation (.713/.829 = .860). The **Reliability Statistics** table also shows the variability attributable to error (**Error Variance** =.116), which when added to the true score variance will be equal to the total amount of variability across all scores (.713 + .116 = .829).

Generally, test–retest or parallel forms reliability of .40 or greater across at least three months is considered acceptable. With respect to the **GSR_Time1** and **GSR_Time2** ratings, given that there was a three month span between assessments, we can say the GSR scale is very reliable over time.

SPLIT-HALF RELIABILITY

For measures with more than one item, reliability can also be estimated by comparing parts of a measure given at a single point in time. This is referred to as the *Internal Consistency* of a measure and can be assessed using either the *Split-Half Reliability* or *Cronbach's Alpha* option. Split-half reliability is obtained by "splitting" the measure into two halves and correlating the sum or average of the scores for one half with sum or average of the scores for the second half. In essence, the split-half approach consists of parallel forms given at single point in time. As with parallel forms, split-half reliability estimates the variability attributable to true score by assessing the consistency in scores between the two halves. However, one assumption of classical measurement theory is that longer tests—tests with more items—are inherently more reliable than shorter tests. Because split–half reliability estimates reliability for a measure after it is split into two halves, the reliability is estimated for a measure that is half the length of the original measure. Therefore, split–half reliability underestimates the reliability of the full test. To estimate the true reliability for the whole measure, it is necessary to use the *Spearman-Brown Prophesy Formula*. Generally, the prophesy formula estimates what the reliability of a test will be if you change the number of items in a test. For split–half reliability, the prophesy formula estimates what the reliability will be if the length of half of the test (split–half) is doubled, therefore estimating the reliability for the full test. SPSS provides a procedure specifically designed to produce split–half reliability and its corresponding Spearman-Brown Prophesy correction.

For our demonstration of obtaining the split–half reliability, we will split the six items of the GSR measure into two groups of three items. The most common method of splitting a measure is to compare the odd items with the even items. We have used this method to test the GSR split half reliability in the following procedure.

PROCEDURE FOR OBTAINING THE ODD VS. EVEN SPLIT-HALF RELIABILITY:

- Select **Analyze** from the pull-down menu.
- Select **Scale**.
- Select **Reliability Analysis...** from the side menu. This will open the **Reliability Analysis** dialogue box.

① Enter the Odd items (**GSR_1**, **GSR_3**, and **GSR_5**) in the **Items:** field by double-clicking each odd variable or left-clicking each odd item while pressing the **Crtl** button and then left-clicking the boxed arrow pointing to the **Items:** field.

② Repeat this procedure for the Even items (**GSR_2**, **GSR_4**, and **GSR_6r**).

  - If you completed steps 1 and 2 correctly, then the odd items will appear first in the list within the **Items:** field and the even items appear at the end of the list.

③ Select the **Split-half** option from the **Model:** drop-down menu.

④ You can add a scale label to the output in the **Scale label:** field. Here, we have typed "GSR: Split-half Reliability: Odd Items vs. Even Items."

⑤ Finally, double-check your variables and options and either select **OK** to run or **Paste** to create syntax to run at a later time.

  If you selected the paste option from the procedure above, you should have generated the following syntax:

```
RELIABILITY
  /VARIABLES=GSR_1 GSR_3 GSR_5 GSR_2 GSR_4 GSR_6r
  /SCALE('GSR: Split-half Reliability: Odd Items vs. Even Items') ALL
  /MODEL=SPLIT .
```

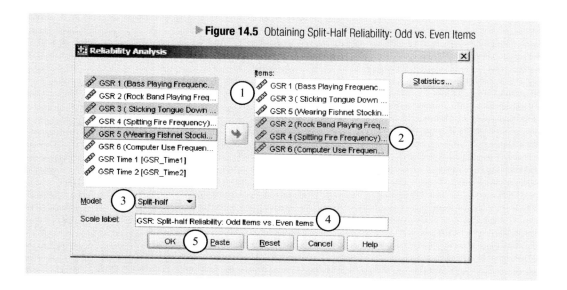

▶ **Figure 14.5** Obtaining Split-Half Reliability: Odd vs. Even Items

READING THE OUTPUT: SPLIT-HALF RELIABILITY FOR ODD VS. EVEN ITEMS

The output generated using the **Split-half** option for the **Reliability Analysis...** consists of two parts: **Case Processing Summary** and **Reliability Statistics**. Only the **Reliability Statistics** table is shown in Figure 14.6 on the following page. The **Reliability Statistics** table presents several different reliability estimates. For the most part, we are only interested in the three that are circled in the figure. First, the split-half reliability is reported in the row labeled **Correlation Between Forms**. For the GSR measure, we have a split-half reliability correlation coefficient of .931. While this is considered very good reliability, it only estimates the reliability for a 3-item questionnaire—half the length of the test. To estimate the true reliability of the complete test, we must look at the Spearman-Brown prophesy correction. In this output, there are two **Spearman-Brown Coefficients**: **Equal Length** and **Unequal Length**. You should use the Equal-Length Spearman-Brown for measures with an even number of items. Conversely, you should use the Unequal-Length Spearman-Brown for measures with an odd number of items. In the current analysis, we have an even number of items (six), so we want to use the first Spearman-Brown estimate, .964. That is, based on the comparison between the odd and even items of the test, we found that 96% of the variance in our measure can be attributed to true score, while 4% of the variance is attributable to error. Internal consistency of .70 or greater is generally considered adequate for personality and attitude measures like the GSR scale. Thus, the evidence supporting the reliability of the GSR is quite strong.

SPLIT-HALF RELIABILITY: A SECOND EXAMPLE

Though the Odd vs. Even split-half reliability correlation coefficient is very large, split-half reliability suffers from a rather powerful limitation. The value of the split-half reliability coefficient can be influenced by the way in which items are grouped. Unreliability can be accentuated or masked depending on the how the items are split. To demonstrate this, we have generated split-half reliability output by grouping the first three items of the GSR with the last three. The output is presented in Figure 14.7 on the following page.

▶**Figure 14.6** Output for Split-Half Reliability: Odd vs. Even Items

Reliability

Scale: GSR: Split-half Reliability

Reliability Statistics

Cronbach's Alpha	Part 1	Value	.460
		N of Items	3[a]
	Part 2	Value	.567
		N of Items	3[b]
	Total N of Items		6
Correlation Between Forms			.931
Spearman-Brown Coefficient	Equal Length		.964
	Unequal Length		.964
Guttman Split-Half Coefficient			.964

a. The items are: GSR 1 (Bass Playing Frequency), GSR 3 (Sticking Tongue Down to Kneecaps Frequency), GSR 5 (Wearing Fishnet Stockings Frequency).

b. The items are: GSR 2 (Rock Band Playing Frequency), GSR 4 (Spitting Fire Frequency), GSR 6 (Computer Use Frequency—scores reversed).

▶**Figure 14.7** Output for Split-Half Reliability: 1st Half vs. 2nd Half

Reliability

Scale: GSR: Split-half Reliability: 1st half vs. 2nd half

Reliability Statistics

Cronbach's Alpha	Part 1	Value	.977
		N of Items	3[a]
	Part 2	Value	.369
		N of Items	3[b]
	Total N of Items		6
Correlation Between Forms			.375
Spearman-Brown Coefficient	Equal Length		.546
	Unequal Length		.546
Guttman Split-Half Coefficient			.494

a. The items are: GSR 1 (Bass Playing Frequency), GSR 2 (Rock Band Playing Frequency), GSR 3 (Sticking Tongue Down to Kneecaps Frequency).

b. The items are: GSR 4 (Spitting Fire Frequency), GSR 5 (Wearing Fishnet Stockings Frequency), GSR 6 (Computer Use Frequency - scores reversed).

When we compare the first half of the measure with the second half, the split-half reliability is .375 and the Spearman-Brown corrected reliability is .546. These values are substantially smaller than the values obtained when the odd and even items were compared. When two split-half reliability estimates for the same measure have very different values, it suggests that one or more items may be inconsistent with the other items of the measure. Split-half statistics alone do not provide specific information about which items may be performing poorly. Fortunately, the procedure for obtaining Cronbach's alpha can provide this information.

CRONBACH'S ALPHA

Cronbach's Alpha is a second measure of internal consistency reliability. Though they have the same name, Cronbach's alpha is quite different from and should not be confused with the alpha level used to determine the significance of a statistical test. Cronbach's alpha is based on the average of the correlations between each item of a measure and each of the other items. These correlations are called inter-item correlations. Generally, you can think of Cronbach's alpha as the average of all possible split-half reliabilities. For this reason, Cronbach's alpha is not subject to the problems associated with a single split-half reliability; it will not mask or overemphasize the effects of unreliable items. Also, because it considers every item in the measure, it is not necessary to use the Spearman-Brown correction with Cronbach's alpha. Further, the output for the Cronbach's alpha procedure will show how individual items contribute to the overall reliability of a measure.

PROCEDURE FOR OBTAINING CRONBACH'S ALPHA STATISTICS:

- Select **Analyze** from the pull-down menu.
- Select **Scale**.
- Select **Reliability Analysis...** from the side menu. This will open the **Reliability Analysis** dialogue box.

1. Enter the scale items (**GSR_1**, **GSR_2**, **GSR_3**, **GSR_4**, **GSR_5**, and **GSR_6r**) in the **Items:** field by double-clicking each variable or left-clicking each item while pressing the **Crtl** button and then left-clicking the boxed arrow pointing to the **Items:** field.

2. Select the **Alpha** option from the **Model:** drop-down menu.

3. You can add a scale label to the output in the **Scale label:** field. Here, we have added the label "GSR: Alpha."

4. To select additional options, left-click the **Statistics...** button. This will open the **Reliability Analysis: Statistics** dialogue box.

5. Select **Correlations** from the **Inter-Item** options, which will produce a matrix of correlations between the items of the scale (called Inter-Item Correlations).

6. Select **Scale if item deleted** from the **Descriptives for** section, which will produce a table of alphas and other statistics that would be obtained if each item were excluded from the measure.

⑦ Left-Click **Continue** to return to the **Reliability Analysis** dialogue box.

⑧ Finally, double-check your variables and options and either select **OK** to run or **Paste** to create syntax to run at a later time.

If you selected the paste option from the procedure above, you should have generated the following syntax:

RELIABILITY
/VARIABLES=GSR_1 GSR_2 GSR_3 GSR_4 GSR_5 GSR_6r
/SCALE('GSR: Alpha') ALL
/MODEL=ALPHA
/STATISTICS=CORR
/SUMMARY=TOTAL .

▶**Figure 14.8** Obtaining Cronbach's Alpha

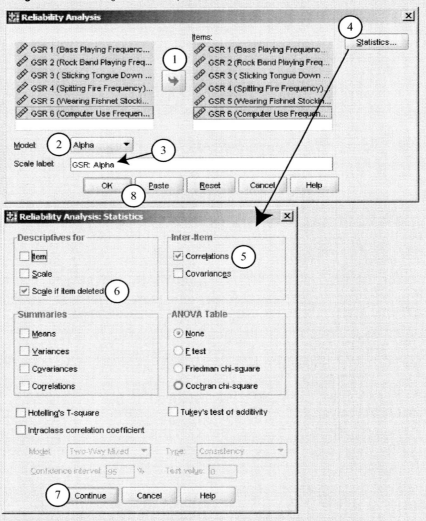

READING THE OUTPUT: ALPHA

The output generated using the **Alpha** option for the **Reliability Analysis...** consists of four parts: **Case Processing Summary**, **Reliability Statistics**, **Inter–Item Correlation Matrix**, and **Item–Total Statistics**. All but the **Case Processing Summary** are shown in Figure 14.9. The first part, labeled **Reliability Statistics**, reports two Cronbach's alpha values: an unstandardized value and a standardized value. The unstandardized alpha value, .791, is the alpha based on the participants' responses. The standardized alpha value, .767, is the alpha based on the participants' responses which have been

▶**Figure 14.9** Output for Cronbach's Alpha Procedure

Scale: GSR: Alpha

Reliability Statistics

Cronbach's Alpha	Cronbach's Alpha Based on Standardized Items	N of Items
.791	.767	6

Inter-Item Correlation Matrix

	GSR 1 (Bass Playing Frequency)	GSR 2 (Rock Band Playing Frequency)	GSR 3 (Sticking Tongue Down to Kneecaps Frequency)	GSR 4 (Spitting Fire Frequency)	GSR 5 (Wearing Fishnet Stockings Frequency)	GSR 6 (Computer Use Frequency — scores reversed)
GSR 1 (Bass Playing Frequency)	1.000	.946	.977	.949	-.232	.000
GSR 2 (Rock Band Playing Frequency)	.946	1.000	.881	.886	-.347	-.149
GSR 3 (Sticking Tongue Down to Kneecaps Frequency)	.977	.881	1.000	.922	-.185	.000
GSR 4 (Spitting Fire Frequency)	.949	.886	.922	1.000	-.244	.000
GSR 5 (Wearing Fishnet Stockings Frequency)	-.232	-.347	-.185	-.244	1.000	.901
GSR 6 (Computer Use Frequency — scores reversed)	.000	-.149	.000	.000	.901	1.000

Item-Total Statistics

	Scale Mean if Item Deleted	Scale Variance if Item Deleted	Corrected Item-Total Correlation	Squared Multiple Correlation	Cronbach's Alpha if Item Deleted
GSR 1 (Bass Playing Frequency)	15.1000	18.989	.872	.997	.666
GSR 2 (Rock Band Playing Frequency)	14.8000	21.067	.727	.982	.711
GSR 3 (Sticking Tongue Down to Kneecaps Frequency)	15.2000	19.511	.854	.993	.673
GSR 4 (Spitting Fire Frequency)	15.1000	20.100	.824	.907	.684
GSR 5 (Wearing Fishnet Stockings Frequency)	15.2000	32.178	-.088	.956	.883
GSR 6 (Computer Use Frequency — scores reversed)	15.1000	29.433	.175	.964	.826

standardized as *Z*-scores. Generally, unless the items of your scale have different response formats (e.g., some use 5-point scales and others use 7-point scales), the unstandardized Cronbach's Alpha is the value reported in research. In this example, the unstandardized alpha is .791, meaning that 79.1% of the variability between scores is attributable to true score. For measures of personality and attitudes, Cronbach's alphas of .70 or greater are generally considered adequate.

The second part of the output reports the **Inter–Item Correlation Matrix**. Like other correlation matrices, the 1.00s on the diagonal represent the correlation between each item and itself. Also, the correlations above the diagonal (upper right-hand portion of matrix) are redundant with those below the diagonal (lower left-hand portion of table). Looking at the values below the diagonal, items 1 through 4 are all very strongly correlated (see the values labeled Ⓐ); the correlations range between .881 and .977. It is quite clear that participants are responding to these items in a consistent manner. In contrast, items 5 and 6 are very poorly correlated with items 1 through 4 (see the values labeled Ⓑ); the correlations range between −.347 and .000. However, 5 and 6 are very highly correlated with each other (.901). This pattern of results suggests that items 5 and 6 may measure something quite different than what is assessed by the other items of the GSR.

The final section of output, labeled **Item–Total Statistics**, is quite useful for deciding what items could be dropped from the measure in order to improve the overall reliability of the measure. The two main columns of interest are the **Corrected Item–Total Correlation** and **Cronbach's Alpha if Item Deleted**. The column labeled **Corrected Item–Total Correlation**, represents the correlation between each item and the average of the scores for the remaining items. Items with item-total correlations less than .30 may need to be dropped from the measure. In this example, items 5 and 6 both have item-total correlations less than .30 (−.088 and .175, respectively), indicating that they should most likely be dropped from the measure. This is the same conclusion suggested by the inter-item correlation matrix.

The last column (**Cronbach's Alpha if Item Deleted**) shows what would happen to the overall scale if each item were deleted. Removing items 1 through 4 from the scale would result in a reduction of the reliability of the scale. Notice that the reduction in alpha that results from dropping an item is proportional to the item-total correlation for that item. Removing items with larger item-total correlations will result in a greater drop in alpha than will removing items with smaller item-total correlations. For example, item 1 has the largest item-total correlation (.872), and deleting item 1 would result in the smallest alpha (.666). This suggests that item 1 makes the greatest contribution to the reliability of this scale.

Alternatively, dropping some items will result in an increase in alpha. Deleting items 5 or 6 will increase the alpha from .791 to .883 and .826, respectively. Also, notice that dropping the item with the lowest item-total correlation (item 5) resulted in the greatest improvement in alpha. This item most strongly undermines the reliability of the measure.

CONCLUDING COMMENTS ON THE GSR SCALE

If we were to evaluate the overall reliability of the Gene Simmons Resemblance scale across time and across items, we would conclude that our measure shows evidence supporting its reliability. The GSR scale has very high levels of reliability over a three month interval. It also shows appropriate levels of internal consistency when evaluated with Cronbach's alpha. However, analysis of the individual items suggests that reliability could be improved substantially if we eliminated item 5 from the GSR.

SUMMARY

This chapter presented procedures for assessing reliability. First, we focused on the reliability of a measure across time: test-retest and parallel forms reliability. Also, we looked at the reliability of items within a measure (internal consistency): split-half reliability and alpha. Some basic procedures available in SPSS for assessing these different forms of reliability were presented. Each of these approaches has unique advantages and drawbacks. Test-retest and parallel forms reliability both provide information about reliability over time, which Cronbach's alpha and split-half reliability cannot do. However, this extra information is more difficult to obtain. Test-retest procedures are easier to develop than parallel forms, but test-retest reliability can be undermined by practice effects. Split-half reliability is easier to understand at the conceptual level than Cronbach's alpha, but split-half reliability can easily over- or underestimate unreliability. Ideally, we would use all of this information when evaluating the reliability of a measure, but a variety of pragmatic considerations makes such situations rare in practice.

PRACTICE EXERCISES

Assume that our researchers are interested in examining other forms of eccentricity that may result from failing to develop children's computer skills. In this case, the researchers have focused on adolescents' affinity for 1980s hair bands. Hair band attitudes were measured with the HBASS (Hair Band Attitudes Self-report Scale), which is a revised version of the Guitar Legend Attitudes Measure for Metal rockers (G.L.A.M.-Metal). The HBASS consists of the following items which are rated for agreement on a 7-point rating scale (1= strongly disagree and 7 = strongly agree):

1. I feel that metal without make-up is like a day without sunshine.

2. I often dress like members of Mötley Crüe and Cinderella for no apparent reason.

3. Big hair and leather is a look we should all embrace.

4. It is my secret hope to be Axl Rose of Guns N' Roses.

5. Poison was right; every rose does have its thorn.

6. We're not gonna' take it. No, we're not gonna' take it. We're not gonna' take it anymore!!!

The data for 10 adolescents who completed the HBASS are presented in Table 14.1 on the following page. For this data, obtain the following:

1. Assume that the HBASS was given at two points in time and that the HBASS at Time 1 and HBASS at Time 2 are the average scores obtained by each adolescent at the two different times. Obtain the test-retest reliability for this measure.

   a) What portion of the variance is attributable to True Score?

   b) What portion of the variance is attributable to Error?

▶**Table 14.1** Practice Exercise Data

Participant	Item 1	Item 2	Item 3	Item 4	Item 5	Item 6	Time 1	Time 2
	Hair Band Attitudes Self Report Scale Items (Given at Time 1)						**HBASS Total Scores**	
1	1	1	4	1	5	1	2.17	2.20
2	2	1	2	2	2	2	1.83	1.00
3	3	3	4	3	4	3	3.33	3.44
4	3	3	5	4	4	3	3.67	3.53
5	4	4	6	4	7	4	4.83	4.90
6	4	4	4	4	4	4	4.00	4.05
7	5	5	3	4	2	5	4.00	3.95
8	5	5	3	5	5	6	4.83	4.81
9	6	7	2	5	1	6	4.50	5.50
10	7	7	4	7	5	7	6.17	6.20

2. Assume that the first six HBASS items were given at a single point in time:

a) Obtain the split-half reliability comparing the odd items with the even items.

b) Obtain the split-half reliability comparing the first three items with the last three.

c) How do these two values compare? What might this indicate?

d) Obtain Cronbach's alpha for this measure.

e) Looking at the Inter-Item Correlation Matrix, what item(s) might be a problem?

f) Looking at the Item-Total Statistics, what item(s) contribute most to the reliability of the HBASS?

g) Looking at the Item-Total Statistics, what item(s) could be dropped from the HBASS to improve reliability?

Factor Analysis

The goal of this chapter is to show you how to explore the relationships among a set of variables using the correlational technique of *Factor Analysis*. Factor analysis is used to determine the number of groupings that are present among a set of variables. It also provides information about the variables belonging to each group. Specifically, the chapter will cover factor extraction using *Principal Components Analysis* and the *Orthogonal Rotation* of factors through the *Varimax* method.

SETTING UP THE DATA

Like Hobbes in Cartoon 15.1, First Year Graduate Student X is interested in human abilities. Specifically, he is interested in measuring the intelligence of college students. To pursue this interest, he puts together a battery of six tasks he thinks will tap the full range of skills and abilities that are predictive of success and happiness in college. He then administers this battery to 60 undergraduates and enters the data into SPSS. The Variable View for the SPSS Data Editor containing these data is presented in Figure 15.1 on the following page. The variables are described below. Variable names are provided in parentheses.

- **Time Management (TimeMang)**: The ability to balance a variety of conflicting activities, including social commitments, television viewing, meal times, and naps.
- **Text Messaging Acronyms (TextMess)**: Assesses general knowledge of the vast number of acronyms currently used in text messaging. Items range in difficulty from such overused standards as "LOL" to the rare, but stomach-turning "GT4DTG."

▶ Cartoon 15.1

▶**Figure 15.1** Variable View for Child Progeny Data

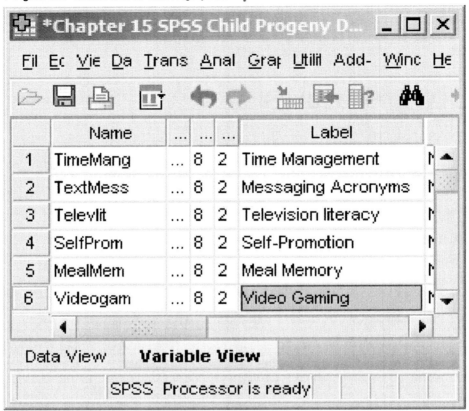

- **Self-Promotion (SelfProm)**: An adaptive behavior pattern with the goal of accruing the greatest amount of credit with the least amount of effort.
- **Television Literacy (Televlit)**: Assesses general awareness of cultural reference points through knowledge of television characters, plots, actors, and, especially, commercials.
- **Menu Memory (MealMem)**: Measures the ability to memorize the cafeteria meal schedule for an entire month.
- **Video Gaming (Videogam)**: Scores are based on the ability to achieve complete and total domination in a wide range of alt-realitied digital environments.

The data collected by Student X are presented in figure 15.2A and figure 15.2B on page 220.

If the tasks Student X has selected are all measures of the same construct—hopefully, in this case, intelligence—then strong correlations should be observed among the scores for each task. The student's advisor, a bit skeptical about the student's choice of tasks, suggests that he might want to consider conducting a factor analysis of the variables.

GOALS OF FACTOR ANALYSIS

Factor analysis is a set of techniques for exploring the relationships among a set of variables. In particular, factor analysis can help to answer two basic questions about the

Figure 15.2A Child Progeny Data (Cases 1–30)

	TimeMang	TextMess	Televlit	SelfProm	MealMem	Videogam
1	63.00	76.00	65.00	72.00	73.00	74.00
2	24.00	64.00	76.00	12.00	63.00	26.00
3	41.00	59.00	55.00	59.00	58.00	27.00
4	66.00	34.00	32.00	63.00	45.00	63.00
5	11.00	25.00	22.00	35.00	35.00	49.00
6	65.00	75.00	69.00	74.00	74.00	72.00
7	23.00	67.00	74.00	11.00	62.00	28.00
8	49.00	64.00	67.00	59.00	68.00	24.00
9	62.00	32.00	37.00	63.00	32.00	66.00
10	14.00	25.00	25.00	38.00	39.00	49.00
11	69.00	58.00	45.00	79.00	47.00	78.00
12	22.00	65.00	77.00	16.00	68.00	28.00
13	42.00	51.00	55.00	58.00	52.00	23.00
14	64.00	40.00	41.00	64.00	42.00	65.00
15	10.00	36.00	39.00	32.00	35.00	47.00
16	65.00	74.00	60.00	72.00	74.00	75.00
17	25.00	68.00	75.00	19.00	69.00	36.00
18	48.00	53.00	53.00	52.00	56.00	28.00
19	64.00	46.00	49.00	65.00	45.00	62.00
20	13.00	36.00	34.00	38.00	32.00	49.00
21	67.00	70.00	64.00	76.00	72.00	75.00
22	23.00	60.00	75.00	15.00	68.00	28.00
23	43.00	55.00	57.00	13.00	57.00	21.00
24	65.00	41.00	45.00	67.00	43.00	60.00
25	13.00	37.00	33.00	36.00	42.00	40.00
26	64.00	75.00	61.00	78.00	74.00	76.00
27	25.00	63.00	75.00	13.00	68.00	26.00
28	46.00	68.00	65.00	52.00	62.00	25.00
29	66.00	48.00	44.00	69.00	44.00	63.00
30	13.00	25.00	29.00	35.00	28.00	48.00

variables in a data set: (a) *"How many constructs have we measured?"* and (b) *"What are these constructs?"* We know that Student X recorded scores for each subject on six variables, but that does not mean he really measured six entirely different things about each person. Factor analysis will tell us how many groupings of variables, *factors,* are present in our original set of variables. In a nutshell, *a factor is a set of variables that are strongly correlated with each other but not strongly correlated with other variables.* Technically, it takes as many factors to account for all of the variance in a set of variables as the number of variables.

▶ **Figure 15.2B** Child Progeny Data (Cases 31–60)

	TimeMang	TextMess	Televlit	SelfProm	MealMem	Videogam
31	64.00	76.00	64.00	72.00	76.00	78.00
32	24.00	61.00	79.00	18.00	58.00	22.00
33	43.00	69.00	64.00	58.00	66.00	25.00
34	64.00	45.00	46.00	64.00	48.00	65.00
35	12.00	23.00	21.00	36.00	35.00	48.00
36	62.00	59.00	57.00	72.00	61.00	79.00
37	29.00	67.00	76.00	11.00	62.00	21.00
38	47.00	35.00	35.00	54.00	38.00	20.00
39	60.00	43.00	45.00	63.00	49.00	65.00
40	14.00	26.00	24.00	38.00	35.00	44.00
41	65.00	78.00	64.00	74.00	76.00	79.00
42	37.00	64.00	75.00	18.00	62.00	23.00
43	48.00	65.00	68.00	50.00	48.00	28.00
44	64.00	44.00	43.00	60.00	49.00	65.00
45	17.00	27.00	25.00	39.00	36.00	48.00
46	69.00	75.00	64.00	78.00	68.00	73.00
47	25.00	61.00	75.00	14.00	68.00	25.00
48	43.00	63.00	66.00	59.00	61.00	28.00
49	67.00	40.00	45.00	63.00	49.00	69.00
50	14.00	37.00	39.00	38.00	35.00	43.00
51	61.00	75.00	64.00	79.00	72.00	75.00
52	26.00	65.00	76.00	13.00	69.00	25.00
53	48.00	58.00	56.00	52.00	55.00	23.00
54	65.00	45.00	43.00	69.00	40.00	64.00
55	14.00	24.00	24.00	38.00	22.00	48.00
56	69.00	75.00	64.00	76.00	79.00	72.00
57	22.00	68.00	78.00	19.00	66.00	28.00
58	45.00	58.00	55.00	58.00	52.00	20.00
59	64.00	43.00	47.00	56.00	43.00	66.00
60	12.00	24.00	25.00	38.00	30.00	49.00

However, it is very often possible to account for a large portion of the total variance for that set of variables with a much smaller number of factors. We will see if that happens for Student X's data set; but before we do that, we will describe briefly the goals for the two major steps in conducting a factor analysis. *Factor extraction* will help us to determine the number of factors we have, and *factor rotation* will help us to name the factors.

HOW MANY CONSTRUCTS? A BRIEF DESCRIPTION OF FACTOR EXTRACTION

Perhaps the most important information we get from factor analysis is a determination of the number of constructs being measured in the set of variables under consideration. In any particular set of variables, the number of constructs assessed may range from *one* (if all the variables were very strongly correlated with each other) to *the number of variables used* (if the correlations among the variables were very close to zero). When we extract a factor from a set of variables, we are specifying the variables that are said to contribute to, or *load on*, that factor. One interesting and challenging thing about factor analysis is that there are a number of different strategies for deciding which variables contribute to which factor, and these different strategies can sometimes produce different answers. Also, given that every variable is going to be correlated to at least some extent with every other variable, all of the variables will contribute at least a little bit to every factor. The job of *factor extraction* is to tell us the extent to which each variable contributes to the measurement of a particular factor.

We are going to show you the most common method for factor extraction within SPSS, *Principal Components Analysis* (PCA). Principal Components Analysis takes the total amount of variance present in the set of variables specified and then constructs a "super-variable" that has the job of accounting for as much of this total variance as possible. Each original variable is assigned a weighting or *factor loading* that specifies the influence that variable has in determining the score or value for this new variable. This new super-variable is the first *factor* extracted by PCA. The further the factor loading for a variable is from zero, the greater the contribution of that variable to the score for this first factor (Factor 1). Specifically, each factor loading represents the correlation of a particular variable with the factor.

After scores for Factor 1 have been determined, SPSS identifies the loadings for a second factor, and then a third factor, and so on until it has calculated the loadings for as many different factors as we have variables. At each step, the rules for calculating a set of factor loadings are (a) the new factor has to account for as much of the total variance as possible, but (b) it can't account for variability that has already been accounted for by an earlier factor. Generally, this means that the first few factors account for large portions of the total variability for the data set, and there's not much left for the last few factors to account for. In this way, PCA is able to boil a large number of variables down to a relatively small number of factors.

Determination of the number of factors is often based on the *eigenvalue* associated with each factor. An eigenvalue is a descriptive property of a factor and represents *the number of variables' worth of variance that has been accounted for by that factor*. Generally, a factor must have an eigenvalue of 1.0 or higher to be considered important enough to work with. In other words, a factor has to account for at least one variable's worth of variability to be considered important. By default, SPSS will include as many factors as have eigenvalues greater than or equal to 1.0.

NAMING THE FACTORS: FACTOR ROTATION

Principal Components Analysis can give us a pretty good idea of how many clusters of variables are present in the data. The next step is to decide which variables are present in each cluster. Unfortunately, the factor loadings provided by PCA are not always helpful. As we will see for Student X's data, the loading of a particular variable on one factor can be pretty close in size to the loading of that same variable on another factor. This can be the case even though that variable is in reality a member of only one cluster of variables. "Rotating" the factors can make it considerably easier to decide which variables load strongly on a particular factor. Basically, *factor rotation rearranges the factor loadings to maximize the degree to which each variable loads strongly on one factor but less strongly on all of the other factors.*

There are a variety of rotation strategies to choose from. The most common choice for rotating factors is the **Varimax method**. The Varimax method is said to be an *orthogonal* rotation strategy because it generates scores for the various factors that are uncorrelated with each other. This means that the constructs described by each factor are independent of each other, which is conceptually appealing to many researchers. Non-orthogonal methods can give us sets of factor loadings that make it easier to assign particular variables to particular factors, but they do so at the price of giving us factors that overlap in terms of the constructs they are measuring. For this example, we are going to ask SPSS to rotate the factors using the Varimax method.

SAVING FACTOR SCORES AS VARIABLES

Because working with a large number of variables makes data analysis more complex, it is useful for researchers to be able to make their analyses more manageable by combining variables. Given that factor analysis identifies factors that are statistically independent of each other, we can ask SPSS to output as data the scores for each subject on each of these factors. These **factor scores** can then be treated as numerical measures of the constructs captured by each factor.

RUNNING A FACTOR ANALYSIS IN SPSS

Figures 15.3 and 15.4 display the various steps described in the procedure below for running a factor analysis.

PROCEDURE FOR RUNNING A FACTOR ANALYSIS:

① Select **Analyze** from pull-down menu.

② Select **Data Reduction**.

③ Select **Factor...** from the side menu. This will open the **Factor Analysis** dialogue box.

④ Enter all the variables interest into the **Variables:** field by selecting each variable and left-clicking on the boxed arrow pointing to the field. In this example, we want to include all six variables in our analysis.

- Now we need to tell SPSS what to give us in terms of output. The options we need are provided by the **Extraction...**, **Descriptives...**, **Rotation...**, and **Scores...** buttons located at the right side of the **Factor Analysis** dialogue box.

SELECTING OPTIONS FOR FACTOR EXTRACTION:

(5) To request a Principal Components Analysis, left-click the **Extraction...** button. This will open the **Factor Analysis: Extraction** dialogue box (displayed at the top of Figure 15.4).

(6) Make sure the default option **Principal components** is selected from the **Method:** drop-down menu.

(7) In the **Display** section, check the **Unrotated factor solution** option.

(8) In the **Extract** section, the default option is **Eigenvalues over: 1**. That is what we are going to use.

(9) Left-click **Continue** to go back to the **Factor Analysis** dialogue box (Figure 15.3).

▶**Figure 15.3** Running Factor Analysis

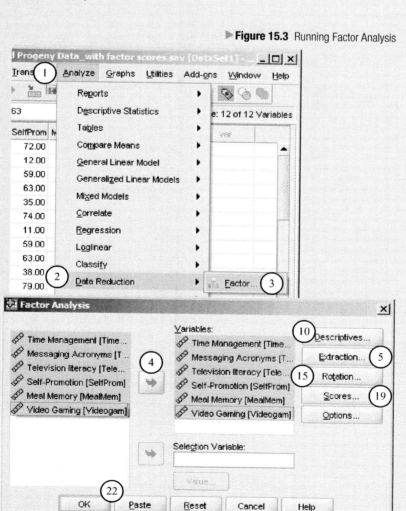

SELECTING OPTIONS FOR DESCRIPTIVE STATISTICS:

⑩ To get descriptive statistics for the variables, as well as a table of correlations among the variables, Left-click on the **Descriptives...** button. This will open the **Factor Analysis: Descriptives (**displayed in the middle of Figure 15.4 on the right-hand side).

• The **Initial solution** option is checked by default.

⑪ Select the **Univariate descriptives** option in the **Statistics** section.

⑫ and ⑬ Select the **Coefficients** and **Significance levels** options in the **Correlation Matrix** section.

⑭ Left-click **Continue** to return to the **Factor Analysis** dialogue box (Figure 15.3).

▶**Figure 15.4** Running Factor Analysis Continued

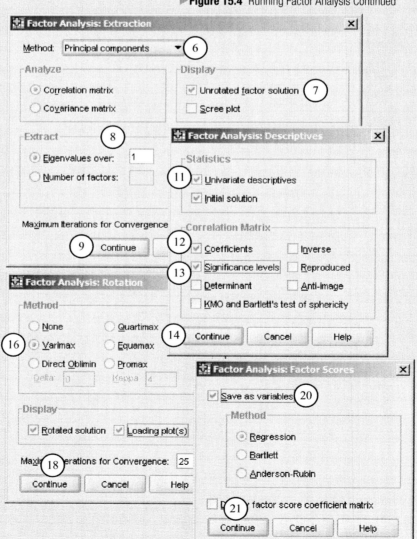

SELECTING OPTIONS FOR FACTOR ROTATION:

(15) To rotate the factors, left-click the **Rotation...** button in the Factor **Analysis** dialogue box (Figure 15.3). This will open the **Factor Analysis: Rotation** dialogue box (displayed at the bottom left-hand corner of Figure 15.4).

(16) Select **Varimax** from the **Method** options.

(17) Among the **Display** options, keep the **Rotated solution** option checked. Also check the **Loading plot(s)** option.

(18) Click **Continue** to return to the **Factor Analysis** dialogue box (Figure 15.3).

SAVING FACTOR SCORES AS VARIABLES:

(19) To save factor scores as variables in the SPSS spreadsheet, left-click the **Scores...** button in the **Factor Analysis** dialogue box (Figure 15.3). This will open the **Factor Analysis: Factor Scores** dialogue box (displayed in the bottom-right corner of Figure 15.4).

(20) Select the **Save as variables** option. Keep the **Regression** option checked as the **Method**.

(21) Left-click **Continue** to return to the **Factor Analysis** dialogue box (Figure 15.3).

(22) Finally, double-check your variables and options and either select **OK** to run or **Paste** to copy the commands for the analysis into a syntax window to run at a later time.

If you choose the paste option from the procedure above, you should have obtained the following syntax:

```
FACTOR
    /VARIABLES TimeMang TextMess Televlit SelfProm MealMem Videogam
    /MISSING LISTWISE
    /ANALYSIS TimeMang TextMess Televlit SelfProm MealMem Videogam
    /PRINT UNIVARIATE INITIAL CORRELATION SIG EXTRACTION ROTATION
    /PLOT ROTATION
    /CRITERIA MINEIGEN(1) ITERATE(25)
    /EXTRACTION PC
    /CRITERIA ITERATE(25)
    /ROTATION VARIMAX
    /SAVE REG(ALL)
    /METHOD=CORRELATION .
```

READING THE SPSS OUTPUT FOR FACTOR ANALYSIS

DESCRIPTIVE STATISTICS

The first information SPSS gives you in the output window are the **Descriptive Statistics** and **Correlation Matrix** tables, which are shown in Figure 15.5. Notice that in the correlations, **Time Management**, **Self Promotion**, and **Video Gaming** are strongly correlated with each other, but none of these variables are strongly correlated with any of the other three variables. Also, the **Messaging Acronyms**, **Television Literacy**, and **Menu Memory** variables are strongly correlated with each other but not with any of the first set of three variables. This pattern provides an initial indication that there might be two relatively independent groupings of variables.

READING THE OUTPUT FOR FACTOR EXTRACTION

Following the descriptive data in the SPSS output, a series of tables are presented that provide information about the extraction of factors from our six original variables. Figure 15.6 displays the first three of these tables, but we have changed the order in which they appear for greater clarity of presentation. The **Total Variance Explained** table shows us the *eigenvalues* for each of the six new factors, or super-variables. The eigenvalue for the first factor is 3.025 [see the section labeled Ⓐ in Figure 15.6]. This means that SPSS has constructed one new variable that can account for 3.025 variables' worth of variance based on a linear combination of the six original variables. This is equivalent to 50.409% of the total variance for the data set. The second factor has an eigenvalue of 2.404, which means that the second factor accounts for an additional 2.404 variables' worth of variance. This second factor accounts for 40.071% of total variance

▶**Figure 15.5** Factor Analysis Output for Child Progeny Data

Descriptive Statistics

	Mean	Std. Deviation	Analysis N
Time Management	42.6500	21.10894	60
Messaging Acronyms	53.0500	16.97598	60
Television literacy	53.4167	17.47278	60
Self-Promotion	48.5333	22.11485	60
Meal Memory	53.9167	14.98167	60
Video Gaming	47.4833	20.64756	60

Correlation Matrix

		Time Management	Messaging Acronyms	Television literacy	Self-Promotion	Meal Memory	Video Gaming
Correlation	Time Management	1.000	.409	.178	.819	.361	.613
	Messaging Acronyms	.409	1.000	.902	.147	.946	.000
	Television literacy	.178	.902	1.000	-.201	.868	-.287
	Self-Promotion	.819	.147	-.201	1.000	.094	.736
	Meal Memory	.361	.946	.868	.094	1.000	.015
	Video Gaming	.613	.000	-.287	.736	.015	1.000
Sig. (1-tailed)	Time Management		.001	.087	.000	.002	.000
	Messaging Acronyms	.001		.000	.131	.000	.500
	Television literacy	.087	.000		.062	.000	.013
	Self-Promotion	.000	.131	.062		.238	.000
	Meal Memory	.002	.000	.000	.238		.453
	Video Gaming	.000	.500	.013	.000	.453	

Figure 15.6 Factor Analysis Output for Child Progeny Data

Total Variance Explained

Component	Initial Eigenvalues			Extraction Sums of Squared Loadings			Rotation Sums of Squared Loadings	Rotation Sums of Squared Loadings	
	Total	% of Variance	Cumulative %	Total	% of Variance	Cumulative %	Total	% of Variance	Cumulative %
1	3.025	50.409	50.409	3.025	50.409	50.409	2.923	48.710	48.710
2	2.404	40.071	90.480	2.404	40.071	90.480	2.506	41.769	90.480
3	.333	5.542	96.022						
4	.154	2.564	98.586						
5	.064	1.070	99.656						
6	.021	.344	100.000						

Extraction Method: Principal Component Analysis.

Communalities

	Initial	Extraction
Time Management	1.000	.865
Messaging Acronyms	1.000	.971
Television literacy	1.000	.962
Self-Promotion	1.000	.905
Meal Memory	1.000	.934
Video Gaming	1.000	.791

Extraction Method: Principal Component Analysis.

Component Matrix [a]

	Component	
	1	2
Time Management	.648	.667
Messaging Acronyms	.951	-.260
Television literacy	.808	-.556
Self-Promotion	.376	.874
Meal Memory	.925	-.280
Video Gaming	.225	.860

Extraction Method: Principal Component Analysis.

a. 2 components extracted.

for the data set. Because the variance accounted for by Factor 2 is independent of what Factor 1 already accounted for, we know that these two factors together can account for 90.48% of all the variability in the scores for the six original variables. In other words, we could account for 100% of the variability by taking six factors into account or 90.48% by taking just these two factors into account. Because none of the remaining factors has an eigenvalue anywhere close to 1.0, we can say that there are only two factors, and that *in this set of six variables, it appears that we only really measured two different constructs.*

The **Communalities** table [Ⓑ in Figure 15.6] provides, logically enough, the *communality* for each original variable. *Communality is the proportion of variability in the scores for an original variable that is accounted for by the meaningful factors (factors with eigenvalues of 1.0 or greater).* The communality for each variable is displayed in the **Extraction** column. SPSS chose to use two factors, so, for example, the communality of .865 for **Time Management** means that the two new factors capture 86.5% of the variability in the original scores for **Time Management**. Obviously, the two new factors do a better job of accounting for the variability in some of the original variables than others, but the high communalities observed in the **Extraction** column indicate that very little information is lost by thinking of the data set in terms of two new "super-variables," rather than the six original variables.

The **Component Matrix** table [Ⓒ in Figure 15.6] shows the factor loadings for every factor with an eigenvalue of 1.0 or higher. Each column (labeled 1 and 2 in this example) represents the meaningful factors. The values for factor loadings are in the same units as those for correlation coefficients. For example, a negative value for a factor loading means that higher scores on the original variable are associated with lower scores for that factor. The further a factor loading is from zero, the more strongly that variable loads on the factor.

We should be able to use the factor loadings to decide which variables contribute most strongly to each factor. Naming the factors would then be a matter of deciding what the variables that load on each factor have in common. However, it is not always obvious which factor a particular variable belongs to when we look at the loadings in the Component Matrix. For example, the variable in the top row, **Time Management**, has a factor loading of .648 for Factor 1 and a loading of .667 for Factor 2. These two values are so close to each other that assigning the variable to one factor or another seems like a toss-up. This is where factor rotation comes in handy. Rotating the factors is designed to maximize the loadings of variables on a single factor and to minimize the size of the loadings on the other factors.

READING THE OUTPUT FOR FACTOR ROTATION

The last section of output, which is shown in Figure 15.7, displays information about the rotation of our two factors. The **Rotated Component Matrix** table provides a new "rotated" set of loading for each factor. You can see that for **Time Management**, the loading for Factor 1, is now .322 and the loading for Factor 2 is now .873, which makes it more obvious that **Time Management** loads more strongly on Factor 2 than it does on Factor 1. The differences between the factor loadings for the other variables are also more pronounced.

Further inspection of the **Rotated Component Matrix** indicates that **Messaging Acronyms**, **Television Literacy**, and **Menu Memory** all load strongly on Factor 1. Having a high score on each of these variables is heavily influenced by the ability to learn and recall a large store of "facts" related to various topics. This seems highly related to what psychologists refer to as "*crystallized intelligence.*" We can also see that the **Time Management**, **Self-Promotion**, and **Video Gaming** variables all load strongly on Factor 2. High levels of performance on these variables is largely a function of the ability to adapt to changing situations and to solve problems. This overall ability is referred to by psychologists as "*fluid intelligence.*" It appears that the six original tasks group together in two factors; one that we might name Crystallized Intelligence and the other that we might name Fluid Intelligence.

The **Component Plot in Rotated Space** presented in the bottom half of Figure 15.6 displays the rotated factor loadings of each variable for Factor 1 plotted against the rotated factor loadings for Factor 2. This provides a visual representation of the same information contained in the Rotated Factor Matrix. From the plot, we can easily see that there are two noticeable groupings of variables, based on the loadings of each original variable for both Factor 1 (the X-axis) and Factor 2 (the Y-axis). One way of thinking about factor rotation is by imagining a process in which the axes in the graph are rotated quite literally so the X- and Y-axes run as close to the centers of these groupings of variables as possible. This is what produces high loadings for a particular variable on one factor but weaker loadings on the other factor(s). The concept of factor rotation is something you will no doubt see covered in considerable detail in your statistics textbook. For now, we want you to know that you can use SPSS to see the results of factor rotation in both numerical (i.e., Rotated Factor Matrix) and pictorial (i.e., Component Plot in Rotated Space) forms.

GETTING AND USING FACTOR SCORES

Finally, we will show you where to find the factor scores we asked SPSS to calculate. Figure 15.8 on page 230 shows the Data View of the SPSS Data Editor containing the data for this example. On the far right side of the spreadsheet, you see that two new variables have been created: **FAC1_1** and **FAC2_1**. The column for **FAC1_1** contains the

▶ **Figure 15.7** Factor Analysis Output Continued

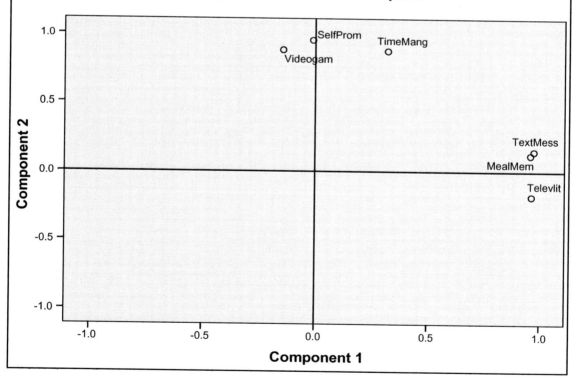

Rotated Component Matrix[a]

	Component 1	Component 2
Time Management	.322	.873
Messaging Acronyms	.974	.148
Television literacy	.964	-.181
Self-Promotion	-.011	.951
Meal Memory	.959	.119
Video Gaming	-.143	.878

Extraction Method: Principal Component Analysis.
Rotation Method: Varimax with Kaiser Normalization.
a. Rotation converged in 3 iterations.

Component Plot in Rotated Space

scores for Factor 1. The column for **FAC2_1** contains the scores for Factor 2. The "1" at the end of the variable name indicates that this is the first set of factor scores we asked SPSS to provide. If you were to run the analysis again, SPSS would generate a second set of factor scores, but the columns containing these scores would be labeled **FAC1_2** and **FAC2_2**. You are certainly free to rename the variables containing these factors' scores if

▶**Figure 15.8** Data View Factor Scores for Child Progeny Data

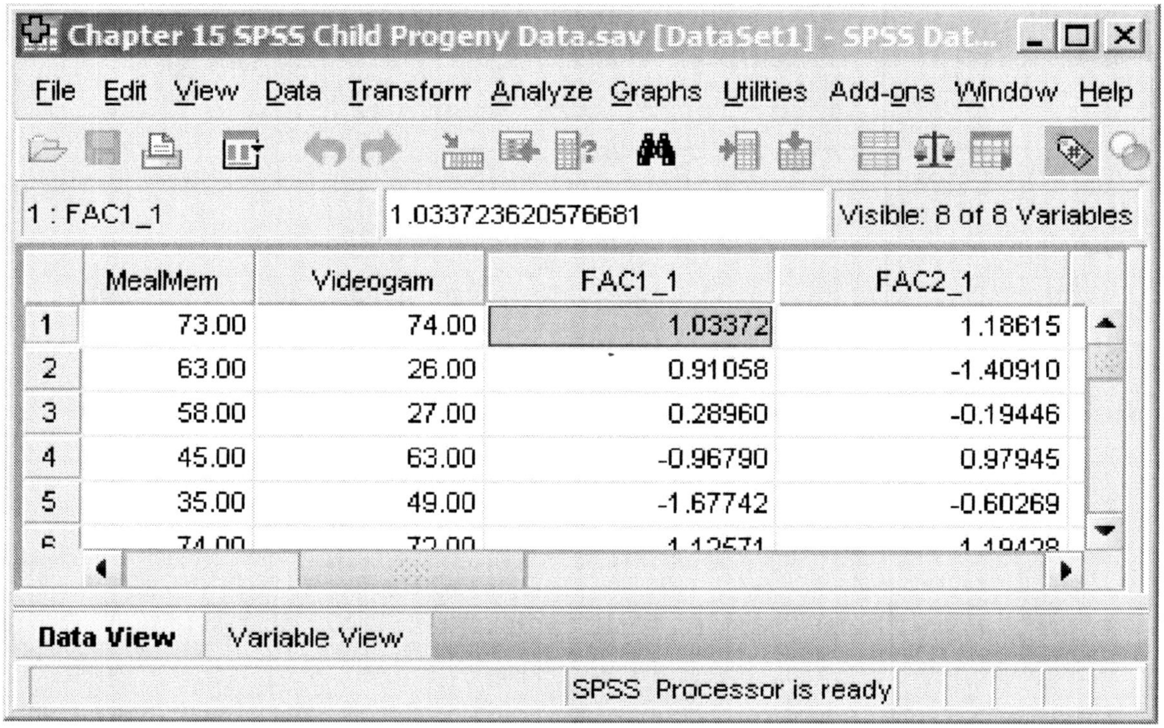

that will make it easier to use them. Whether you rename them or not, these two new variables can be used in the same ways you would use any variable. For example, you might compare male and female college students on these new measures of crystallized and fluid intelligence using independent-samples t-tests.

SUMMARY

In this chapter, we learned how to request results for the extraction of factors using the Principal Components Analysis procedure and for the rotation of these factors using the Varimax method. In addition, we discussed the reasoning a researcher would go through in naming the factors identified by SPSS. Finally, we covered the procedure for adding factor scores to the SPSS Data Editor.

These are the basics of conducting a factor analysis using SPSS. We presented a general overview of the reasoning behind factor analysis but did not describe the computational procedures SPSS used to generate the results. We suggest that you consult a more comprehensive textbook for this information.

PRACTICE EXERCISES

1. Chapter 14 uses data from the Gene Simmons Resemblance Scale. Analysis for the six items in the scale showed that items 1–4 were correlated with each other but not with items 5 and 6. Use the data from that chapter (see Figure 14.2) to conduct

a factor analysis. Specifically, using the factor analysis procedures described in this chapter:

a. Compute descriptive statistics for the scores for each item, as well as the correlation matrix for all six items.

b. Conduct a Principal Components Analysis. How many factors are identified? What are the eigenvalues for each factor?

c. Rotate the factors using the Varimax method. On the basis of the rotated factor matrix, what names seem appropriate for each factor?

d. Export factor scores for each factor to the SPSS spreadsheet for this data set.

e. Use SPSS to determine the correlation(s) among the factor scores. Why did you get the correlation(s) that you did? Remember, the Varimax method is an orthogonal rotation scheme.

2. Conduct a factor analysis on the Hair Band Attitudes Self-report Scale data from the practice exercise at the end of Chapter 14. Complete the same five steps that are listed in Practice Exercise 1 above.

3. Make up your own data from a study that has at least four variables and 40 subjects. Make sure the variables are as goofy and devoid of pedagogical value as possible (write us and let us know what you come up with). Play with the data to create first a two-factor solution and then a three-factor solution.